“Isabella is the best teacher and a most talented chef. I adore her fennel pasta and think about how delicious it is all the time. It was such an honour to be in the Future Dreams House kitchen with her for a very special supper and got to see the wonderful *Pasta Therapy* in action.”

Melissa Hemsley, cookbook author & *Sunday Times* bestseller

"Isabella's *Pasta Therapy* workshops have become a cornerstone of our community offerings. They are highly anticipated for many of our members, providing a place not just for learning, but for healing and connecting. We've seen first-hand how these sessions brighten spirits and build bonds. They are a testament to the power of sharing and healing together."

Sam Jacobs, CEO *Future Dreams Charity*

Isabella Barbato

Over 100 nourishing recipes for relaxation, calm and healing

PASTA therapy

To my parents, Giovanna and Riccardo:
For teaching me that love is best shared around the table.
And to everyone who finds solace in the kitchen,
may you discover your own recipe for healing.

PASTA THERAPY
Isabella Barbato

First published in the UK and USA in 2026 by
Nourish, an imprint of Watkins Media Limited
Unit 11, Shepperton House, 83–93 Shepperton Road,
London N1 3DF

enquiries@nourishbooks.com

Editorial Director: Ella Chappell
Managing Editor: Brittany Willis
Project Editor: Gigi St John
Head of Design: Karen Smith
Design concept: Francesca Corsini
Typesetting: Glen Wilkins/Eleri Stanton
Layouts: Karen Smith
Photography: Isabella Barbato
Photography on page 14, and select photos on pages 12 and 13: Akshay Kiran
Head of Production: Uzma Taj

A CIP record for this book is available from the British Library

ISBN: 978-1-84899-449-2 (Hardback)
ISBN: 978-1-84899-450-8 (eBook)

10 9 8 7 6 5 4 3 2

Typeset in Sofia Pro
Printed in China

Publisher's note
While every care has been taken in compiling the recipes for this book, Watkins Media Limited, or any other persons who have been involved in working on this publication, cannot accept responsibility for any errors or omissions, inadvertent or not, that may be found in the recipes or text, nor for any problems that may arise as a result of preparing one of these recipes. If you are pregnant or breastfeeding or have any special dietary requirements or medical conditions, it is advisable to consult a medical professional before following any of the recipes contained in this book.

Notes on the recipes
Unless otherwise stated:
Use medium fruit and vegetables
Use medium (US large) organic or free-range eggs
Use fresh herbs, spices and chillies
Use granulated sugar (Americans can use ordinary granulated sugar when caster sugar is specified)
Do not mix metric, imperial and US cup measurements:
1 tsp = 5ml 1 tbsp = 15ml 1 cup = 240ml

nourishbooks.com

The manufacturer's authorised representative in the EU for product safety is: eucomply OÜ - Pärnu mnt 139b-14, 11317 Tallinn, Estonia, hello@eucompliancepartner.com, www.eucompliancepartner.com

Contents

FOREWORD
by Melissa Hemsley

I first met Isabella in the kitchen of the Future Dreams House, where we cooked a special supper for a group of media and influencers. It was such a lovely evening, relaxed, warm and full of good food, and it was clear from the start that Isabella had created something really thoughtful with *Pasta Therapy*.

She has a way of making you feel completely at ease in the kitchen. Her approach to pasta is practical, hands-on and filled with heart. There's no fuss, no pressure. It's not about chasing perfection. It's about enjoying the process, being present and finding a bit of calm through something as simple as flour and water. That's the beauty of it. You get to switch off from everything else, just for a while, and lose yourself in the rhythm of it.

The idea for *Pasta Therapy* came from Isabella's own life when, after facing illness and subsequent grief, she found herself turning to food, not just for nourishment, but to feel grounded again. Pasta-making became her calming ritual in the middle of everything else. A way to slow down, focus and take comfort in small, familiar movements. Over time, she began sharing it with others, first through her writing and online community, then in small workshops and supper clubs, and now through this beautiful book.

I still remember the fennel pasta she made that night. It was simple, unfussy and completely delicious, one of those dishes that stays with you. That's Isabella's gift. Her food isn't just about flavour, but also about how it makes you feel.

Whether you're completely new to making pasta or just looking for more joy in the kitchen, I hope you enjoy these recipes and the feeling that comes with them. Calm, connection and something truly satisfying at the end of it.

Author's Note

There are many reasons people write cookbooks. For me, it all started with a question: *Could I have done something differently?*

In 2022, I lost both my parents to cancer, just months apart. Years earlier, I had gone through it too: my own diagnosis, my own reckoning with fear and fragility. I had always felt the need to be strong: the daughter who had survived, who had travelled the world, made a career, lived boldly. But when they were gone, I was left with a grief so raw it tore through every part of me. And beneath that grief was something heavier: guilt. Not logical, not deserved, but persistent. A constant wondering: *Did I leave too soon? Was I too far away? Should I have seen it coming? Done more? Been more?*

As time passed, I began to reflect more gently. My parents had lived a simple life in Sicily. My mother, the kindest soul I've ever known, carried a quiet sadness that I had turned my back on my roots. I left Sicily when I was 18, eager to explore the bigger world. I lived in places she'd never dreamed of visiting . . . until she did. In the last decade of her life, she and my father travelled farther than they ever thought possible: to Southeast Asia, North America, the UK and the Middle East. They embraced unfamiliar cultures, tried dishes they couldn't name and welcomed every experience with open hearts. They did it for me and my sister. And they did it bravely. But they longed for home. Their food. Their kitchen. Their loud, messy, wonderful Sundays.

Now that they're gone, I realize something. I can't change the past, but I can preserve what mattered most to them: their legacy, their love, the recipes that filled our table.

This book is how I come home. Every recipe is a memory. A gesture of return. A way to say, *I remember.* A way to feel their hands still guiding mine, even when the signs are silent. This is how I keep them with me: by writing it all down.

It's just a cookbook. But it's also the most sacred thing I've ever made.

If you've ever felt grief that words can't hold, or lost someone who was your compass, I hope this book makes you feel a little less alone.

Because this is more than pasta. It's therapy.

Ch. 1

INTRODUCTION TO *Pasta Therapy*

We all begin somewhere. This chapter is your starting point. It doesn't begin with a recipe but with a few essential tools, notes and techniques that will help you feel more at ease as you move through the book. You'll find tips on how to mix and knead dough, how to shape and cook pasta, and what to do when things don't go to plan. There's also a short note on how the book is organised.

Each chapter has a theme, whether emotional or practical, and the recipes are grouped with that in mind. Some focus on technique, others on comfort, some on healing or family traditions. You can follow the order or skip around. There is no right or wrong way to approach it.

You'll also find a bit of personal context here. A story about how I found myself turning to pasta during one of the most difficult times in my life, and how something as ordinary as flour and water gave me a sense of focus when everything else felt chaotic. The heavier parts of that story sit in the pages that follow, but this chapter helps frame what the book is, and what it isn't. There are no tests here. No rules to follow too strictly. Just an invitation to slow down and try.

Top to bottom: family meals in Sicily in the summer; my mamma Giovanna; nonna Maria and me; zia Rita, my father Riccardo and my uncle Gianni.

WHERE IT ALL BEGAN

Growing up in Sicily, Sundays were sacred. Not in the traditional sense of attending church, but in the way our family gathered around food. Meals weren't just meals; they were a ritual, a chance to reconnect, to laugh, to share. In the lead up each week, my mamma (mother), zia (aunt) and nonna (grandma) would spend hours on the phone, debating who would bring what, each eager to contribute their signature dish.

My mamma Giovanna was the queen of Ricotta Ravioli with Sugo (My Sugo Finto version is on page 59), each perfectly shaped piece rolled with a delicate touch and paired with her slow-cooked tomato sauce with pork belly and sausage. Other favourites included her saffron-infused *penne gialle* ("yellow penne"), her *penne del bandito* ("outlaw's penne") with its decadent tomato, egg and bacon sauce, and her comforting Timballo di Patate, a nutmeg-scented potato pie. Meals often ended with her indulgent Tronchetto Roulade, filled with chocolate and sweet ricotta. But it was her Scaccia (page 79) that she was famous for, even beyond the family. Thin layers of bread dough folded over a savoury filling. To this day, I've never met anyone who can roll the dough as thin as she did.

My zia Rita was equally a force to be reckoned with in the kitchen, as she prepared her Sunday Lasagna (page 76) and her crispy *cotolette*. I still remember her loud laughter echoing through the house as she breaded and fried the cutlets, filling the air with the smell of home. She was the youngest of my dad's siblings and many mistook us for mother and daughter as I resembled her so strikingly.

Meanwhile, my nonna Maria brought the flavours of her native Benghazi to our table, contributing dishes that felt foreign to my childhood palate. Her Pasta Al Forno Con Broccoli (page 83) was my first encounter with red chillies and a dish of comfort, but it was her 7 Vegetable Couscous (page 72), with spices that spoke to the North African coast where she grew up, that made me feel connected to something larger. And her Spaghetti Alla Carrettiera (page 75), a simple dish of fresh tomatoes and garlic, reminded me that sometimes the simplest meals are the most evocative, and the most potent.

My younger sister Paola and I would hang around the kitchen, stealing bits of dough when we thought no one was looking, invariably getting caught and admonished. According to adults' wisdom, eating raw pasta dough would give us a stomach ache, though it never did. The kitchen was a place of magic for us: flour-dusted countertops, the rhythmic bubbling of sauce on the hob/stovetop, the loud chatter of women and the even louder volume of the TV persistently in the background. It was in those moments that I realized I was witnessing something special, something that would stay with me forever.

MY FATHER, RICCARDO

While the women in my family shaped my love for food, my papà (father), Riccardo, shaped my approach to life. He was the dreamer in our family, always encouraging me to aim higher and believe that nothing was out of reach. While my mother's practicality kept me grounded, my father's optimism lifted me. From leaving home at age 18 to study in Venice, to travelling the world and settling in Singapore, building a successful career, to moving to England to pursue a new job, his belief in me was a constant in my life.

He never got to see this book – nor did mamma, zia or nonna – but I know how much it would have meant to him. He would have shared it proudly, bragging about it to anyone who'd listen, probably to the point of embarrassment, his face lighting up with joy. His pride in our family heritage and his unshakeable belief in me shaped everything I've done. This book is a tribute to him, his faith in me, his love for our Sicilian roots and his insistence that no dream was too big.

A NEW CHAPTER

In 2018, food and cooking took on a different, more profound role in my life. What had always been a source of joy became a lifeline when, on the eve of my 38th birthday, I received news that would change everything: I had breast cancer. That moment shattered everything I thought I knew about myself. The four years that followed were filled with treatments, surgeries, recovery, a global pandemic and the unbearable loss of both my parents, Giovanna and Riccardo, to the same disease.

It was during these darkest times that I found refuge in an unexpected but familiar place: the kitchen. Amidst flour, eggs and the comforting bubbling away of tomato sauce, I discovered a therapy in pasta making. Each strand of dough, each imperfectly shaped ravioli became a way to reclaim control and normalcy. The kitchen became my sanctuary as I navigated illness and unendurable grief. The repetitive actions of kneading and shaping pasta grounded me, helping me process emotions that felt too heavy to bear.

But this journey isn't just mine. It reflects the experiences of many who have turned to the kitchen during difficult times, finding solace in the simple act of creating something with their hands. Whether facing daily stresses or profound challenges, cooking can heal, connect and ground us.

Top to bottom: me and my younger sister Paola; my nonna Peppina, my mum and me on my first birthday; my father making tomato sauce; my mama and papá.

Photos from my time in Sicily.

HOW IT ALL STARTED

Out of this personal journey came something I never anticipated: *Pasta Therapy*, a series of workshops I created for Future Dreams, a charity supporting people affected by breast cancer. In March 2023, I started monthly sessions, inviting women to knead dough, roll pasta and, in the process, heal. It was more than just cooking lessons; it was a safe, nurturing space where the act of making pasta provided comfort, community and connection among women who were going through the worst of times.

The response has been humbling. Over 200 women have joined me so far, crafting pasta shapes like tagliatelle and pappardelle, paired with simple, seasonal sauces. I wanted these sessions to always be accessible to everyone, no matter their health, skills or circumstances. For many, the workshops brought something they hadn't felt in a long time: a sense of normalcy, a shared experience and a moment of joy during a tough time.

This idea that pasta making can be a form of therapy, a way to heal through the act of creation, is what brought me here, to this book. And I wonder: What if *Pasta Therapy* became more than just a workshop, or a book? What if it became a movement? A way for people globally to come together, to heal and connect through the shared joy of cooking?

Pasta making, after all, is a universal language. It's tactile, requiring you to be present in the moment, and needs patience. It's a way to quiet the mind and focus on something simple but profound. And in that quiet, I believe we can find peace, even amidst life's storms.

PASTA THERAPY: A MOVEMENT

This book is an invitation to explore the therapeutic power of food. Imagine *Pasta Therapy* spreading beyond the workshops, becoming a movement where communities gather to cook, heal and share. It could be a way for people everywhere to connect, create and find solace, just as I have.

Pasta has always been a testament to transformation. From a simple mixture of flour and water, we can create something that feeds our bodies and our spirits. The act of making pasta is grounding, offering a tactile connection to the present moment and a sense of accomplishment that nourishes the soul.

As you turn these pages, I hope you feel inspired to not just cook, but to create, to heal and to connect with those you love. Whether you are an experienced cook or just starting out, *Pasta Therapy* offers a space to find comfort, joy and a bit of peace in the process.

Welcome to *Pasta Therapy*: a therapeutic journey of healing through the art of pasta making.

HOW TO READ THIS BOOK

Every recipe in this book is marked with two icons to help you decide what to cook, when to cook it and what to serve alongside. These markers appear at the top of each recipe and reflect two things:

■ **Dietary:** This is a meat- and seafood-free cookbook, so you'll find recipes marked as:

vegan

vegetarian

gluten-free

egg-free

If a recipe is marked as vegetarian and it includes cheese, you may need to use a similar vegetarian cheese alternative (that doesn't contain animal rennet) to ensure it is suitable.

■ **Difficulty level:** All the recipes are easily explained, but some are a little easier to follow for beginners, and so you'll see a rolling pin symbol on each recipe telling you how hard the recipe is, from 1–3 (3 being the hardest).

■ **Season:** While most recipes can be made year-round, I've suggested the best time of year to enjoy them based on ingredient seasonality and flavour. Look for symbols for **spring**, **summer**, **autumn** or **winter** to guide your cooking with the rhythm of the seasons.

BASIC EQUIPMENT

Making pasta by hand doesn't require much: just a good wooden board, a rolling pin and your hands. In my family, no one used fancy gadgets. My nonna rolled out sheets of dough with a long, heavy *mattarello* (rolling pin), worn smooth by years of use, and cut tagliatelle with a simple kitchen knife. The kitchen table was her workspace, dusted with flour and scattered with shapes in various stages of completion. Today, I still believe in keeping things simple. You don't need a cupboard full of tools to make beautiful pasta. But there are a few essentials that can make the process easier, especially if you're just getting started.

THE ESSENTIALS

- **A good wooden board or surface:** Ideally, a large, untreated wooden board or table with enough space to knead, roll and shape. Wood is forgiving and naturally textured, which helps the dough grip ever so slightly as you work it.

- **Rolling pin:** For hand-rolling pasta, I recommend a long, cylindrical, handleless rolling pin. It allows for better control and even pressure. Avoid the thick, short rolling pins with handles, which are used for pastry.

- **Pasta machine:** While not essential, a manual pasta machine, like the Marcato Atlas 150, is a worthwhile investment. It's durable, easy to use and helps you roll out even sheets, especially for stuffed pastas. Many affordable models work just as well, and with proper care, they'll last you decades.

- **Attachments and cutters:** If you use a pasta machine, consider picking up a few extra cutters or attachments for shapes like tagliolini, fettuccine or even ravioli. Most machines come with a few basic cutters included.

- **Ravioli stamps or wheels:** Traditional brass or wooden ravioli stamps come in many shapes: round, square, heart, flower. But don't worry if you don't have one. You can use a glass, a cookie cutter or even just a knife to trim and seal your ravioli. A fork can help crimp the edges and keep the filling secure.

- **Gnocchi board/paddle (*rigagnocchi*):** A small, ridged board made from wood is traditionally used to give gnocchi their signature grooves and can be used to make other shapes too like garganelli, rigatoni or cavatelli. But the back of a fork or even a cheese grater works just as well. What matters most is having texture to catch the sauce.

- ***Ferretto*:** A thin metal rod traditionally used in Sicily to shape pasta such as busiate. It resembles a long knitting needle and is rolled diagonally along small pieces of dough to create the pasta's signature spiral shape. If you don't have a *ferretto*, a thin wooden skewer or knitting needle works just as well.

- **Knife or dough cutter:** A sharp kitchen knife or bench scraper is useful for cutting sheets of pasta, trimming edges and dividing dough.

- **Clean dish towels and trays:** To rest and dry your pasta, use dish towels to cover the dough and prevent it from drying out while you work. Lay shaped pasta on flour-dusted trays before cooking.

NICE-TO-HAVES (BUT NOT NECESSITIES)

As you grow more comfortable with pasta-making, you might find yourself curious about other tools. These aren't essential, but they can add variety and a little fun to your process, especially if you enjoy experimenting with different shapes and textures.

- **Pasta wheel (*rotella*):** A small tool with a fluted or straight edge, perfect for cutting decorative edges on tagliatelle or ravioli. It gives your pasta a beautiful, professional look with very little effort.

- ***Chitarra*:** A traditional Abruzzese tool made with fine wire strings stretched over a wooden frame. Sheets of pasta are pressed through the wires to create square-edged spaghetti, known as tonnarelli. It's tactile, musical and a joy to use, but takes up quite a bit of space, so it's not for everyone.

- **Drying rack:** Particularly handy if you're making long shapes like tagliatelle, fettuccine or pappardelle and want to dry them slightly before cooking or storing. You can also use a clean broom handle balanced between two chairs, as my nonna sometimes did.

- **Stackable pasta drying trays:** Shallow, ventilated trays used to air-dry short pasta shapes like orecchiette, gnocchi, trofie or malloreddus. They're especially useful when making large batches, as they save space and allow air to circulate around the pasta to prevent sticking. I was tempted to include these in the essentials, as I find them incredibly useful. They can be disassembled and stacked away neatly when not in use, making them ideal even for small kitchens like mine.

- **Tortellini or gnocchi boards with multiple cavities:** These help produce uniform shapes quickly, though I still prefer shaping by hand for the rhythm and mindfulness it brings.

- **Piping bag:** Useful for filling ravioli or cappellacci cleanly and evenly, especially if your filling is on the softer side. That said, I normally just use a teaspoon to distribute the filling equally. Simple, fuss-free and it does the job perfectly well.

Remember: these are simply tools to support your hands, not replace them. As you become more confident, you'll find your favourite tools and maybe even pass them down one day, just like my mamma's ravioli cutter, which I've used many times in this book.

BASIC TECHNIQUES

Pasta-making begins with simple ingredients, but it's guided by a combination of instinct and technique. Your hands become your most trusted tools: sensing the texture of the dough, adjusting the pressure as you knead and recognizing when it's ready just by touch. While much of this comes with practice and feel, there are also a few reliable rules you can learn. These foundational methods will form the backbone of your pasta-making journey. With practice, they'll become second nature.

Mixing and Kneading: Always lightly dust your work space with flour before you get started. Then make a well of flour on your board and pour the water or eggs into the middle. Draw the flour in gradually with your fingers or a fork, working slowly until it forms a shaggy dough. Then comes the kneading. Use the heel of your hand to push the dough away, then fold it back over itself and repeat. Eventually, after 5–7 minutes, the dough should spring back slightly when pressed with a finger and it should no longer stick to your hands or the board. That's when you know it's ready.

Resting: Once the dough is kneaded, wrap it in a clean dish towel or cover it with an upturned bowl and let it rest for at least 30 minutes. This allows the gluten to relax, making the dough easier to roll and shape. Resting is just as important as kneading, and it's the perfect moment to prepare your filling or sauce or simply pause and breathe.

Rolling: If you're using a rolling pin, start from the middle and push outward, turning the dough occasionally to keep it even. For a pasta machine, begin on the widest setting and pass the dough through several times, folding it in half between passes until it becomes smooth and consistent. Then gradually reduce the thickness setting, one notch at a time, until you reach your desired thinness. Sprinkle with a little flour if needed, but don't overdo it. The dough should stay supple and slightly tacky, not dry.

Shaping: Some shapes are quick and rustic, like hand-rolled cavatelli or orecchiette pressed with a thumb. Others, like ravioli or tortellini, require more precision and care. No matter the shape, take your time. Imperfections are part of the charm. If you're cutting ribbons like tagliatelle, make sure your dough is well-floured and rolled thin. For filled pasta, seal the edges firmly and remove any air bubbles to prevent them from bursting in the water.

Cooking: Fresh pasta cooks quickly – usually in just 2–4 minutes. Use a large pot of well-salted water, and don't overcrowd it. Stir gently to prevent sticking, and taste as you go. We sometimes add a little oil to the cooking water to prevent sticking but using a bigger pot with plenty of water will work just fine. Pasta should be al dente – tender but still with a bit of bite. Always reserve a splash of the cooking water to help loosen and bind your sauce.

CUPBOARD INGREDIENTS

Pasta might be the heart of a dish, but the real magic comes from what you put with it. In our kitchen, the cupboard was always stocked with a few essential ingredients that could turn a simple bowl of pasta into something memorable. We always had extra virgin olive oil, and used it generously. Onions, carrots and celery were the starting point of every soffritto, and fresh herbs like parsley, basil and mint were picked from pots on the windowsill – never dried, not for pasta at least.

There were always jars of capers and bowls of olives, adding bursts of flavour to sauces or simply eaten with bread when the wait for the water to boil was too long. Dried red chillies lived in a small paper package tucked into the spice drawer, ready to be crumbled over *aglio e olio* or infused into oil. And, of course, there were good-quality canned tomatoes, along with my mum's homemade tomato sauce, which she would prepare with the ripest September tomatoes to last until the next tomato season. These were the backbones of our kitchen. Here are the ingredients I always try to keep in my kitchen:

OILS, SAUCES & CONDIMENTS

- Extra virgin olive oil
- White wine vinegar
- Red wine vinegar
- Capers in salt or brine
- Tomato purée/paste (for smooth sauces)
- Tomato passata/*polpa di pomodoro* (finely chopped tomatoes, for chunkier sauces)
- Peeled canned tomatoes/*pelati*

AROMATICS & FLAVOUR BUILDERS

- Garlic
- Red and white onions
- Shallots
- Dried red chillies
- Black pepper (whole and ground)
- Sea salt or fine salt
- Nutmeg

HERBS & SPICES

- Fresh parsley
- Fresh basil
- Fresh mint
- Fresh dill or wild fennel
- Rosemary (fresh or dried)
- Bay leaves
- Fennel seeds
- Dried oregano

CANNED & JARRED GOODS

- Olives (green and black)
- Artichokes in oil
- Sun-dried tomatoes

DRY GOODS

- Semola
- 00 flour
- Plain/all-purpose flour (for some doughs and sauces)
- Whole-wheat/wholemeal flour (use plain/all-purpose)
- Other flours like spelt, quinoa, gluten-free flour blends
- Breadcrumbs (homemade or plain, not seasoned)
- Dried pasta (as a backup)

CHEESES & PRESERVED ITEMS

- Grana Padano or Parmigiano Reggiano (wedge or grated)
- Pecorino
- Ricotta Salata
- Butter (unsalted)

LENTILS & PULSES

- Borlotti beans
- Chickpeas/garbanzo beans
- Brown lentils
- Broad/fava beans
- Peas

GETTING STARTED: FOUR DOUGHS AND ONE SAUCE

Before we move on to shapes and fillings, I want to share a few basic recipes. These are the essentials I return to most often in my own kitchen, and many of the dishes in this book begin here.

THERE ARE FOUR DOUGHS

- A soft, elastic egg dough used for tagliatelle, tortelli or lasagne
- A firmer semola and water dough typical of the south
- A tomato dough with added depth and colour
- A spinach dough for freshness and vibrancy

And one sauce: my mum Giovanna's tomato sauce. It's simple and comforting.

These are the starting points. Once you're comfortable with them, everything else becomes easier.

SIMPLE FRESH EGG PASTA DOUGH

Pasta all'uovo

A basic recipe for creating the most common fresh pasta dough, perfect for shaping into tagliatelle, pappardelle or fettuccine. This is a foundational recipe to build confidence. It's made with just flour and eggs and is the easiest dough to work with: soft, elastic and reliable. While in the south we often use semola and water doughs, this egg-based version is typical of central and northern Italy and widely used across the country. The ratio is simple: 100g/3½oz/¾ cup of flour and 1 egg per person. It scales easily, yields generous portions and forms a versatile base for many recipes. Once you've mastered this dough, you'll be ready to roll, cut and shape with confidence.

Serves: 4

Preparation time: approx. 10 minutes, plus 30 minutes resting

Cooking time: depends on the shape

Ingredients:

* 400g/14oz/3 cups 00 flour
* 4 eggs

Make the Dough: On a clean work surface, make a mound with the flour and create a well in the middle. Crack in the eggs and whisk gently with a fork, gradually incorporating the flour from the edges until a rough dough forms. If the dough feels too dry and crumbly, add a teaspoon of water; if it sticks to your hands, sprinkle in a little more flour.

Knead the Dough: Once the dough has formed, begin kneading it with your hands. Use the heel of your hand to push the dough away from you, then fold it back over itself. Continue kneading for about 5–7 minutes, until the dough is smooth and elastic. It should spring back slightly when pressed. Cover the dough with a clean dish towel and let it rest at room temperature for at least 30 minutes.

Roll and Cut the Pasta: After resting, lightly dust a work surface with flour and cut the dough into 2–4 pieces. Depending on the type of pasta you are making, roll the dough into thin sheets or shape it directly by hand. For ribbon shapes like tagliatelle, pappardelle or fettuccine, roll each piece using a pasta machine or rolling pin until it reaches a smooth, even thickness (typically around 1–1.5mm though this may vary depending on the shape). For hand-formed pastas like cavatelli, busiate or orecchiette, there's no need to roll the dough into sheets; instead, cut and shape it directly from smaller pieces.

When choosing your shape, think about the sauce you'll pair it with. Pastas with texture or ridges are perfect for holding on to richer, heartier sauces. Smoother shapes like tagliolini suit lighter, more delicate sauces that gently coat the surface. A good match enhances both the pasta and the sauce.

Cook the Pasta: Bring a large pot of salted water to a rolling boil. It's essential to use a large pot to ensure the pasta doesn't stick together. The cooking time will depend on the shape and size but fresh pasta cooks quickly, so keep an eye on it. You'll know it's done when it floats to the top and has a firm, yet tender texture. Since fresh pasta is delicate, it's best not to drain it in a colander; instead, use a slotted spoon to transfer it directly into a large pan or plate with your sauce. Mix gently to coat the pasta evenly.

Store the Fresh Pasta: If you're not cooking the pasta right away, shape it and place on a floured plate or tray, ensuring that the pieces don't touch and stick together. Transfer the tray to the freezer. After a few hours, once the pasta is frozen, transfer it to a ziplock bag and store in the freezer for up to 2 months. Cook the pasta in boiling water straight from frozen, adding a minute or two to the cooking time.

SIMPLE SEMOLA & WATER DOUGH

Pasta di semola

A rustic pasta dough made from semola and water, perfect for hearty shapes like orecchiette, cavatelli or strozzapreti. This is the pasta of the south, the kind we made at home – rough, rustic and full of character. It requires a little more effort to knead but rewards you with a firm dough that holds its shape beautifully. Semola is finely milled durum wheat flour, not to be confused with coarser semolina, and has a golden colour and slightly gritty feel that softens as you knead. It's the base for orecchiette, busiate and cavatelli: pasta meant to catch sauce in its grooves and ridges. If you've never made pasta before, this is a wonderful place to start. The process is easy to remember too: a ratio of 2:1 semola to water is all you need to create this dough.

Serves: 4

Preparation time: approx. 10 minutes, plus 30 minutes resting

Cooking time: depends on the shape

Ingredients:

* 400g/14oz/3 cups semola
* 200ml/7fl oz/scant 1 cup lukewarm water

Make the Dough: On a clean work surface, make a mound with the semola and create a well in the middle. Gradually add the lukewarm water, mixing with your fingers or a fork to incorporate the semola until a rough dough forms. If the dough feels too dry, resist adding more water right away; knead it instead, as the dough will soften after resting. If it remains too crumbly, add water just a spoonful at a time, kneading continuously.

Knead the Dough: Once the dough has come together, knead it with your hands. Push the dough away with the heel of your hand, then fold it back over itself, repeating this motion for about 5–7 minutes until the dough is smooth, elastic and slightly firm. It should have a soft bounce when pressed. Cover the dough with a clean dish towel and let it rest at room temperature for at least 30 minutes.

Roll and Shape the Pasta: After resting, lightly dust a work surface with semola and divide the dough into 2–4 pieces. From here, cut it into smaller pieces and shape according to the pasta variety you wish to make. For example, roll them into orecchiette by pressing your thumb into each piece, or create cavatelli by rolling each piece along a grooved surface. The possibilities are endless.

Cook the Pasta: Bring a large pot of salted water to a rolling boil. It's essential to use a large pot to ensure the pasta doesn't stick together. Fresh semola pasta cooks quickly, so keep an eye on it. You'll know it's done when it floats to the top and has a firm, yet tender texture. Use a slotted spoon to carefully transfer the pasta to a pan with your sauce and mix gently to coat.

Store the Fresh Pasta: If not used right away, shape the pasta, place it on a floured (or semola-dusted) plate or tray, ensuring the pieces don't touch, and freeze for a few hours. Once frozen, transfer to a ziplock bag and store in the freezer for up to 2 months. Cook the pasta in boiling water straight from frozen, adding a minute or two to the cooking time.

TOMATO DOUGH

Impasto al pomodoro

A colourful pasta dough enriched with tomato purée/paste, perfect for rustic shapes like garganelli, malloreddus or cavatelli. This dough is a playful twist on the classic southern semola-and-water base, with the subtle sweetness and colour of tomato folded in. It's just as sturdy and versatile, but with a beautiful hue that brings extra warmth to your plate. You can use it for any shape that benefits from a bit of visual drama and a hint of tomato richness. The ratio remains the same – 2:1 semola to liquid – with a small adjustment to account for the tomato purée/paste.

Serves: 4

Preparation time: approx. 10 minutes, plus 30 minutes resting

Cooking time: depends on the shape

Ingredients:

* 400g/14oz/3 cups semola
* 2 tbsp tomato purée/paste
* 180ml/6fl oz/¾ cup lukewarm water

Make the Dough: On a clean work surface, make a mound with the semola and create a well in the middle. In a small bowl or jug, mix the tomato purée/paste into the lukewarm water until dissolved. Gradually pour the tomato water into the well, mixing with your fingers or a fork to incorporate the semola until a rough dough forms. If the dough feels too dry, don't add more water right away; start kneading, as the dough will hydrate further with time and soften after resting. If it remains too crumbly, add a spoonful of water at a time.

Knead the Dough: Once the dough has come together, knead it with your hands. Push it away using the heel of your hand, then fold it back over itself, repeating the motion for about 5–7 minutes until the dough is smooth, elastic and slightly firm, with a soft bounce when pressed. Cover the dough with a clean dish towel and let it rest at room temperature for at least 30 minutes.

Roll and Shape the Pasta: After resting, lightly dust a work surface with semola and divide the dough into 2–4 pieces. Shape according to the pasta variety you're making. This dough works especially well for ridged or indented shapes like foglie d'ulivo, malloreddus or garganelli, as the tomato colour accentuates their texture.

Cook the Pasta: Bring a large pot of salted water to a rolling boil. Use a big pot so the pasta cooks evenly and doesn't stick together. Tomato dough cooks quickly; it is done when the pasta floats to the surface and has a firm yet tender texture. Transfer to your sauce with a slotted spoon and toss gently to coat.

Store the Fresh Pasta: If not cooking immediately, shape and lay the pasta on a floured (or semola-dusted) plate or tray in a single layer, ensuring the pieces don't touch. Freeze for a few hours, then transfer to a ziplock bag and store in the freezer for up to 2 months. Cook the pasta in boiling water straight from frozen, adding a minute or two to the cooking time.

SPINACH DOUGH

Impasto agli spinaci

A vibrant green dough, as beautiful as it is delicious. It builds on the classic fresh egg base, with finely chopped or puréed cooked spinach added for vibrant colour and a hint of flavour. It's traditionally used for dishes like lasagne verdi or spinach tagliatelle and works beautifully for filled pastas too. The addition of spinach makes the dough slightly softer and more delicate to work with, but the technique is the same.

Serves: 4

Preparation time: approx. 10 minutes, plus 30 minutes resting

Cooking time: depends on the shape

Ingredients:

* 400g/14oz/3 cups 00 flour
* 100g/3½oz/⅔ cup cooked spinach, squeezed dry and finely chopped
* 4 eggs

Make the Dough: On a clean work surface, make a mound with the flour and create a well in the middle. Add the chopped spinach and crack in the eggs. Whisk the eggs and spinach gently with a fork, gradually incorporating the flour from the edges until a rough dough forms. If the dough feels too wet, add a little more flour a spoonful at a time. If it's too dry, wet your hands lightly and start kneading.

Knead the Dough: Once the dough has come together, knead it with your hands for about 5–7 minutes. Use the heel of your hand to push it away from you, then fold it back and repeat. The spinach may make the dough appear slightly speckled at first, but it will become smooth and uniform as you knead. It will eventually become elastic and spring back slightly when pressed. Cover with a dish towel and rest at room temperature for at least 30 minutes.

Roll and Cut the Pasta: After resting, lightly dust a work surface with flour and divide the dough into 2–4 pieces. Roll it out using a pasta machine or rolling pin and cut into your desired shape. Spinach dough is especially beautiful when used for tagliatelle or lasagne sheets, and it pairs wonderfully with creamy or buttery sauces that let the colour shine. For filled pasta, be sure to roll the dough thin and seal the edges well.

Cook the Pasta: Bring a large pot of salted water to a rolling boil. Use a big pot so the pasta cooks evenly and doesn't stick together. Fresh spinach pasta cooks quickly, usually in 2–4 minutes. Use a slotted spoon or tongs to carefully transfer the pasta to a pan with your sauce and toss gently to coat.

Store the Fresh Pasta: If not cooking immediately, shape and lay the pasta on a floured plate or tray in a single layer, ensuring the pieces or strands don't touch. Freeze for a few hours, then transfer to a ziplock bag and store in the freezer for up to 2 months. Cook the pasta in boiling water straight from frozen, adding a minute or two to the cooking time.

GIOVANNA'S TOMATO SAUCE

Salsa di pomodoro

A cherished family recipe, this sauce takes me straight back to my mum, Giovanna, and the comforting smell that would fill our home whenever she made it. I remember her standing by the hob/stovetop, stirring the pot with care, tasting the sauce until it was just right. She knew how to turn the simplest ingredients into something special, and her tomato sauce is one of my most treasured reminders of her love and warmth. Even though she's no longer with us, this sauce keeps her close, and every time I make it, I feel like she's right there with me, watching over my shoulder.

Serves: 10–12

Preparation time: 15 minutes

Cooking time: 2 hours 50 minutes

Ingredients:

* 3kg/6.6lbs ripe tomatoes – use the best quality, local, ripe, in-season tomatoes; Roma, San Marzano or beefsteak varieties work well
* 1 onion, quartered
* 3 garlic cloves, lightly crushed
* 3 tbsp extra virgin olive oil
* 8–10 fresh basil leaves
* Salt and pepper, to taste

Prepare the Tomatoes: Roughly chop the tomatoes and add them to a large pot. Using your fist or palm, press down on the tomatoes in the pot to release their juices. This step allows the tomatoes to break down and cook without the need to add any water.

Start the Sauce: Add the onion, garlic and some salt and pepper. Cover the pot with a lid and place it over a medium-low heat. Do not add any additional ingredients at this stage; just bring the sauce to a simmer gently. Remove the lid occasionally to stir, ensuring nothing sticks to the bottom.

Simmer and Reduce: After about 30 minutes of simmering, the tomatoes will have started to release their liquid. Continue simmering gently for around 2 hours, stirring occasionally. The sauce will gradually reduce by half, and you'll see it thicken as the flavours concentrate.

Add the Olive Oil and Basil: Once the sauce has reduced, add the olive oil and basil leaves. Stir well and let it cook for an additional 20 minutes, allowing the basil to infuse its aroma into the sauce.

Blend and Finish the Sauce: While the sauce is still hot, run it through a vegetable mill in batches or use a hand-held/immersion blender to grind the skins and seeds, creating a smooth consistency. Transfer the sauce to a clean pot or bowl as you work through the batches.

Store the Sauce: If using immediately, serve with your favourite pasta. To store, transfer the sauce to sterilized jars and keep in the refrigerator for up to a week. For longer storage, vacuum-seal the jars to keep them at room temperature for several months.

Ch. 2

THE ART OF *Pasta Making*

Pasta has been a staple of Mediterranean culture for centuries, woven into the fabric of daily life and traditions. Its origins are the subject of much debate: some say it travelled along the Silk Road from Asia, while others believe it emerged naturally from local grains and creativity. Regardless of where it began, pasta found a home in the Mediterranean, where the interplay of climate, fertile soil and a melting pot of influences shaped its endless varieties. From the rolling hills of Tuscany to the coastal breeze of Sicily, pasta evolved not just as a food but as an expression of place and people.

Growing up in Sicily, I watched my mother transform flour and water into something extraordinary. With her hands dusted in flour, she worked the dough as if it itself held stories – stories of our family, our land and the passage of time. Her gestures were acts of love and preservation, linking her to the generations that came before.

Each region, each village, even each family has its own take on pasta: a different shape, a secret ingredient, a time-honoured technique passed down through generations. Its versatility reflects my beloved Mediterranean landscape, where simple, local ingredients like olive oil, tomatoes and fresh herbs are transformed into something so precious. This chapter is not just about learning the basic techniques of pasta but about connecting to this timeless tradition and embracing the process, finding comfort, joy and a little bit of magic in every strand.

TAGLIATELLE WITH MUM'S TOMATO SAUCE

Tagliatelle al sugo della mamma

Hand-cut tagliatelle made with semola and whole eggs, served with the slow-cooked tomato sauce that is the beating heart of this book. I could not have started this book with anything else. This dish is where it all begins: my love of cooking, my sense of belonging, my first memories of family gathered around the table. The sauce, slow-cooked with care, is the same one I described in the opening pages: our end-of-summer ritual, bottling the ripe tomatoes to last through winter. And the pasta? Golden, resilient, honest. These tagliatelle ribbons are rolled and cut by hand, the way our nonnas did, the way I still do. A reminder that tradition isn't static. It lives on in the way we shape it.

Serves: 4

Preparation time: 30 minutes (if you have made the sauce), plus 30 minutes resting

Cooking time: 3–4 minutes

For the Dough:

* 400g/14oz/3 cups semola
* 4 eggs

To Serve:

* 700ml/24fl oz/3 cups Giovanna's Tomato Sauce (page 26)
* Ragusano DOP or Parmigiano Reggiano, to serve
* Fresh basil leaves, to garnish

Make the Dough: On a clean work surface, make a mound with the semola and create a well in the centre. Crack in the eggs and whisk gently with a fork, gradually incorporating the semola until a rough dough forms. Knead for 5–7 minutes until smooth and elastic. Cover with a dish towel and let rest for 30 minutes.

Roll and Cut the Tagliatelle: Lightly dust a work surface with semola. Divide the rested dough into 2–3 portions. Roll each piece into a thin sheet, about 1mm thick (setting 5 on a Marcato). Dust with semola, then fold the sheets loosely lengthways into thirds or quarters, just enough to handle easily. Slice into ribbons about 6–8mm/⅓in wide. Unfold and toss with semola to prevent sticking.

Cook and Serve: Warm Giovanna's Tomato Sauce in a wide pan. Meanwhile, bring a large pot of salted water to the boil. Cook the tagliatelle for around 3–4 minutes, or until al dente. Using tongs, lift the pasta directly into the pan with the sauce and toss gently to combine, adding a splash of the cooking water if needed to help the sauce cling evenly. Serve immediately with a generous grating of Ragusano or Parmigiano and a few basil leaves.

PAPPARDELLE WITH BROWN BUTTER, LEMON & PARMESAN

Pappardelle al burro, limone e parmigiano

A beginner-friendly recipe that lets the simplicity of handmade pasta and the brightness of lemons shine. Citrus fruits hold a special place in Mediterranean culture, particularly in Sicily. This dish offers a moment of sunshine on the plate and in the soul, bringing the brightness of lemons into every bite.

Serves: 4

Preparation time: 20 minutes, plus 30 minutes resting

Cooking time: 4 minutes

For the Pappardelle:

* 400g/14oz/3 cups 00 flour
* 4 eggs

For the Sauce:

* 5 unwaxed lemons, plus the juice of ½ lemon
* 50g/1¾oz/3½ tbsp unsalted butter
* Freshly grated Parmigiano Reggiano cheese (approx. 60g/2oz/½ cup, or to taste), plus extra to serve
* Fresh parsley, finely chopped
* Salt, to taste

Make the Dough: On a clean work surface, form the flour into a mound and create a well in the centre. Add the eggs, then gradually incorporate the flour using a fork until a rough dough forms. Knead the dough until smooth and elastic. Wrap in cling film/plastic wrap, or cover with a clean dish towel, and let rest for 30 minutes.

Roll the Pasta: Once the dough has rested, lightly flour a clean surface to prevent sticking. Cut the dough into 4 smaller pieces to make it more manageable.

If making by hand, take one piece and flatten it with your hands. Using a rolling pin, roll the dough away from you, applying even pressure. Rotate the dough a quarter-turn every few rolls to keep it as round and even as possible. Continue rolling until you achieve a 1–2mm-thick dough. Repeat with the remaining dough pieces.

If using a pasta machine, take one piece and flatten it with your hands. Set your machine to the widest setting and pass the dough through. Fold the dough in thirds, like an envelope, and pass it through again. Repeat this folding and rolling 2–3 times to build the dough's elasticity. Gradually reduce the machine setting one notch at a time, passing the dough through once at each setting, until it reaches the desired thinness (1–2mm). Repeat with the remaining dough pieces.

Cut the Pappardelle: Once your pasta sheets are ready, dust them lightly with flour to prevent sticking. If the sheets are long, cut them into manageable lengths (30cm/12in each). Roll each sheet up loosely, like a log, and use a knife to slice into wide ribbons (about 3cm/1¼in wide). Carefully unroll to reveal the pappardelle.

Drying the Pasta: Once cut, dust lightly with flour to prevent them from sticking again. You can either hang the pasta over a clean surface or create loose nests on a floured tray while you prepare the rest of the pasta and sauce.

Prepare the Sauce: Zest 3 of the lemons and set the zest aside. In a large pan, melt the butter over a medium heat. Add the lemon zest and allow it to brown gently for 1–2 minutes, infusing the butter with citrusy aroma. Remove from the heat.

Cook the Pasta: Bring a large pot of salted water to the boil. Remove the skin from one of the remaining lemons with a peeler and add it to the boiling water to infuse. Add the pappardelle and cook for around 4 minutes, until al dente. Cooking time may vary depending on the pasta thickness, but you know it's done when it starts floating. Reserve a ladle (approx. 60ml/2fl oz/¼ cup) of the water before draining.

Finish the Sauce: Return the pan with the browned butter and lemon zest to a low heat. Add the reserved pasta water and the lemon juice, stirring to combine. Toss in the pappardelle and parsley and add the grated Parmigiano Reggiano. Adjust the salt. Stir well, ensuring the pasta is well coated with the lemony butter.

Serve: Divide the pappardelle among plates and top with more grated Parmigiano Reggiano and zest from the remaining lemon. Garnish with parsley and serve.

WHOLEMEAL/WHOLE-WHEAT FETTUCCINE WITH MUSHROOM, TALEGGIO & THYME

Fettuccine integrali ai funghi, taleggio e timo

Serves: 4

Preparation time: 20 minutes, plus 30 minutes resting

Cooking time: 15 minutes

For the Dough:

* 250g/9oz/2 cups wholemeal/whole-wheat flour
* 150g/5¼oz/1¼ cups 00 flour
* 4 eggs

For the Sauce:

* 50g/1¾oz/3½ tbsp salted butter
* 300g/10½oz/4 cups porcini mushrooms, sliced, or 60g/2oz/scant 1 cup dried porcini, soaked in warm water and drained, then chopped roughly
* 2–3 fresh thyme sprigs, leaves picked, or 1 tsp dried thyme
* 100ml/3½fl oz/scant ½ cup double cream/heavy cream
* 150g/5⅟₄oz/½ cup Taleggio cheese, chopped (including the rind)
* Salt and pepper, to taste
* Fresh sprigs of thyme, chopped, to garnish
* Finely grated Parmigiano Reggiano, to serve (optional)

This earthy dish brings together the rich flavours of mushrooms with the grounding essence of wholemeal/whole-wheat pasta, connecting us to the earth and the nourishment it offers. Making this dough always brings me back to moments when the world felt too loud and the act of kneading was the only thing that made sense. Rolling and cutting pasta by hand becomes a calming ritual, one that pulls me into the present. I love the ruggedness of wholemeal/whole-wheat flour in that it mirrors life's imperfections. The sauce is just as grounding: earthy porcini, woodsy thyme, soft melting Taleggio. It's a meal that wraps around you like a warm embrace. If Taleggio isn't available where you live, substitute with a soft, bloomy-rind cheese like brie (rind removed) or camembert.

Make the Dough: On a clean work surface, mix the wholemeal/whole-wheat and 00 flours into a mound. Create a well in the centre and crack in the eggs. Gently whisk with a fork, gradually incorporating the flour until a rough dough forms. Knead for 5–7 minutes until smooth and elastic. Cover with a dish towel and let rest for 30 minutes.

Make the Sauce: Melt the butter in a large pan over a medium heat. Add the mushrooms and sauté for 6–8 minutes, until golden and tender. Add the thyme and cook for 1–2 minutes more. Stir in the cream and Taleggio, season with salt and pepper and simmer for another 1–2 minutes until melted and well combined.

Roll and Cut the Fettuccine: Lightly dust a work surface with flour. Divide the rested dough into 2–4 pieces. Roll each piece into a thin sheet about 1mm thick (setting 5 on a Marcato). Dust lightly with flour, then fold the sheet loosely lengthways into thirds or quarters, just enough to handle easily, and cut into ribbons about 1cm/⅓in wide. Toss with flour to prevent sticking.

Cook the Fettuccine: Bring a large pot of salted water to the boil. Cook the fettuccine for 2–3 minutes, or until al dente.

Combine and Serve: Using tongs, lift the pasta directly into the pan with the sauce. Toss gently to coat, adding a splash of cooking water if needed to help the sauce cling evenly. Garnish with thyme and finish with a generous grating of Parmigiano Reggiano, if desired. Serve immediately.

TROFIE WITH PESTO GENOVESE, POTATO & GREEN BEANS

Trofie al pesto con patate e fagiolini

Serves: 4

Preparation time: 45 minutes, plus 30 minutes resting

Cooking time: 10 minutes

For the Dough:

* 400g/14oz/3 cups semola
* 200ml/7fl oz/scant 1 cup lukewarm water

For the Pesto Genovese:

* 1 garlic clove
* 50g/1¾oz/2 cups packed fresh basil leaves
* 30g/1oz/¼ cup pine nuts
* 60ml/2fl oz/¼ cup extra virgin olive oil, plus more if needed
* 30g/1oz/¼ cup Parmigiano Reggiano, finely grated (optional)
* 30g/1oz/¼ cup Pecorino, finely grated (optional)
* Salt, to taste

To Assemble:

* 2 potatoes, peeled and diced into 8–10 pieces each
* 150g/5¼oz green beans, trimmed and cut into 2.5cm/1in pieces
* Fresh basil leaves and grated unwaxed lemon zest, to garnish (optional)
* Finely grated Parmigiano Reggiano or Pecorino, to serve (optional)

This is the kind of pasta you find in Liguria's homes and trattoria. It's simple, seasonal and built on ingredients that speak to both land and tradition: hand-rolled trofie, tender green beans, soft potato and a basil pesto that's fragrant and alive. Making it is a sensory experience: from the feel of the dough under your palm to the perfume of basil crushed in a mortar. Every element has its place, and the result is a dish that feels balanced and generous. If you prefer to skip the cheese and keep the pesto dairy-free and vegan, go right ahead. The beauty lies in its adaptability, not in strict rules.

Make the Dough: On a clean work surface, make a mound with the semola and create a well in the centre. Gradually add the water, mixing with your fingers or a fork to incorporate the semola until a rough dough forms. Knead for 5–7 minutes until smooth and elastic. Cover with a dish towel and let rest for 30 minutes.

Make the Pesto Genovese: Crush the garlic with a pinch of salt using a mortar and pestle. Gradually add the basil, working in a circular motion until fragrant and broken down. Add the pine nuts and continue grinding for 3–5 minutes, until smooth. Drizzle in the olive oil slowly, stirring until creamy. Add the cheeses, if using, and adjust the seasoning with salt. Set aside. If you prefer to use a blender or food processor, pulse the garlic, basil, pine nuts and a little oil in short bursts to avoid overheating the basil. Add the remaining oil gradually and finish by stirring in the cheeses, if using.

Shape the Trofie: Lightly dust a tray and work surface with semola. Cut the rested dough into small pieces, about the size of a hazelnut. Working one at a time, place a piece on a wooden board or work surface. Using the side of your palm, especially the outer edge near your pinkie finger, press down and roll the dough diagonally across the surface, dragging it gently toward you. This creates a tapered, twisted shape with pointed ends and a thicker middle. It takes a bit of practice, but once you find the right pressure and angle, it becomes second nature. Place the finished trofie on the tray as you go and keep covered as you work.

Cook the Vegetables and Trofie: Bring a large pot of salted water to the boil. Add the diced potatoes and cook for 5 minutes, then add the green beans. After 1–2 minutes, add the trofie. Cook for 2–3 minutes or until the pasta floats and the potatoes and beans are fork-tender.

Combine and Serve: Using a slotted spoon, lift the pasta and vegetables directly onto the serving dish with the pesto and toss to combine, adding a splash of the cooking water if needed to help the sauce cling evenly. Garnish with fresh basil, lemon zest and extra cheese, if desired. Serve immediately.

BUSIATE WITH SICILIAN RED PESTO

Busiate con pesto trapanese

Twisted pasta with a bold tomato, almond and basil pesto from Trapani, on Sicily's western coast, where locals reimagined pesto using ingredients that grow abundantly in the region. Unlike the Genovese version, Pesto Trapanese combines tomatoes, almonds, garlic and basil into a vibrant and textured sauce. I like to use datterino tomatoes for their natural sweetness, but any ripe cherry-size variety will work. The pasta shape itself is named after the *busa*, a reed traditionally used to twist each strand into a spiral. This recipe is a celebration of simplicity and resourcefulness, capturing deep flavour with just a few ingredients and a bit of care.

Serves: 4

Preparation time: 30 minutes, plus 30 minutes resting

Cooking time: 10 minutes

For the Dough:

* 400g/14oz/3 cups semola
* 200ml/7fl oz/scant 1 cup lukewarm water

For the Pesto Trapanese:

* 300g/10½oz/2 cups datterino or ciliegino tomatoes, chopped
* 85g/3oz/½ cup almonds, blanched and peeled
* 1 garlic clove
* 50g/1¾oz/2 cups packed fresh basil leaves
* 80ml/2¾fl oz/⅓ cup extra virgin olive oil, plus extra to serve
* Salt and pepper, to taste
* Finely grated Pecorino, to serve (optional)

Make the Dough: On a clean work surface, make a mound of semola and create a well in the centre. Gradually add the water, mixing with your fingers or a fork to incorporate the semola until a rough dough forms. Knead the dough for about 5–7 minutes until smooth and elastic. Cover with a dish towel and let rest for 30 minutes.

Make the Pesto Trapanese: In a food processor, combine the datterino tomatoes, almonds, garlic and basil leaves. Pulse until the ingredients are roughly chopped. With the processor running, slowly drizzle in the olive oil until the mixture reaches a smooth but still slightly chunky consistency. Season with salt and pepper to taste. For a deeper flavour, add a little extra olive oil if desired. Set aside.

Shape the Busiate: Lightly dust a tray and work surface with semola. Cut off a small piece of rested dough, about the size of a golf ball, and roll it into a rope about the thickness of a pencil. Cut into 4–5cm/1¾in lengths. Roll each piece diagonally around a thin wooden skewer, knitting needle or traditional *ferretto* to form a spiral. Slide it off gently, dust with semola and place on the prepared tray, keeping them covered as you work. Repeat with the remaining dough.

Cook the Busiate: Bring a large pot of salted water to the boil. Add the busiate and cook for 8–10 minutes, or until al dente.

Combine and Serve: Using a slotted spoon, lift the pasta directly onto a serving plate with the pesto. Toss gently to coat, adding a splash of cooking water if needed to help the sauce cling evenly. Serve with a sprinkle of grated Pecorino, if desired, and an extra drizzle of olive oil.

Note: For an added twist, try lightly toasting the almonds before blending them. This adds a rich, nutty depth to the pesto, enhancing the natural sweetness of the tomatoes.

ORECCHIETTE WITH BROCCOLI RABE & ZESTY PANGRATTATO

Orecchiette alle cime di rapa e pangrattato alle zeste

A classic southern Italian dish where humble broccoli rabe meet bright, zesty breadcrumbs for a perfectly balanced and comforting meal. This dish hails from the southern Italian region of Puglia, where *cime di rapa* (broccoli rabe) reigns as a beloved staple. In Sicily, however, we often use other wild and bitter greens, like *cavolicelli* (wild broccoli greens), *bietole* (chard), *nivia* (chicory/endives), *lassini* or *sinapu* (both kinds of wild mustard). These earthy, slightly bitter greens have long been cherished for their health benefits and their ability to bring depth to simple dishes. If *cime di rapa* aren't available where you are, this recipe adapts beautifully with local alternatives like Tenderstem or purple sprouting broccoli, or even regular broccoli, using the small florets and leaves. The citrus-flavoured breadcrumbs in this version aren't traditional but add a zesty note that brightens the bitterness, creating a balanced, flavourful dish. *Orecchiette* is one of the most iconic hand-shaped pastas: a simple yet essential shape to master, making it a perfect starting point for anyone learning the art of pasta making.

Serves: 4

Preparation time: 30 minutes, plus 30 minutes resting

Cooking time: 10 minutes

For the Dough:

* 400g/14oz/3 cups semola
* 200ml/7fl oz/scant 1 cup lukewarm water

For the Sauce:

* 4 tbsp extra virgin olive oil
* 2 garlic cloves, thinly sliced or minced
* 1–2 small red chillies, chopped, to taste
* 1 large bunch of broccoli rabe (*cime di rapa*) or any bitter green of your preference, trimmed and rinsed
* Salt, to taste

For the Zesty Breadcrumbs:

* 2 tbsp extra virgin olive oil
* 50g/1¾oz/½ cup breadcrumbs
* Zest of 1 unwaxed lemon
* Zest of 1 orange
* Salt, to taste

Make the Dough: On a clean work surface, make a mound with the semola and create a well in the centre. Gradually add the water, mixing with your fingers or a fork to incorporate the semola until a rough dough forms. Knead for 5–7 minutes until smooth and elastic. Cover with a dish towel and let rest for 30 minutes.

Sauté the Broccoli Rabe: In a large frying pan, heat the olive oil over a medium heat. Add the garlic and chilli and sauté for 2 minutes until fragrant. Add the broccoli rabe and salt to taste and toss everything together until the greens are wilted. Set aside.

Prepare the Zesty Breadcrumbs: In a small pan, heat the olive oil over a medium heat. Add the breadcrumbs and toast for 3–5 minutes, stirring frequently, until golden and crisp. Add the lemon and orange zests and stir for another minute until fragrant. Season with a pinch of salt and set aside.

Shape the Orecchiette: Lightly dust a tray and work surface with semola. Cut the rested dough into 4 equal pieces and roll each into long ropes about 1cm/⅓in thick. Cut the ropes into small pieces, roughly the size of a thumbnail. You should get around 80–100 pieces in total. Press each piece with a butter knife, dragging it slightly toward you to form a coin-size disc, then turn it inside-out to create the traditional "ear" shape. Place the orecchiette on the tray to prevent sticking and keep covered as you work.

Cook the Orecchiette: Bring a large pot of salted water to the boil. Cook the orecchiette for 3–4 minutes, or until they float to the surface for al dente pasta, or leave for another minute for a more tender texture.

Combine and Serve: Remove the pasta from the pan with a slotted spoon or drain gently in a colander, reserving a ladleful of pasta water, and add directly to the broccoli rabe. Toss well to combine, adding a splash of cooking water if needed to help the sauce cling evenly. Season with salt to taste. Divide the orecchiette between plates, topping each with the zesty breadcrumbs. Serve immediately.

FARFALLE WITH COURGETTE/ ZUCCHINI, PEAS & MINT

Farfalle con zucchine, piselli e menta

Serves: 4

Preparation time: 40 minutes, plus 30 minutes resting

Cooking time: 15 minutes

For the Dough:

* 400g/14oz/3 cups 00 flour
* 4 eggs

For the Sauce:

* 2 tbsp extra virgin olive oil, plus extra to serve
* 1 garlic clove, finely chopped
* 1 courgette/zucchini, thinly sliced
* 150g/5¼oz/1 cup fresh or frozen peas
* Zest of 1 unwaxed lemon
* 30g/1oz/¼ cup Pecorino, finely grated, plus extra to serve
* A handful of fresh mint leaves, finely chopped
* Salt and pepper, to taste

Master the art of shaping farfalle by hand while embracing the bright, delicate flavours of seasonal vegetables. There's something joyful about farfalle. Their delicate ruffled edges and pinched centres make them feel whimsical, as if they were always meant for light, fresh flavours. This dish reminds me of long summer evenings, when courgettes/zucchini are at their sweetest and mint grows wild in the garden. The farfalle are hand-shaped, their soft curves catching just enough of the sauce: a simple medley of courgette, peas and a touch of lemon, bound together with olive oil and Pecorino. It's the kind of meal that feels effortless but lingers in your memory, bright and full of life.

Make the Dough: On a clean work surface, make a mound with the flour and create a well in the centre. Crack in the eggs and whisk gently with a fork, gradually incorporating the flour until a rough dough forms. Knead for 5–7 minutes until smooth and elastic. Cover with a dish towel and let rest for 30 minutes.

Cook the Sauce: Heat the olive oil in a large frying pan over a medium heat. Add the garlic and sauté for 30 seconds until fragrant. Stir in the courgette/ zucchini and cook for 3–4 minutes until just tender. Add the peas and a splash of water, seasoning with salt and pepper. Let everything cook together for another 2–3 minutes, just until the peas are bright green and tender. Set aside.

Shape the Farfalle: Lightly dust a tray and work surface with flour. Roll out the rested dough into a thin sheet, about 1.2–1.5mm thick (setting 4 on a Marcato). Using a fluted pasta cutter or a knife, cut the dough into small rectangles, about 4 x 3cm/1½ x 1¼in. Pinch each rectangle in the centre to form the classic farfalle shape. Lightly dust with flour and set on the tray, and keep covered as you work.

Cook the Farfalle: Bring a large pot of salted water to the boil. Cook the farfalle for around 3–4 minutes, or until they float and are al dente.

Combine and Serve: Using a slotted spoon, lift the farfalle directly into the pan with the courgette and peas. Toss gently to coat, adding a splash of cooking water if needed to help the sauce cling evenly. Stir in the lemon zest, Pecorino and fresh mint, mixing gently so everything is well coated. Drizzle with a little extra olive oil and scatter over more Pecorino. Serve immediately.

SPAGHETTI PUTTANESCA WITH BURRATA

Spaghetti alla puttanesca con burrata

Serves: 4

Preparation time: 20 minutes, plus 30 minutes resting

Cooking time: 25 minutes

For the Dough:

* 400g/14oz/3 cups 00 flour
* 4 eggs

For the Sauce:

* 3 tbsp extra virgin olive oil, plus extra to finish
* 2 garlic cloves, unpeeled, lightly crushed (*in camicia*)
* 1–2 red chillies, sliced lengthways, to taste
* 2 tbsp capers in brine, rinsed
* 2 tbsp raisins
* 500ml/17fl oz/2 cups tomato passata
* 100g/3½oz/½ cup pitted black or green olives
* 1 tsp sugar
* Salt, to taste

To Serve:

* 1 large ball burrata, torn
* A handful of fresh basil leaves (optional)

A homemade egg pasta with a spicy, chunky Southern Italian sauce and a big fat burrata to finish, because . . . why not? My dad hated olives. He hated them so much that whenever we brought them to the table, he would put a hand over his nose and, in the most theatrical way, cry out, "Take them away! Take them away!" His aversion became a family joke. At big gatherings, someone (typically my uncle Salvatore) would slide a plate of olives under his nose just to watch his reaction. I, on the other hand, adore them. I loved olives enough for both of us. So naturally, *puttanesca* became one of my favourite sauces. This version draws on different Southern interpretations. It's rustic, bold and finished with a soft cloud of burrata that melts into the sauce. This dish is messy and unapologetic, and it's just the way I like it.

Make the Dough: On a clean work surface, make a mound with the flour and create a well in the centre. Crack in the eggs and gently whisk with a fork, gradually incorporating the flour until a rough dough forms. Knead for 5–7 minutes until smooth and elastic. Cover with a dish towel and let rest for 30 minutes.

Make the Sauce: Heat the olive oil in a large frying pan over a medium heat. Add the garlic *in camicia*. This traditional method gently perfumes the oil without letting the garlic burn or overpower the sauce. Sauté for about 30 seconds, then add the sliced chillies and cook for another 30 seconds, until fragrant. Stir in the rinsed capers, season lightly with salt and sauté for 1–2 minutes. Add the raisins and reduce the heat slightly, allowing them to soften in the oil for about 30 seconds. Add the passata, olives, sugar and about half a ladle of water. Cover and simmer gently for 12–15 minutes, stirring occasionally. Add a splash more water if needed.

Roll and Cut the Spaghetti: Lightly dust a tray and work surface with flour. Divide the rested dough into 4–6 portions. Roll each piece into a thin sheet, about 1mm thick (setting 5 on a Marcato). If you have a spaghetti cutter attachment for your pasta machine, pass the sheets through, dust lightly with flour and place them on the tray. If cutting by hand, fold the sheet loosely and slice into very thin strands, about 3mm/⅛in wide, keeping the thickness as even as possible for uniform cooking. Gently separate the strands, dust with flour and arrange on the tray, and keep covered as you work.

Cook and Serve: Bring a large pot of salted water to the boil. Cook the spaghetti for 2–3 minutes, or until al dente. Before you combine the pasta and sauce, remove the whole garlic cloves from the sauce. Then, using tongs, lift the pasta directly into the pan with the sauce. Toss gently to coat, adding a splash of cooking water if needed to help the sauce cling evenly. Divide between plates, top each portion with torn burrata and a few basil leaves, if desired, and drizzle a little extra olive oil over the burrata. Serve immediately.

PICI WITH CARROT TOP PESTO

Pici con pesto di foglie di carota

A naturally vegan dish, this recipe combines hand-rolled pici (one of the easiest hand-rolled pasta shapes) with a bright, sustainable carrot top pesto. The art of pasta making is about finding beauty in simplicity, and pici is a perfect example. This Tuscan pasta requires just flour, olive oil, water and patience, transforming these humble ingredients into thick, rustic strands. But it's the carrot top pesto that makes this dish special: an inventive way to use ingredients that are often discarded. Carrot tops have a fresh, herbal taste that's slightly reminiscent of parsley, while toasted almonds and a hint of lemon balance and brighten the flavour. This dish is a celebration of both tradition and creativity, making use of every part of the vegetable in a deliciously mindful way. For this recipe, we're using 0 flour, which is slightly coarser than 00 flour. If 0 isn't available, a blend of 00 flour and semola works beautifully.

Serves: 4

Preparation time: 30 minutes, plus 30 minutes resting

Cooking time: 10 minutes

For the Dough:

* 400g/14oz/3 cups 00 flour (or 270g/9½oz/2 cups 00 flour + 130g/4½oz/1 cup semola)
* 1 tbsp extra virgin olive oil
* 200ml/7fl oz/scant 1 cup lukewarm water

For the Carrot Top Pesto:

* 100g/3½oz/2 cups loosely packed carrot tops, tough stems removed
* 40g/1½oz/¼ cup toasted almonds, plus extra (chopped) to garnish
* Zest and juice of 1 small unwaxed lemon
* 1 garlic clove, minced
* 60ml/2fl oz/¼ cup extra virgin olive oil
* Salt and pepper, to taste
* A few small carrot tops and/or fresh basil leaves, to garnish

Make the Dough: On a clean work surface, make a mound with the flour and create a well in the centre. Add the olive oil and gradually add the water, mixing with your fingers or a fork until a rough dough forms. Knead for 5–7 minutes until smooth and elastic. Cover with a dish towel and let rest for 30 minutes.

Prepare the Carrot Top Pesto: In a food processor, combine the carrot tops, toasted almonds, lemon zest, lemon juice and minced garlic. Pulse until coarsely chopped. With the processor running, slowly drizzle in the extra virgin olive oil until the pesto reaches a smooth, slightly chunky consistency. Season with salt and pepper to taste. Set aside.

Shape the Pici: Lightly dust a tray and work surface with flour. Divide the rested dough into small portions roughly the size of a golf ball, and roll each portion into long, thick strands about 3mm/⅛in in diameter, similar to spaghetti but thicker. Keep the strands dusted lightly with flour and set on the floured tray. Keep covered as you work.

Cook the Pici: Bring a large pot of salted water to the boil. Cook the pici for 5–7 minutes, or until al dente.

Combine and Serve: Using tongs, lift the pasta directly into a large bowl with the pesto. Toss gently to coat, adding a splash of cooking water if needed to help the sauce cling evenly. Divide the pici among plates, and garnish with extra chopped toasted almonds and a few small carrot tops and/or basil leaves. Serve immediately.

MALTAGLIATI WITH ASPARAGUS, LEMON & PECORINO CRISPS

Maltagliati con asparagi, limone e cialde di pecorino

Serves: 4

Preparation time: 20 minutes, plus 30 minutes resting

Cooking time: 15 minutes

For the Dough:

* 400g/14oz/3 cups 00 flour
* 4 eggs

For the Pecorino Crisps & Sauce:

* 100g/3½oz/1 cup Pecorino, finely grated
* 2 tbsp extra virgin olive oil, plus extra to finish
* 1 garlic clove, finely chopped
* 1 bunch of asparagus (300g/10½oz), trimmed and cut into bite-size pieces
* Zest of 1 unwaxed lemon, plus juice of ½ lemon
* Salt and pepper, to taste

An effortlessly rustic pasta shape paired with crisp Pecorino wafers and the delicate flavours of spring. Maltagliati, which means "badly cut," originated in Emilia-Romagna to use the leftover trimmings from more precise pasta shapes like tagliatelle. These scraps were never wasted but rather gathered and transformed into a meal in their own right. Today, maltagliati stands on its own as a celebration of rustic tradition: irregular, playful and full of charm. In this version, the simplicity of the shape meets the elegance of crisp Pecorino wafers and the brightness of asparagus and lemon. It's a dish that proves even the humblest cuts can carry extraordinary flavour.

Make the Dough: On a clean work surface, make a mound with the flour and create a well in the centre. Crack in all the eggs and whisk gently with a fork, gradually incorporating the flour until a dough forms. Knead for 5–7 minutes until smooth and elastic. Cover with a dish towel and let rest for 30 minutes.

Make the Pecorino Crisps: Heat a large, non-stick frying pan over a low heat. Add small mounds of the grated Pecorino (about 1 tablespoon each) and flatten them slightly with the back of a spoon. Cook gently (in batches) for 4–5 minutes until melted and golden around the edges. Leave to cool in the pan for a few seconds before transferring to a plate to crisp up.

Cook the Sauce: Heat the olive oil in a large pan over a medium heat. Add the garlic and sauté for 30 seconds until fragrant. Stir in the asparagus and cook for 3–4 minutes until just tender. Add the lemon zest and juice, season with salt and pepper, and remove from the heat.

Shape the Maltagliati: Lightly dust a tray and work surface with flour. Divide the rested dough into 4–6 portions. Roll each piece into a thin sheet, about 1.2–1.5mm thick (setting 4 on a Marcato). Using a knife or pasta cutter, cut into irregular, uneven shapes: triangles, rhombuses, strips . . . whatever feels natural. Lightly dust with flour and set on the tray, and keep covered as you work.

Cook the Maltagliati: Bring a large pot of salted water to the boil. Drop in the maltagliati and cook for 2–3 minutes, or until al dente.

Combine and Serve: Using a slotted spoon, lift the pasta directly into the pan with the asparagus. Toss gently to coat, adding a splash of cooking water if needed to help the sauce cling evenly. Drizzle with a little extra olive oil and gently toss everything together. Divide the pasta between plates, add broken up pieces of the Pecorino crisps and serve immediately.

CREAMY TAGLIOLINI WITH MONK'S BEARD, LEMON & PECORINO

Tagliolini con barba di frate, limone e pecorino

A silky, citrus-scented sauce wraps around every strand of tagliolini. The monk's beard brings a touch of bitterness, the lemon lifts it and the Pecorino brings it all home. Monk's beard, or *barba di frate*, is a curious green. Slightly grassy, a little bitter, often tangled and unruly, and yet when cooked gently and given the right companions, it becomes something elegant. I discovered it while living in London, sold in small bunches at Italian delis in early spring and I've loved it ever since, sautéed in pasta or folded into an omelette. My mum never cooked with it, which makes it feel like a small adventure every time I do. This dish is about celebrating seasonal finds and letting a few good ingredients speak for themselves.

Serves: 4

Preparation time: 20 minutes, plus 30 minutes resting

Cooking time: 15 minutes

For the Dough:

* 400g/14oz/3 cups semola
* 4 eggs

For the Sauce:

* 200g/7oz/2 cups loosely packed monk's beard, trimmed and rinsed
* 1½ tbsp unsalted butter
* 100ml/3½fl oz/scant ½ cup double cream/heavy cream
* Zest and juice of 1 unwaxed lemon
* 1 red chilli, finely chopped, or a pinch of dried chilli/hot pepper flakes
* 60g/2oz/⅔ cup Pecorino, finely grated, plus extra to serve
* Salt and pepper, to taste

Make the Dough: On a clean work surface, make a mound with the semola and create a well in the centre. Crack in the eggs and whisk gently with a fork, gradually incorporating the semola until a rough dough forms. Knead for 5–7 minutes until smooth and elastic. Cover with a dish towel and let rest for 30 minutes.

Prepare the Sauce: Bring a medium saucepan of salted water to the boil and blanch the monk's beard for 1–2 minutes, just until tender. Drain and set aside. In a wide pan, melt the butter over a low heat. Add the cream, most of the lemon zest (set some aside for garnish), the lemon juice and chilli. Simmer gently for 2–3 minutes, then stir in the grated Pecorino. Season with salt and pepper and keep warm.

Shape the Tagliolini: Lightly dust a tray and work surface with semola. Divide the rested dough into 4–6 portions. Roll each piece to about 1mm thick (setting 5 on a Marcato), then cut into fine ribbons of 3mm/⅛in width using either a tagliolini cutter or by hand with a sharp knife. Dust with semola and set on the tray, and keep covered as you work.

Cook the Tagliolini: Bring a large pot of salted water to the boil. Cook the tagliolini for 1–2 minutes, until al dente.

Combine and Serve: Using tongs, lift the pasta directly into the pan with the sauce. Add the cooked monk's beard and toss gently to coat everything in the sauce, adding a splash of cooking water if needed to help the sauce cling evenly. Plate immediately with an extra grating of Pecorino and the reserved lemon zest.

CLASSIC GNOCCHI ALLA SORRENTINA

Gnocchi alla sorrentina

Serves: 4

Preparation time: 40 minutes

Cooking time: 1 hour 15 minutes

For the Dough:

* 800g/1¾lb floury potatoes (about 4 medium-large), preferably old
* 200g/7oz/1½ cups plain/all-purpose flour
* 1 egg, lightly beaten

For the Sauce:

* 3 tbsp extra virgin olive oil
* 1 small garlic clove, lightly crushed
* 400g/14oz/2 cups canned peeled tomatoes, crushed by hand or with a fork
* A few fresh basil leaves, torn
* Salt, to taste

To Finish:

* 200g/7oz/1½ cups mozzarella, torn into small pieces
* 40g/1½oz/⅓ cup Parmigiano Reggiano, finely grated

Soft, hand-rolled potato gnocchi baked in a bubbling tomato and mozzarella sauce. A dish that comforts deeply and teaches you how to slow down. Gnocchi wasn't something my mother made often. It wasn't part of our usual repertoire, which made it all the more surprising when I first served this dish to my dad and discovered he had never tried it. Though born and raised in Sicily, his roots were Campanian, and yet this classic had somehow escaped him. When he tasted it, not long before he passed away, he was genuinely taken aback. I can still see the look on his face as it stirred something in him, something unexpected and warm. That memory makes this dish bittersweet for me. I always carry a trace of that moment with me when I make it. And I make it often. This was the very first recipe I taught at my *Pasta Therapy* workshops, and it's still one I return to again and again. It's simple, yes, but also special. Old potatoes work best for gnocchi, as they are drier and starchier than fresh. Their lower water content means you need less flour to form the dough, resulting in light, fluffy gnocchi rather than dense and heavy ones.

Prepare the Gnocchi: Boil the potatoes with their skins on until extremely soft, about 40–45 minutes. Drain, then while still warm, peel and mash them until smooth, using a ricer if you have one. Leave to cool slightly. Add the flour and egg. Mix quickly and lightly until just combined; do not overwork. Lightly dust a tray and work surface with flour. Roll the dough into ropes and cut into bite-size pieces. If you like, roll them gently against the tines of a fork. Dust lightly with flour and set on the tray, and keep covered as you work.

Make the Sauce: Heat the olive oil in a pan over a medium-low heat and sauté the garlic gently until golden, about 3–4 minutes. Add the tomatoes and a pinch of salt. Simmer, uncovered, for 15–20 minutes, until thickened. Stir in the torn basil, discard the garlic, then remove from the heat.

Cook the Gnocchi: Bring a large pot of salted water to the boil. Drop in the gnocchi in batches and cook for 2–3 minutes. They're ready when they float to the surface. Remove with a slotted spoon and transfer to a large bowl.

Assemble and Bake: Preheat the oven to 200°C/400°F/Gas Mark 6. In a baking dish, layer the gnocchi with spoonfuls of the tomato sauce, some mozzarella and a sprinkle of Parmigiano. Repeat until everything is used up, finishing with a bit of Parmigiano on top. Bake for 15–20 minutes, until bubbling and golden.

Serve: Let rest for a couple of minutes before serving, just enough time to let the cheese settle, but not so much that it stops stringing.

RICOTTA & SPINACH GNUDI WITH BUTTER & SAGE

Gnudi di ricotta e spinaci al burro e salvia

Soft, pillowy dumplings made with ricotta and spinach, lightly floured and served in a classic sage-infused butter. There's something deeply satisfying about gnudi. No machines, no fancy technique, no pasta sheets to roll. Just a bowl of filling and your hands. Anyone can shape these little dumplings. You don't even need a table: just your palms. I like to blend the spinach because it gives a smooth, almost creamy texture and a vibrant green colour. But some people just chop it up with a knife and call it a day. Honestly, do whatever feels right. That's the beauty of this dish. It's simple and deeply comforting, with nothing to prove.

Serves: 4

Preparation time: 30 minutes, plus 30 minutes chilling

Cooking time: 10 minutes

For the Dough:

* 250g/9oz/1 cup ricotta, well drained
* 250g/9oz/1½ cup cooked spinach, squeezed dry and finely chopped or puréed, according to your preference
* 40g/1½oz/⅓ cup Parmigiano Reggiano, finely grated
* 1 egg
* 1–2 tbsp plain/all-purpose flour
* Freshly grated nutmeg, to taste
* Salt and pepper, to taste

For the Sage Butter:

* 80g/2¾oz/⅓ cup unsalted butter
* 10–12 fresh sage leaves
* Salt, to taste
* Finely grated Parmigiano Reggiano, to serve

Make the Gnudi: In a bowl, combine the ricotta, spinach, Parmigiano, egg and a tablespoon of flour. Season with some nutmeg and salt and pepper. Mix gently until just combined. If the mixture is very soft, add a touch more flour, but keep it light.

Shape the Gnudi: Dust your hands and a tray with flour. Scoop out small spoonfuls of the mixture and shape into walnut-size balls. Roll each one lightly in flour and place on the tray. Chill for 30 minutes to help them firm up.

Make the Sage Butter: Melt the butter in a wide frying pan over a medium-low heat. Add the sage leaves and fry gently until the butter turns golden and the sage is crisp, about 2–3 minutes. Season with salt.

Cook the Gnudi: At the same time, bring a large pot of salted water to the boil. Gently lower the gnudi into the water and cook until they float to the surface, about 2–3 minutes. Let them bob there for another minute, then remove with a slotted spoon straight onto serving plates.

Serve: Spoon the sage butter over the gnudi. Finish with a dusting of Parmigiano.

Ch. 3

THE THERAPY of Tradition

What I remember most about growing up in Sicily are the little things. My dad's hands smelling of oranges. My mum doing the dishes, half-turned toward the TV. In summer, the blinds stayed closed and the kitchen door was left ajar, though it never helped much: the sun was too harsh, and we didn't have air conditioning. The smell of tomato sauce simmering on the hob/stovetop, and mum's voice rising above the TV. There were always the same things on the table: bread, fresh ricotta and provolone, a jar of olives, marinated aubergines/eggplants and *capuliato* (sun-dried tomato relish). Coffee came after, sometimes with *pasticcini* (small assorted Italian pastries): a gift from dad, not for any special occasion but just because.

My maternal nonna Peppina doesn't feature much in this book. She had a stroke before I was born and lived with us but couldn't speak, move or cook. Yet I remember her stern but affectionate look as she held me. I remember patting her legs shouting, "*Cammina! Cammina!*" ("Walk! Walk!"), not comprehending why she wouldn't rise from her wheelchair. Her recipes lived on through my mamma Giovanna, who carried them forward, sometimes adapting them.

Some recipes in this chapter come from my other nonna Maria, who brought her loud presence and the flavours of her native Benghazi into our kitchen. Others come from zia Rita, who had an authority in the kitchen that nobody questioned. My papà, Riccardo, features too. He rarely cooked, but the way he treated a well-prepared meal made it feel sacred.

These are the recipes I reach for when I want to feel anchored. When everything feels uncertain, I stir a pot of something that's been made a hundred times and think of the people who've cooked it before me. Now that the most important people in my life are gone, these dishes carry more than flavour. They hold memories, voices and laughter I thought had faded.

If you've ever cooked something that reminded you of a loved one, you know that sense of closeness. If you're grieving or missing home, make something that ties you to those memories. It doesn't have to be perfect. It just has to be yours.

MUM'S RICOTTA RAVIOLI WITH SUGO FINTO

Ravioli della mamma con sugo finto

Sweet ricotta-filled ravioli from Ragusa, served with a spiced, meatless sauce. This is the dish my mum made whenever our relatives came over. Ravioli always shared the spotlight with tagliatelle; both served together and covered in sauce and copious quantities of grated caciocavallo cheese. If there were any leftovers (rare), they'd be pan-fried on Monday into something we called pasta fritta.

The ricotta filling is traditional to my hometown, Ragusa. My mum made these with a slow-cooked pork and sausage sauce, but here I use a version that skips the meat and keeps the depth. *Sugo finto*, or "fake ragù", uses onion, carrot, celery, fennel seeds and chilli to bring out the flavours you'd expect from sausage, without the heaviness. The sweet filling and the spicy sauce balance each other beautifully.

Serves: 4

Preparation time: 40 minutes, plus 30 minutes resting

Cooking time: 1 hour 45 minutes

For the Dough:

* 400g/14oz/3 cups semola
* 4 eggs

For the Ricotta Filling:

* 500g/17½oz/2 cups ricotta, well drained
* 2 tbsp chopped fresh marjoram (optional)
* 1½ tsp sugar
* Salt, to taste

For the Sugo Finto:

* 4 tbsp extra virgin olive oil
* ½ red onion, finely chopped
* ½ brown onion, finely chopped
* 1 carrot, finely chopped
* 1 celery stalk, finely chopped
* 1 bay leaf
* 60ml/2fl oz/¼ cup white wine
* 400g/14oz/2 cups tomato passata or polpa di pomodoro
* 1 tsp fennel seeds
* 1 small red chilli, minced
* 1 tsp sugar
* Salt, to taste

To Serve:

* Finely grated caciocavallo or Parmigiano Reggiano (optional)
* Fresh basil leaves, to garnish

Make the Dough: On a clean work surface, make a mound with the semola and create a well in the centre. Crack in the eggs and whisk gently with a fork, gradually incorporating the semola until a rough dough forms. Knead for 5–7 minutes until smooth and elastic. Cover with a dish towel and let rest for 30 minutes.

Prepare the Ricotta Filling: Ensure the ricotta is well drained of all water. In a bowl, mix the drained ricotta with the chopped marjoram, if using, the sugar and a pinch of salt. Taste and adjust the seasoning if needed. Set aside in the refrigerator while the dough rests.

Make the Sugo Finto: In a large saucepan, heat the olive oil over a medium heat. Add the red and brown onions, carrot, celery and bay leaf, and sauté gently until softened, about 10 minutes. Add the white wine and stir until it evaporates. Stir in the passata, fennel seeds, chilli and sugar. Season with salt and bring to a gentle simmer. Let the sauce cook, uncovered, over a low heat for 1–1½ hours, stirring occasionally, until it thickens and the flavours are well developed.

Roll and Fill the Ravioli: Lightly dust a tray and work surface with semola. Divide the rested dough into 4–6 portions. Roll each piece into a long thin sheet about 1mm thick (setting 5 on a Marcato).

Starting from the right-hand side of the sheet, leaving about 2cm/¾in from the edge, place a teaspoon of ricotta filling. Continue adding dollops of filling along the sheet, spacing them 3–4cm/1½in apart until you reach the other end. Fold the sheet over itself horizontally so the filling is enclosed. Using the sides of both hands, gently press the dough around each mound of ricotta to seal and space them out. This helps remove any air and ensures the ravioli hold together when cooked. Use a ravioli stamp to cut out each raviolo. I use a round, sun-shaped stamp that belonged to my mum and was in her hands for more than 50 years. If you don't have a stamp, a glass, cookie cutter, pastry wheel or even a small knife will do the job just fine. Place the finished ravioli on the tray and keep covered as you work.

Cook the Ravioli and Serve: Bring a large pot of salted water to the boil. Gently drop the ravioli into the water and cook for 2–3 minutes, until they float and the texture is al dente. Before you combine the pasta and sauce, remove the bay leaf from the sauce. Then, use a slotted spoon to lift the ravioli directly into the warm sauce and toss gently to coat. Serve immediately with a generous amount of grated caciocavallo, if desired, and some fresh basil to garnish.

ANGEL HAIR WITH MUM'S DILL & CAPER PESTO

Capelli d'angelo al pesto di aneto e capperi della mamma

A bright, aromatic dish with dill and capers that carries the very essence of Mediterranean flavours. Capers are one of Sicily's treasures, especially those from the island of Pantelleria, where they develop an intense, briny flavour thanks to the sun and sea. My mum had a special recipe for caper pesto, which she made just for me, knowing how much I loved bold flavours. But she hated dill! She was forced to eat it as a child and it left a lasting trauma, but even so, she made this pesto.

This pesto has become one of my favourites. The dill adds a fresh, aromatic twist to the capers, balancing their bold, briny flavours with the bright, sweet notes of the herb. It's a dish that always reminds me of my mum and the lengths she would go to make me happy, putting our family first and herself second. It's a reflection of the sacrifices she made and the special bond we will always share.

Serves: 4

Preparation time: 30 minutes, plus 30 minutes resting

Cooking time: 5 minutes

For the Dough:

* 200g/7oz/1½ cups 00 flour
* 200g/7oz/1½ cups semola
* 6 egg yolks, plus 1 whole egg

For the Pesto:

* 50g/1¾oz/2 cups packed fresh dill, thick stems removed, plus extra leaves to garnish
* 45g/1½oz/3 tbsp capers, rinsed
* 60g/2oz/½ cup pine nuts, toasted, plus extra to garnish
* 1 small garlic clove (optional)
* Zest and juice of 1 unwaxed lemon, plus extra zest to garnish
* 4 tbsp extra virgin olive oil
* Salt and pepper, to taste

Make the Dough: On a clean work surface, make a mound with the flour and semola and create a well in the centre. Add the egg yolks and whole egg into the well and whisk gently with a fork, gradually incorporating the flour and semola until a rough dough forms. Knead for 5–7 minutes until smooth and elastic. Cover with a dish towel and let rest for 30 minutes.

Prepare the Pesto: In a food processor, combine the dill, capers, toasted pine nuts and garlic, if using. Pulse until coarsely chopped. Add the lemon zest and juice and slowly drizzle in the olive oil while blending until the pesto reaches a smooth, slightly chunky consistency. Season with salt and pepper to taste. Set aside.

Cut the Angel Hair: Lightly dust a tray and work surface with flour. Divide the rested dough into 4–6 portions. Roll each piece into a very thin sheet, about 0.8–1mm thick (setting 6 on a Marcato). Cut the sheets into long, fine strips about 1mm wide with a sharp knife. Dust with flour and set aside on the tray. Keep covered as you work.

Cook the Angel Hair: Bring a large pot of salted water to the boil. Cook the angel hair for 2–3 minutes, or until al dente.

Combine and Serve: Using tongs, lift the pasta directly into a large bowl. Toss the angel hair with the dill and caper pesto. Add a splash of pasta water if needed to help the sauce cling evenly and mix gently until combined. Garnish the angel hair with extra lemon zest, dill and pine nuts for added texture and brightness.

SPELT TAGLIATELLE WITH SUN-DRIED TOMATO PESTO

Tagliatelle al pesto degli iblei

Serves: 4

Preparation time: 30 minutes, plus 30 minutes resting

Cooking time: 5 minutes

For the Dough:

* 400g/14oz/3 cups spelt flour
* 4 eggs

For the Pesto:

* 60g/2oz/½ cup sun-dried tomatoes, soaked and drained
* 1 tbsp tomato purée/paste
* 50g/1¾oz/½ cup almonds, blanched
* 20g/¾oz/1 cup loosely packed fresh dill or wild fennel fronds
* 4–5 fresh oregano leaves
* 2–3 large fresh basil leaves
* ½ tsp fennel seeds
* 50g/1¾oz/½ cup Pecorino, finely grated
* 80ml/2¾fl oz/⅓ cup extra virgin olive oil
* Salt, to taste

Every ingredient in this dish takes me back to Sicily. The sun-dried tomatoes, with their pungent, tangy aroma, remind me of hot summers spent drying them on the roof, their scent filling the house. Fennel seeds, that familiar spice, bring to mind both sweet and savoury dishes (from spicy sausages to the fragrant Sicilian doughnuts called *sfinci*). Then there's dill, or aneto, a sweet herb woven through many Sicilian dishes. And the almonds are a taste of my dad's province, Siracusa, an area famous for producing some of the finest nuts. For the pasta, I use spelt flour (farro), one of Sicily's *grani antichi* (ancient grains – this variety is called *perciasacchi* back home), prized for its wholesome flavour and deep connection to the island's agricultural roots. I chose tagliatelle, just like my mum used to make for our Sunday gatherings, to celebrate these flavours, each one holding a piece of home and memory.

Make the Dough: On a clean work surface, make a mound with the flour and create a well in the centre. Crack in the eggs and whisk gently with a fork, gradually incorporating the flour until a rough dough forms. Knead for 5–7 minutes until smooth and elastic. Cover with a dish towel and let rest for 30 minutes.

Make the Pesto: In a food processor or blender, combine the sun-dried tomatoes, tomato purée/paste, almonds, all the herbs, fennel seeds and half of the Pecorino. Pulse to form a coarse paste. Gradually add the olive oil while pulsing until the pesto reaches a smooth consistency. Season with salt to taste. Set aside.

Roll and Cut the Tagliatelle: Lightly dust a tray and work surface with flour. Divide the rested dough into 2–4 pieces. Roll each piece into a thin sheet, about 1mm thick (setting 5 on a Marcato). Cut into long strips about 6–8mm/⅓in wide to form tagliatelle. Dust with flour and set on the tray, and keep covered as you work.

Cook the Tagliatelle: Bring a large pot of salted water to the boil. Add the tagliatelle and cook for about 3–5 minutes, or until al dente.

Combine and Serve: Using tongs, lift the pasta directly into a large bowl with the pesto. Toss gently to coat, adding a splash of cooking water if needed to help the sauce cling evenly. Adjust the seasoning if necessary. Serve topped with the remaining grated Pecorino.

PAOLA'S PISTACHIO SPAGHETTI ALLA CHITARRA

Spaghetti alla chitarra con pistacchi e capperi

Serves: 4

Preparation time: 30 minutes, plus 30 minutes resting

Cooking time: 5 minutes

For the Dough:

* 400g/14oz/3 cups semola
* 4 eggs

For the Sauce:

* 3 tbsp extra virgin olive oil
* 1 garlic clove, minced
* 1 tbsp capers in brine, rinsed and finely minced
* 60g/2oz/½ cup ground pistachios
* Salt, to taste

For Garnish:

* Chopped pistachios or unwaxed lemon zest (optional)

A five-ingredient sauce from my sister Paola. While I cook with instinct and a pinch of chaos, she brings science, technique and order into the kitchen (she's a scientist by trade, after all). She came up with this pasta one day, and I've been obsessed with it ever since. It's so simple it feels like cheating: just a few pantry staples, a swirl of olive oil and pistachios.

Spaghetti alla chitarra are made by rolling fresh pasta dough into sheets and cutting them on a special wooden frame strung with fine wires, like guitar strings (*chitarra* means guitar). The wires cut the dough into square-edged strands. If you don't have a chitarra, you can buy an attachment for your pasta machine to make this shape quickly.

Pistachios, by the way, aren't just any old nut in Sicily. The best ones grow on the lava-rich slopes of Mount Etna, near Bronte. They're our pride, and this dish is proof that a handful can go a very long way.

Make the Dough: On a clean work surface, make a mound with the semola and create a well in the centre. Crack in the eggs and gently whisk with a fork, gradually incorporating the semola until a rough dough forms. Knead for 5–7 minutes until smooth and elastic. Cover with a dish towel and let rest for 30 minutes.

Roll and Cut the Spaghetti: Lightly dust a tray and work surface with semola. Divide the rested dough into 4 pieces. Roll each piece into a sheet about 3mm/⅛in thick (setting 3 on a Marcato). For spaghetti alla chitarra, the dough should be slightly thicker than for tagliatelle (1mm) to give the strands their signature bite.

Place the rolled pasta sheet over the strings of a chitarra wooden frame. Using a rolling pin, press and roll firmly over the dough until the strands fall through the wires. Alternatively, you can use the appropriate attachment for your pasta machine. The result is square-cut spaghetti with a firm texture and rustic edges. Dust with flour and set aside on the tray, and keep covered as you work.

If you don't have a chitarra, you can use a spaghetti alla chitarra attachment for your pasta machine, which cuts a similar shape.

Alternatively, roll the dough out as above, fold it gently and use a sharp knife to cut thin ribbons by hand, about 2–3mm/⅛in wide, to form tagliolini. They won't be square, but they'll still be fresh and satisfying.

Cook the Spaghetti: Bring a large pot of salted water to the boil. Cook the spaghetti alla chitarra for about 2–3 minutes, or until al dente.

Make the Sauce and Serve: While the pasta cooks, heat the olive oil in a wide pan over a medium heat. Add the garlic and cook until just golden, about 30 seconds. Stir in the capers and cook for another minute. Using tongs, lift the pasta directly into the pan with the sauce, along with the ground pistachios. Toss well, loosening with a splash of pasta water until creamy and well coated. Season with salt to taste. Serve immediately, topped with extra pistachios or lemon zest, if desired.

NONNA'S TAGLIATELLE WITH CAULIFLOWER & OLIVES

Tagliatelle con cavolfiore e olive

A simple and nourishing vegan dish with homemade semola tagliatelle, sautéed cauliflower, citrusy breadcrumbs, sultanas/golden raisins and pine nuts. This recipe, passed down by my nonna Maria, holds a special place in my heart. She believed that eating cauliflower kept us healthy and free from disease, and perhaps she was right: she lived a long, vibrant life. In our family, recipes weren't carefully recorded in notebooks but passed on by memory or jotted down on scraps of paper, hidden in the pages of photo albums or found tucked in old textbooks. This dish reflects those memories: a simple but flavourful combination of tender cauliflower, pungent olives, citrusy toasted breadcrumbs, sweet sultanas/golden raisins and rich pine nuts, made even more special with homemade semola tagliatelle. This dish, like my nonna, is humble yet full of wisdom, offering nourishment and a reminder of the healing power of food. Each bite is a tribute to the belief that what we eat can protect and strengthen us, just as it did for her.

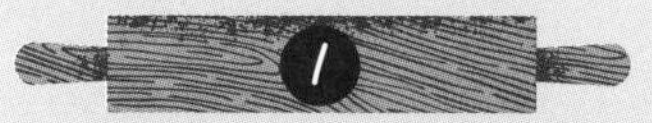

Serves: 4

Preparation time: 25 minutes, plus 30 minutes resting

Cooking time: 25 minutes

For the Dough:

* 400g/14oz/3 cups semola
* 200ml/7fl oz/scant 1 cup lukewarm water

For the Cauliflower Sauce:

* 4 tbsp extra virgin olive oil (divided)
* 100g/3½oz/1 cup breadcrumbs
* Zest of 1 orange
* 3 garlic cloves, thinly sliced
* 1 cauliflower, broken into small florets
* 50g/1¾oz/⅓ cup sultanas/ golden raisins
* 50g/1¾oz/¼ cup pitted black or green olives
* 40g/1½oz/⅓ cup pine nuts, toasted
* 1 dried red chilli, crushed/ hot pepper flakes (optional)
* Salt and pepper, to taste
* Fresh parsley, chopped, to garnish

Make the Dough: On a clean work surface, make a mound with the semola and create a well in the centre. Gradually add the water, mixing it with the semola until a rough dough forms. Knead for 5–7 minutes until smooth and elastic. Cover with a dish towel and let rest for 30 minutes.

Prepare the Breadcrumbs: In a small frying pan, heat 2 tablespoons of the olive oil over a medium heat. Add the breadcrumbs and toast them, stirring frequently, until they are golden and crispy, about 5 minutes. Stir in the orange zest and a pinch of salt. Set aside.

Sauté the Cauliflower: In a large pan, heat the remaining 2 tablespoons of olive oil over a medium heat. Add the garlic and sauté until fragrant but not browned, about 1–2 minutes. Add the cauliflower florets, sultanas/golden raisins, olives and pine nuts, seasoning with salt and pepper. Sauté the cauliflower, stirring occasionally, until tender but still slightly crunchy, about 10–15 minutes. For a bit of heat, add the crushed red chilli/hot pepper flakes, if desired.

Roll and Cut the Tagliatelle: Lightly dust a tray and work surface with semola. Divide the rested dough into 2–4 pieces. Roll each piece into a thin sheet, about 1mm thick (setting 5 on a Marcato). Cut the dough into long strips about 6–8mm/⅓in wide to form tagliatelle. Dust with semola and set on the tray, and keep covered as you work.

Cook the Tagliatelle: Bring a large pot of salted water to the boil. Add the tagliatelle and cook for 3–4 minutes, or until al dente.

Combine and Serve: Using tongs, lift the pasta directly into the pan with the cauliflower, tossing everything together. If needed, add a little cooking water to help the sauce cling evenly. Stir in the toasted breadcrumbs, saving a handful for garnish. Taste and adjust the seasoning as needed. Serve the tagliatelle topped with the remaining breadcrumbs and a sprinkle of fresh parsley for a burst of colour and freshness.

DAD'S PASTA "MARITATA" (MARRIED PASTA)

A simple, soulful dish that speaks of home and of my father. There weren't many things my dad cooked, but this was his signature. He'd call it pasta maritata, "married pasta", with a sense of pride, as though he'd invented the combination himself. Just ricotta, tomato sauce and pasta. But not just any ricotta: he would go out of his way to bring home the freshest he could find, still warm from the farm, tucked into its *fascedda/fuscella*, the traditional cheese mould used in Sicily. And the sauce, of course, was always my mum's.

He liked things simple, comforting and done right. And this dish was exactly that. I can still picture him standing at the hob/stovetop, swirling the pasta into the sauce, spooning in the ricotta with care. I make it with *maccheroni al ferretto*, rolled on a brass rod the old way, just as it should be. This is the dish that reminds me of him most, along with the Broccoli e Ricotta Soup (page 89).

Serves: 4

Preparation time: 30 minutes (if you have pre-made the sauce), plus 30 minutes resting

Cooking time: 5 minutes

For the Dough:

* 400g/14oz/3 cups semola
* 200ml/7fl oz/scant 1 cup lukewarm water

For the Sauce:

* 500ml/17fl oz/2 cups Giovanna's Tomato Sauce (page 26)
* 400g/14oz/1½ cups ricotta, at room temperature

To Serve:

* A drizzle of extra virgin olive oil

Make the Dough: On a clean work surface, make a mound with the semola and create a well in the centre. Gradually add the water, mixing with your fingers or a fork to incorporate the semola until a rough dough forms. Knead for 5–7 minutes until smooth and elastic. Cover with a dish towel and let rest for 30 minutes.

Shape the Maccheroni: Lightly dust a tray and work surface with semola. Cut off a small piece of rested dough, roughly the size of a golf ball, and roll it into a rope about the thickness of a pencil. Cut into 4–5cm/2in lengths. Roll each piece around a traditional brass *ferretto*, or a thin metal or wooden BBQ skewer, pressing gently and rolling back and forth to lengthen the tube. Slide it off carefully and set aside on the tray, and keep covered as you work. Repeat with the remaining dough. The pasta should be hollow, slightly ridged from the rolling and rustic in shape.

Cook the Maccheroni: Bring a large pot of salted water to the boil. Cook the maccheroni for 4–5 minutes, or until al dente.

Combine and Serve: Meanwhile, warm Giovanna's Tomato Sauce in a wide pan. Using a slotted spoon, lift the pasta directly into the sauce. Toss gently to coat, adding a splash of cooking water if needed to help the sauce cling evenly. In a separate bowl, gently loosen the ricotta with a splash of pasta water and mix well. Serve the pasta and top each plate with a few spoonfuls of warm ricotta. Drizzle the ricotta with a little olive oil and serve.

MUM'S COURGETTE/ZUCCHINI CARBONARA WITH BUSIATE

Busiate alla carbonara di zucchine

Serves: 4

Preparation time: 30 minutes, plus 30 minutes resting

Cooking time: 10 minutes

For the Dough:

* 400g/14oz/3 cups semola
* 200ml/7fl oz/scant 1 cup lukewarm water

For the Sauce:

* 3 tbsp extra virgin olive oil
* 2 courgettes/zucchini, thinly sliced into rounds
* 4 large eggs
* 50g/1¾oz/½ cup Parmigiano Reggiano, finely grated, plus extra to serve
* Salt, to taste
* Freshly ground black pepper, to taste, plus extra to serve

This dish, along with pasta maritata, was one of our go-to lunches on school days. Both my parents worked and usually got home just after me and my sister. That's why we learned to cook so young: we'd start lunch, so it was ready for everyone.

At home we loved courgette/zucchini. They were affordable, always in the refrigerator and we found ways to use them in everything. This carbonara was one of my mum's favourites. It's not traditional, of course: there's no pancetta, just golden courgette rounds sautéed in olive oil, tossed with eggs and a bit of Parmigiano. Quick, light and so satisfying.

My mum usually made this with store-bought spaghetti to save time, but for the book I've paired it with fresh busiate, which the sauce clings to beautifully, elevating the dish without complicating it.

Make the Dough: On a clean work surface, make a mound with the semola and create a well in the centre. Gradually add the water, mixing with your fingers or a fork to incorporate the semola until a rough dough forms. Knead for 5–7 minutes until smooth and elastic. Cover with a dish towel and let rest for 30 minutes.

Shape the Busiate: Lightly dust a tray and work surface with semola. Cut off a small piece of rested dough, roughly the size of a golf ball, and roll it into a rope about the thickness and length of a pencil. Roll each piece diagonally around a thin wooden skewer, knitting needle or traditional brass *ferretto* to form a tight spiral. This may take a little practice, but you'll get there. Slide it off gently, dust with semola and set on the tray, and keep covered as you work. Repeat with the remaining dough.

Prepare the Courgette/Zucchini: Heat the olive oil in a large pan over a medium heat. Add the courgette slices and sauté for 8–10 minutes, until golden and soft. Season with salt and pepper, then remove from the heat and set aside.

Beat the Eggs: In a small bowl, beat the eggs with the grated Parmigiano. Season lightly with salt and pepper.

Cook the Busiate: Bring a large pot of salted water to the boil. Cook the busiate for 4–5 minutes, or until al dente.

Combine and Serve: Using tongs, lift the pasta directly into the pan with the courgette. Toss gently to coat, adding a splash of cooking water if needed to help loosen. Pour in the egg mixture, stirring quickly to create a silky sauce from the heat of the pasta. Add a splash of pasta water if needed to help the sauce cling evenly. Serve immediately with extra Parmigiano and black pepper.

NONNA MARIA'S 7 VEGETABLE COUSCOUS

Couscous 7 verdure di nonna Maria

Serves: 4

Preparation time: 15 minutes

Cooking time: 1 hour

For the Sauce:

* 3 tbsp extra virgin olive oil
* 2 onions, finely julienned
* 2 large carrots, cut into batons
* 2 potatoes, peeled and cut into large chunks
* 1 yellow courgette/zucchini, cut into batons
* 1 green courgette/zucchini, cut into batons
* 2 large tomatoes, grated
* 150g/5¼oz/1 cup fresh broad/fava beans, shelled
* 1 tsp ground cinnamon
* ½ tsp black pepper
* 1 tsp sweet paprika
* ½ tsp ground nutmeg
* 600ml/20fl oz/2½ cups water
* Salt, to taste

For the Couscous:

* 300g/10½oz/2 cups couscous
* 1 tbsp extra virgin olive oil
* 1 large onion, finely grated
* A small handful of fresh parsley, finely chopped
* Salt and pepper, to taste

For the Tfaya:

* 3 tbsp extra virgin olive oil
* 1 large onion, thinly sliced
* 1 tbsp pine nuts
* 2 tbsp raisins
* Salt, to taste

For Garnish:

* Fresh parsley and dill, chopped

My nonna Maria was born in Benghazi, Libya, where her parents had moved after the First World War. One of five siblings, she grew up in a nun's orphanage but always spoke of Libya with affection. In her late teens she moved to Sicily, bringing a traditional couscoussier and a cherished recipe with her. Years later I found that recipe tucked inside one of her old books, faded and incomplete. When I cook this dish now, I do it her way, with heart and instinct.

Couscous may be more often linked to North Africa, but it holds a rightful place in Sicilian tradition, especially in the west, where centuries of Arab influence left their mark. This version is made with seven seasonal vegetables and the gentle spices of our land such as cinnamon, nutmeg, black pepper and paprika.

Prepare the Sauce: In the base of a couscoussiere or a large, heavy pot, heat the olive oil over a medium heat. Add the onions and sauté for 5–7 minutes until soft. Add the carrots, potatoes, courgette/zucchini, tomatoes, broad/fava beans and the dry spices, stir and season with salt. Pour in the water and bring to the boil, then reduce to a gentle simmer and cook, covered, for 30–40 minutes, until the vegetables are tender but not falling apart. Set aside while the couscous cooks.

Prepare the Couscous: Place the couscous in a large bowl. Add the olive oil, then wet your hands 3–4 times, each time sprinkling the water over the couscous and fluffing it with your hands. Let it sit for 10 minutes, then fluff again. Add the onion, parsley and some salt and pepper and mix well.

If You Have a Couscoussier: Transfer the couscous to the top tier of the couscoussiere and steam over the bubbling sauce for 15–20 minutes. Return it to the bowl, fluff again and repeat the steaming once or twice more, for a total of 40–45 minutes, until the grains are light and tender.

If You Don't Have a Couscoussier: Place the couscous in a large sieve/fine-mesh strainer set over the pot of simmering sauce, making sure it doesn't touch the liquid. Cover tightly with foil and a lid to trap the steam. Steam for 15–20 minutes, then transfer the couscous to a large bowl, fluff gently with a fork to separate the grains, then return to the colander for a second steaming of 10–15 minutes. This two-step steaming gives the couscous a light, airy texture close to the traditional method. Alternatively, you can follow standard couscous package directions using hot stock or water, but steaming yields the most authentic result.

Make the Tfaya: In a small pan, heat the olive oil over a medium-low heat. Add the onion, pine nuts and a pinch of salt, and cook gently for 15–20 minutes, until deeply golden and soft. Add the raisins and cook for 5 more minutes, until they plump and absorb the flavour of the onion.

Serve: Spread the steamed couscous into a large, shallow platter, forming a soft mound. Neatly arrange the vegetables on top in clusters by type, keeping their large, rustic shape. Spoon over some of the sauce. Place the tfaya in the centre and garnish with fresh herbs. Serve warm, with extra sauce on the side.

NONNA'S TAGLIOLINI ALLA CARRETTIERA

Tagliolini alla carrettiera della nonna

Raw tomatoes, garlic and basil. Simple, fresh and full of memories. There are many versions of spaghetti alla carrettiera, and they vary across regions: some use cooked tomatoes, others don't; some use breadcrumbs, some use cheese, some don't even use tomatoes. Even within Sicily the interpretations are endless. But this is how I remember it, the way my nonna Maria made it.

For some reason, this dish is tied to a specific memory. I was in primary school, and my mum had taken a job in another city, so we'd go to our grandparents' after school. One day, the school bus broke down. There were no mobile phones back then. My sister and I were among the last children to be dropped home, what felt like hours late. When we finally arrived, I saw my nonna sitting on the stairs outside, head in her hands, wearing a bright pink scarf. She had been crying, worried sick. I've never forgotten that image.

Maybe she had made this pasta for lunch that day and that's why I remember? Olive oil, lots of raw minced garlic, cherry tomatoes blanched and pressed with a fork, and fresh basil. Simple, fresh and uncomplicated . . . unlike life, sometimes.

Serves: 4

Preparation time: 30 minutes, plus 30 minutes resting

Cooking time: 5 minutes

For the Dough:

* 400g/14oz/3 cups 00 flour
* 4 eggs

For the Sauce:

* 300g/10½oz/2 cups cherry tomatoes
* 3 tbsp extra virgin olive oil
* 2 garlic cloves, minced
* A handful of fresh basil leaves, plus extra to garnish
* Salt, to taste
* Freshly ground black pepper, to taste (optional)

Make the Dough: On a clean work surface, make a mound with the flour and create a well in the centre. Crack in the eggs and gently whisk with a fork, gradually incorporating the flour until a rough dough forms. Knead for 5–7 minutes until smooth and elastic. Cover with a dish towel and let rest for 30 minutes.

Prepare the Sauce: Meanwhile, bring a medium saucepan of water to the boil. Score the cherry tomatoes and blanch them for 10–15 seconds, just enough to loosen the skins. Drain them, and, if desired, gently press with a fork to crush them slightly. In a large bowl, combine the olive oil with the minced garlic and a pinch of salt. Add the tomatoes and tear in the basil leaves. Let the mixture sit at room temperature while you make and cook the pasta to allow the flavours to mingle.

Roll and Cut the Tagliolini: Lightly dust a tray and work surface with flour. Divide the rested dough into 2–4 pieces. Roll each piece into a thin sheet, about 1mm thick (setting 5 on a Marcato). Lightly flour and fold the sheets, then cut into very thin ribbons, about 2–3mm/⅛in wide, using a sharp knife or tagliolini cutter. Unfold the strands, dust with flour and set on the tray, and keep covered as you work.

Cook the Tagliolini and Serve: Bring a large pot of salted water to the boil. Cook the tagliolini for 2–3 minutes, or until al dente. Using tongs, lift the pasta directly into the bowl with the sauce. Toss well to coat. Serve immediately, with a little more basil, and a grind of black pepper, if you like.

ZIA RITA'S SUNDAY LASAGNA

Lasagne della domenica di zia Rita

Serves: 6–8

Preparation time: 45 minutes, plus 30 minutes resting

Cooking time: 1 hour 45 minutes

For the Dough:

* 400g/14oz/3 cups 00 flour
* 4 eggs

For the Vegetarian Ragù:

* 150g/5¼oz/1½ cups textured vegetable protein (TVP)
* Hot vegetable stock, for soaking
* 3 tbsp extra virgin olive oil
* 1 small red onion, finely chopped
* 1 carrot, finely chopped
* 1 celery stalk, finely chopped
* 2 tbsp tomato purée/paste
* 120ml/4fl oz/½ cup red wine
* 700ml/24fl oz/3 cups tomato passata
* 2 bay leaves
* Salt and pepper, to taste

For the Béchamel:

* 60g/2oz/4 tbsp unsalted butter
* 60g/2oz/½ cup plain/all-purpose flour
* 700ml/24fl oz/3 cups whole milk
* Freshly grated nutmeg, to taste
* Salt and pepper, to taste

To Assemble and Serve:

* 100g/3½oz/1 cup Parmigiano Reggiano, finely grated, plus extra to serve
* Olive oil or butter, for greasing
* Parsley, chopped, to serve

A slow-cooked vegetarian ragù layered with silky pasta sheets and béchamel, inspired by the warmth and joy of Sunday lunch at zia Rita's. There was nothing quite like being invited to her house. She was loud, always laughing and loved with her whole heart. My dad adored her. They were the youngest of four and thick as thieves, talking about movies all through lunch, then moving to the sofa with coffee in hand, ready for a film and a running commentary.

Her home had a particular scent of coziness. She was a wonderful cook, and her lasagna was always the star of the table. This version is a tribute to her, made with a vegetarian ragù that still delivers the comfort of the classic. It's rich, generous and celebratory, just like her.

Make the Dough: On a clean work surface, make a mound with the flour and create a well in the centre. Crack in the eggs and whisk gently with a fork, gradually incorporating the flour until a rough dough forms. Knead for 5–7 minutes until smooth and elastic. Cover with a dish towel and let rest for 30 minutes.

Prepare the Vegetarian Ragù: Rehydrate the textured vegetable protein (TVP) in just enough hot vegetable stock to cover. Let it sit for 10–15 minutes, then drain well and set aside. In a large pan, heat the olive oil over a medium heat. Add the onion, carrot and celery, and sauté for 8–10 minutes until soft and fragrant. Stir in the tomato purée/paste and cook for 1 minute. Add the drained TVP and stir to coat. Pour in the red wine and let it reduce for 2–3 minutes. Add the passata, bay leaves and some salt and pepper. Simmer over a medium-low heat for 30–40 minutes, stirring occasionally, until thick and flavourful. Remove the bay leaves.

Make the Béchamel: In a saucepan, melt the butter over a medium heat. Add the flour and whisk into a smooth paste, then cook for 2–3 minutes until slightly golden. Gradually add the milk, whisking constantly to prevent lumps. Cook until thickened, about 8–10 minutes. Season with nutmeg, salt and pepper to taste.

Roll and Cut the Lasagna Sheets: Lightly dust a work surface with flour. Divide the rested dough into 2–4 pieces. Roll each piece into a thin sheet, about 1mm thick (setting 5 on a Marcato). Cut into rectangles to fit your baking dish.

Cook the Lasagna Sheets (Optional): If you prefer a softer texture, blanch the sheets for 30 seconds or so in a pan of salted boiling water, 1–2 at a time, then transfer to a dish towel to dry. Otherwise, you can assemble the lasagna with raw sheets making sure they are evenly covered with hot béchamel and ragù for even baking.

Assemble the Lasagna: Preheat the oven to 180°C/350°F/Gas Mark 4. Lightly grease a baking dish. Spread a spoonful of béchamel on the base of your dish, then layer pasta sheets, ragù, béchamel and a sprinkle of Parmigiano. Repeat until you've used up all the ingredients, finishing with past sheets, béchamel and Parmigiano on top.

Bake and Serve: Bake for 35–40 minutes until golden and bubbling. Let rest for 10–15 minutes before garnishing with the extra Parmigiano nd chopped parsley, before serving. Even better the next day, just like zia Rita would have insisted.

SCACCIA (LAYERED FLATBREAD FROM RAGUSA)

The folded flatbread that defines a city. This recipe belongs to my other nonna, Peppina. She lived with us, but by the time I was born she could no longer speak or move after a stroke. Still, her presence filled the house, and her love was felt in silence. Scaccia is Ragusa's most iconic dish, found in every bakery and home, with countless mostly vegetarian fillings from tomato and cheese, to aubergine/eggplant and tomato, spinach and garlic, or ricotta and broad/fava beans. My favourites are the two my mum and nonna made most often: classic with tomato sauce, and parsley, garlic and caciocavallo. Peppina was a single mother in 1960s Sicily who found strength in the kitchen and comfort in feeding others. It may not be pasta, but it belongs at our table all the same.

Makes: 8 (serves 4, with leftovers)

Preparation time: 45 minutes, plus 1–2 hours resting

Cooking time: 1 hour 20 minutes

For the Dough:

* 12g/½oz fresh brewer's yeast or 4g/½ tbsp fast-action/ instant active dried yeast
* 400ml/14fl oz/1⅔ cups lukewarm water
* 1kg/2¼lb/7½ cups semola
* 2 tsp salt
* 4 tbsp extra virgin olive oil, plus extra for brushing

For the Parsley & Garlic Filling:

* 2 large bunches of fresh parsley, leaves picked and stems discarded
* 5–6 garlic cloves, minced
* Extra virgin olive oil, for drizzling
* 400g/14oz/3 cups caciocavallo, sliced 3mm/⅛in thick
* Salt and pepper, to taste

For the Tomato & Onion Filling:

* 8 tbsp extra virgin olive oil (divided), plus extra for drizzling
* 700ml/24fl oz/3 cups tomato passata
* Fresh basil leaves, to taste
* 2 large onions, thinly sliced
* 1 tsp sugar
* Salt and pepper, to taste

Make the Dough: Dissolve the yeast in the water and let sit for 5 minutes to activate. In a large bowl, mix the semola and salt. Add the olive oil and the yeast mixture. Stir to combine into a rough dough, then knead on a floured surface for about 10 minutes, until smooth and elastic. Place in a greased bowl, cover with a dish towel and let rise in a warm place for 1–2 hours, until doubled in size.

Make the Parsley and Garlic Filling: Combine the parsley and garlic in a bowl. Season with olive oil, salt and pepper. Let the mixture sit to infuse while the dough rises.

Make the Tomato and Onion Filling: In a saucepan, warm 4 tablespoons of olive oil over a medium heat and add the tomato passata. Season with salt and a few torn basil leaves. Simmer, covered, over a low heat for 40 minutes, or until the oil separates. In a separate pan, warm the remaining olive oil over a medium-low heat. Add the sliced onions with a pinch of salt and pepper and cook slowly for 10–15 minutes until soft and translucent. Once soft, stir in the sugar and cook for 2–3 more minutes. Leave both fillings to cool before using.

Roll and Fill the Scaccia: Preheat the oven to 200°C/400°F/Gas Mark 6. Line one or two large baking sheets with baking parchment. Work with one piece of dough at a time, keeping the remaining dough covered to prevent drying out. On a well-floured surface, roll a piece of dough into a thin, large rectangle, about 40 x 30cm (16 x 12in). The dough should be paper-thin and almost transparent.

Fold the Scaccia: For the parsley and garlic scaccia, drizzle with olive oil, spread a layer of the parsley and garlic mixture on top and add a few slices of caciocavallo. For the tomato and onion scaccia, drizzle with olive oil, spread a layer of the tomato sauce on top to fully cover the surface and top with caramelized onions.

Fold the two long sides inward toward the centre (like folding a letter) to encase the filling. Spread another thin layer of filling over the folded dough, then fold the short sides inward into thirds (one over the top) to create a compact rectangular bundle, about the size of a brick. Spread a final thin layer of filling over the top to keep the surface moist during baking. Transfer to the baking sheet, leaving space between the scacce. Repeat with the remaining pieces of dough and the fillings.

Bake and Serve: Pierce the top of each scaccia with a fork and brush generously with olive oil. Bake for 30–40 minutes, or until golden brown and crisp. Leave to cool slightly before slicing. Store at room temperature for up to 3 days or refrigerate during warmer months. They also freeze for 2–3 months once cooled.

ZIA RITA'S BAKED PASTA WITH MUSHROOMS

Pasta al forno ai funghi di zia Rita

Serves: 4

Preparation time: 15 minutes

Cooking time: 1 hour

For the Pasta:

* 2 tbsp extra virgin olive oil, plus extra for drizzling
* 1 garlic clove, minced
* 500g/17½oz/4 cups mixed mushrooms (like chestnut/cremini, button or porcini, frozen work too), roughly chopped
* 400g/14oz/4 cups mezze maniche or rigatoni
* 250g/9oz/2 cups mozzarella, chopped
* 100g/3½oz/1 cup Parmigiano Reggiano, finely grated
* Butter, for greasing and topping
* Salt and pepper, to taste

For the Béchamel:

* 60g/2oz/4 tbsp unsalted butter
* 60g/2oz/½ cup plain/all-purpose flour
* 700ml/24fl oz/3 cups whole milk
* Freshly grated nutmeg, to taste
* Salt and pepper, to taste
* Parsley, chopped, to garnish

A baked pasta dish layered with creamy béchamel, mixed mushrooms, mozzarella and loads of grated cheese. Cosy, comforting and full of Sunday memories. While her classic lasagna was the showstopper, zia Rita always made a second meal for those who preferred something a little different. This was that dish. My cousin Giusy fondly remembers it sitting next to the bubbling lasagna on the table: creamy, golden and irresistible. Zia Rita never did things by halves. Her pasta al forno was always generous, filled with layers of béchamel sauce, stretchy mozzarella and *funghi misti* (mixed mushrooms), whatever was in season. While she made hers with homemade lasagna sheets, I like to prepare it with mezze maniche instead: a shape that holds the sauce beautifully and makes for a slightly quicker Sunday lunch.

Zia Rita made food that made people feel welcome, like there was nowhere else in the world they should be.

Prepare the Mushrooms: Heat the olive oil in a large pan over a medium heat. Add the garlic and cook for 1 minute until fragrant. Add the chopped mushrooms, season with salt and pepper and sauté for 10–12 minutes, until softened and golden. Set aside.

Make the Béchamel: In a saucepan, melt the butter over a medium heat. Add the flour and whisk into a smooth paste, then cook for 2–3 minutes until slightly golden. Gradually add the milk, whisking constantly to prevent lumps. Cook until thickened, about 8–10 minutes. Season with nutmeg, salt and pepper to taste.

Cook the Pasta: Bring a large pot of salted water to the boil. Cook the mezze maniche until very al dente (2 minutes less than the package directions suggest). Drain and toss with a drizzle of olive oil to prevent sticking.

Assemble the Pasta al Forno: Preheat the oven to 190°C/375°F/Gas Mark 5. Lightly butter a large baking dish. In a large bowl, combine the cooked pasta with the sautéed mushrooms, half of the béchamel, half of the mozzarella and half of the grated Parmigiano. Mix gently. Spoon the mixture into the baking dish. Top with the remaining béchamel, mozzarella and Parmigiano. Add a few small knobs of butter on top if you like a crispier crust. Bake for 25–30 minutes until golden and bubbling on top. Let rest for 10 minutes before garnishing with the chopped parsley and serving.

Note: If you'd like to make a handmade version of mezze maniche, you can use a classic semola dough (400g/14oz/3 cups semola + 200ml/7fl oz/scant 1 cup lukewarm water). Roll the dough into small logs and cut into 2cm/¾in pieces. Using a gnocchi board and a thin dowel or knitting needle, press and roll each piece into a short tube. It won't be perfectly uniform, but it will have beautiful ridges and a rustic charm; plus, it holds sauce exceptionally well.

NONNA'S BAKED PASTA & BROCCOLI

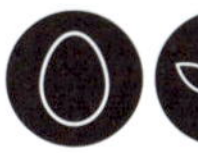

Pasta al forno con broccoli della nonna

If there's one dish I could eat for the rest of my life, this is it. It's humble, unassuming and deeply comforting. My nonna Maria would make it often, especially when the whole family was gathered. I remember her kitchen so clearly. She had moved the hob/stovetop and oven out to the balcony to make more space indoors, and in my memory, it was always filled with sunlight.

This dish is also an ode to my nonno Pasquale . . . Pasqualino, as everyone called him. A man of few words and a severe look, but he adored my nonna. I remember him sitting in his usual chair in the corner of the kitchen, hands cold and folded in his lap, just watching her move about like she was dancing. I used to rest my little hand on his and kiss his cheek. He would speak in riddles, sometimes in Latin, and he loved this pasta. She would make it with Sicilian fennel sausage, but as I don't use meat in this book, I find that just using the spices (fennel seeds and a little chilli) brings all the same warmth.

I make mine with rigatoni, like she did; though I use the rigatoni press on my KitchenAid. It's still her dish, through and through.

Serves: 4

Preparation time: 15 minutes

Cooking time: 45 minutes

Ingredients:
* 1 large head of broccoli, cut into small florets
* 2–3 tbsp extra virgin olive oil
* 2 large shallots or 1 onion, finely sliced
* 1 garlic clove, minced
* 1 tsp fennel seeds
* 1 small fresh red chilli, finely chopped, or ½ tsp dried chilli/hot pepper flakes
* 400g/14oz/4 cups rigatoni
* 100g/3½oz/1 cup caciocavallo or Parmigiano Reggiano, grated, plus extra to finish
* 2 tbsp breadcrumbs
* Butter, for greasing and topping
* Salt and pepper, to taste

Cook the Broccoli: Bring a large pot of salted water to the boil. Add the broccoli florets and cook for 5–6 minutes, until soft but not falling apart. Remove with a slotted spoon and set aside, reserving the cooking water.

Sauté the Aromatics: In a wide pan, heat the olive oil over a medium heat. Add the shallots and cook for 8–10 minutes until soft and golden. Add the garlic, fennel seeds and chilli and cook for another 2 minutes until fragrant.

Add the drained broccoli to the pan with the shallots and spices. Season with salt and pepper and cook together for another 5–10 minutes, gently mashing some of the florets with the back of a spoon until creamy and well combined.

Cook the Pasta: In the same water used for the broccoli, cook the rigatoni until very al dente (about 2 minutes less than the package suggests). Drain and transfer directly to the pan with the broccoli mixture.

Assemble the Dish: Toss the pasta well, adding the grated caciocavallo. Taste and adjust the seasoning. Transfer everything to a greased baking dish. Top with more grated caciocavallo, the breadcrumbs and a few dots of butter.

Finish Under the Grill/Broiler (optional): If desired, place under a hot grill/broiler at the maximum temperature for 5–10 minutes, until the top is golden and crisp, but the base remains moist. Serve.

Note: If you'd like to make your own rigatoni, use a classic semola dough (400g/14oz/3 cups semola + 200ml/7fl oz/scant 1 cup lukewarm water) and a rigatoni pasta press attachment or bronze die. If you don't have one, you can make rustic tubes by rolling small pieces of dough over a gnocchi board with a dowel or knitting needle.

MAMMA GIOVANNA'S COURGETTE/ ZUCCHINI SOUP

Minestra di zucchine della mamma

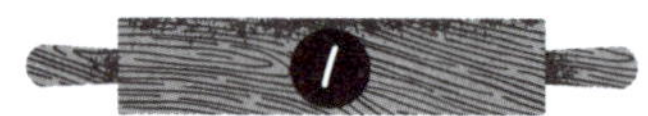

Serves: 4

Preparation time: 15 minutes, plus 30 minutes resting

Cooking time: 25 minutes

For the Dough:

* 200g/7oz/1½ cups semola
* 90ml/3fl oz/6 tbsp lukewarm water

For the Soup:

* 2 tbsp extra virgin olive oil
* 1 small onion, finely chopped
* 1 small carrot, finely chopped
* 1 celery stalk, finely chopped
* 3 courgettes/zucchini, sliced into half moons
* 200ml/7fl oz/scant 1 cup tomato passata or polpa di pomodoro
* Salt and pepper, to taste

Optional Toppings (per portion):

* 1 triangle of cream cheese
* Finely grated Parmigiano Reggiano
* A spoonful of plain yogurt

This was one of those recipes my mum made every single week. It was quick, nourishing and comforting – a midweek bowl that felt like a hug. Perfect for the kind of days when no one wanted to think too much about what was for dinner, but everyone still wanted something warm and familiar. We called it simply *la minestra*. It's one of those dishes that takes you straight back to childhood. I still eat it the same way I did then, with a triangle of cream cheese stirred in at the end. You can judge me, but I'm never going to have it any other way!

What makes this soup special is the pastina: tiny pieces of pasta. Not the store-bought kind, but a simple semola dough, rested in the refrigerator until firm, then grated directly into the pot on the coarse side of a cheese grater. Pasta making can't get any easier than that. It cooks in under 2 minutes and tastes of care and home.

Make the Pastina Dough: Add the semola to a large bowl. Gradually add the water and mix with your fingers or a fork until a rough dough forms. Knead for 5–7 minutes until smooth and elastic. Cover with a dish towel and rest in the refrigerator for 30 minutes.

Once the dough is rested and firm, lightly dust a tray with semola and grate the dough using the coarse side of a cheese grater onto it. Separate the shreds gently with your fingers and toss in some flour to prevent sticking. Set aside until ready to use and keep covered as you work.

Make the Soup: Heat the olive oil in a large pot over a medium heat. Add the onion, carrot and celery and sauté for 5–6 minutes until softened. Add the courgette/zucchini and cook for another 5 minutes until softened. Stir in the passata and season with salt and pepper. Add a splash of water if needed and simmer gently, covered, for 10–15 minutes until the vegetables are meltingly tender.

Cook the Pastina and Serve: Bring the soup to a gentle boil. Add the fresh pastina and cook for 1–2 minutes, until just tender. Ladle into bowls and serve hot, with your topping of choice: cream cheese stirred through, a dusting of Parmigiano or a dollop of yogurt.

ZIA MARIETTA'S PASTA & RICE SOUP

Minestra di pasta e riso di zia Marietta

Serves: 4

Preparation time: 10 minutes

Cooking time: 20 minutes

Ingredients:

* 3 tbsp extra virgin olive oil, plus extra to serve
* 1 small onion, finely chopped
* 1 carrot, finely chopped
* 1 celery stalk, finely chopped
* 1.5l/52fl oz/6½ cups vegetable stock
* ½ head of broccoli, broken into small florets
* 90g/3¼oz/½ cup white rice, preferably the Carnaroli or Arborio variety
* 100g/3½oz/½ cup ditalini or any small pasta
* 2 egg yolks
* 500g/17½oz/2 cups ricotta
* Salt and white pepper, to taste

A simple soup that carries a family's warmth across continents. Zia Marietta was my mum's aunt, nonna Peppina's sister. While I don't have many memories of nonna Peppina, I remember Marietta clearly. We would visit her often – my mum, my sister and I – and her home always felt calm, warm and lived-in. Two of her three sons, Giovanni and Giuseppe, had left Sicily to build a new life in the United States. My mum would talk fondly of them as if they were big brothers to her.

When they'd come back to visit, they never came empty-handed. We'd wait in excitement for the strange and colourful gifts they brought from America: Wrigley's gum in all kinds of flavours (Juicy Fruit was my favourite) and bright red twisted liquorice sticks called Red Vines. I don't think I'd ever seen anything like that in Sicily.

While working on this book, I reached out to Giovanni, now in his eighties, asking if he remembered any special family recipe I could include. He gave me this. A humble bowl of rice and pasta, thick with ricotta and sweet with memories. It might not look like much, but it feels special.

Make the Soup: Heat the olive oil in a large pot over a medium heat. Add the finely chopped onion, carrot and celery. Sauté for 5–7 minutes until soft and fragrant, stirring occasionally. Pour in the vegetable stock and bring to the boil. Add the broccoli florets and rice. Season with salt and white pepper. Lower the heat slightly and simmer for 4–5 minutes.

Add the pasta and cook for another 5–7 minutes, or until both the rice and pasta are tender and the broccoli florets are soft.

Finish and Serve: Remove from the heat. Whisk in the egg yolks and ricotta until fully combined and the soup is thick and creamy. Add a drizzle of olive oil and stir again. Taste and adjust the seasoning. Serve warm in deep bowls.

PAPÀ RICCARDO'S FAVOURITE SOUP

Minestra di broccoli e ricotta

A gentle bowl from a gentleman. This was one of the few recipes my dad would make himself. He wasn't usually the one in the kitchen, but when he was, it was always for something simple and comforting. He made it without ceremony, but always with care.

Purple broccoli, a spoonful of ricotta, pastina and a drizzle of olive oil. That was it. I don't think he ever measured a thing. But somehow, it always came out tasting just right. I remember the way he'd ladle it out slowly, as if it deserved his full attention, and how he would always go for the extra dollop of ricotta. This is a soup that asks for very little but gives back so much.

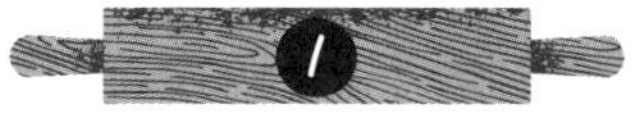

Serves: 4

Preparation time: 10 minutes

Cooking time: 15 minutes

Ingredients:

* 1.5l/52fl oz/6½ cups vegetable stock
* 1 small head of purple sprouting broccoli or regular broccoli, cut into small florets
* 100g/3½oz/½ cup pastina or other tiny soup pasta (see page 84)
* 500g/17½oz/2 cups ricotta
* Salt, to taste
* Freshly ground black pepper, to taste, plus extra to serve
* Extra virgin olive oil, to serve

Make the Soup: Bring the vegetable stock to the boil in a large pot. Add the broccoli florets and cook for 8–10 minutes until tender. Season with salt and pepper.

Cook the Pastina: Add the pastina to the pot and simmer for another 5–7 minutes, or according to the package directions.

Finish and Serve: Turn off the heat. The broccoli should be very soft and starting to break apart. Taste and adjust the seasoning if needed. Add a few spoonfuls of the ricotta (you can stir the ricotta in until it dissolves if you prefer). Drizzle each bowl with a thread of good olive oil before serving. Serve hot, with an extra scrunch of black pepper.

NONNA PEPPINA'S HAND-ROLLED PASTA WITH BROAD/FAVA BEAN SOUP

Lolli col macco

Serves: 4

Preparation time: 30 minutes, plus 30 minutes resting

Cooking time: 1 hour 30 minutes

For the Dough:

* 400g/14oz/3 cups semola
* 200ml/7fl oz/scant 1 cup lukewarm water

For the Macco (Broad/Fava Bean Purée):

* 3 tbsp extra virgin olive oil, plus extra to serve
* 1 onion, finely chopped
* 1 carrot, finely chopped
* 1 celery stalk, finely chopped
* 1 tsp tomato purée/paste
* 1 tsp fennel seeds
* 300g/10½oz/1½ cups dried broad/fava beans without skin
* 1l/35fl oz/4¼ cups water or vegetable stock, plus more as needed
* Salt, to taste
* Freshly ground black pepper, to taste, plus extra to serve
* Fresh fennel fronds or dill, to garnish

Of the four soups in this chapter, this one is my favourite. There's something satisfying about the combination of tender hand-rolled pasta and the earthy creaminess and slight bitterness of macco, a purée made from dried broad/fava beans. It's simple, filling and powerful like many of the best Sicilian dishes.

Broad beans are a cornerstone of Sicilian cuisine, especially in my province, Ragusa. They come in three main forms: fresh green (available only in spring); dried decorticate (peeled) beans, which are used in this recipe; and dried beans with the skin, used in heartier versions of macco, or deep-fried and eaten as salty snacks.

This soup is typical of Modica, known for its world-famous chocolate and vibrant food culture. Modica has a way of elevating the humble without forgetting its roots and this dish is no exception. The lolli are one of the easiest pasta shapes. And the macco is the definition of comfort.

Make the Dough: On a clean work surface, make a mound with the semola and create a well in the middle. Gradually add the water, mixing with your fingers or a fork until a rough dough forms. Knead for 5–7 minutes until smooth and elastic. Cover with a dish towel and let rest for 30 minutes.

Make the Macco: In a large pot, heat the extra virgin olive oil over a medium heat. Add the onion, carrot and celery, and sauté for about 10 minutes until soft and fragrant. Stir in the tomato purée/paste and fennel seeds, cooking for an additional 2 minutes. Add the broad/fava beans and enough water to cover them. Bring to the boil, then reduce the heat to low and let the beans simmer for about 1–1½ hours, or until very tender. Season with salt and pepper. Once the beans are soft, use a hand-held/immersion blender or food processor to purée them to a smooth, thick consistency. If the macco is too thick, add more water to adjust the texture. Keep warm.

Shape the Lolli: Lightly dust a tray and work surface with semola. Roll the rested dough into ropes about 1cm/⅓in thick. Cut into 3–4cm/1½in pieces. Using your index, middle and ring fingers, press firmly on the dough while dragging it toward you against the surface. This rolling motion creates ridges from your fingers and causes the dough to curl slightly into a small, rustic tube. Set the shaped lolli on the tray and keep covered as you work. Repeat with the remaining dough.

Cook the Lolli: Bring a large pot of salted water to the boil. Add the lolli and cook for 5–7 minutes, or until they float and the texture is al dente.

Combine and Serve: Using a slotted spoon, lift the pasta directly into the macco and gently warm everything together over a low heat. If the mixture is too thick, add a bit of water to loosen it to your desired consistency. Ladle the *lolli col macco* into bowls and drizzle with extra virgin olive oil. Garnish with freshly ground black pepper and a handful of fresh fennel fronds for a burst of fresh, herbal flavour. Serve hot.

Ch. 4

MEDITERRANEAN Mosaic

The Mediterranean is where history, culture and cuisine intersect. Nowhere is this more evident than in Sicily, the southern reaches of Italy and the islands. The influence of the many cultures that have passed through – Greek, Arab, Norman, Spanish and more – is deeply woven into the fabric of our cuisine. Sicily sits at the crossroads of the Mediterranean, and our cooking bears the imprint of the region. Nothing is wholly original, yet everything is distinctly ours. From the fragrant spices brought by the Arabs to the age-old methods of preserving, fermenting and layering flavour, our cooking is a rich mosaic of influences from across the sea.

Growing up in Sicily, I often felt this connection to the broader Mediterranean world. It started with the flavours passed down by my nonna and deepened through my studies in Venice. Living and learning in a city shaped by centuries of exchange taught me to stay curious and open to people, cultures and the many ways in which belonging is built over time.

That curiosity has stayed with me. Cooking is a way of recognizing and celebrating the richness that migrant communities bring with them, just as my own Sicilian ancestors did when they made new lives elsewhere and created something that wasn't entirely Sicilian anymore, yet somehow still was.

Today, in the kitchens of London or Venezia, in Tunis or Palermo, I see echoes of that same exchange. Food becomes a place where different stories meet, where something familiar takes on new meaning through integration and influence. When I use mint, sumac or preserved lemon, I feel connected to both my roots and to the journeys of others. I feel gratitude for those who came before us and those who will come after, each contributing to this ever-evolving expression of food and identity.

This chapter celebrates the Mediterranean's vegetarian flavours: recipes rooted in the rhythms of the land and the pleasure of communal meals. From homemade harissa to burnt aubergine/eggplant sauces, from orzo with lemon cream to *fideuà* with saffron, these dishes are an invitation to gather and experience the generous spirit that defines Mediterranean culture.

CAVATELLI WITH MUSHROOM & SUMAC RAGÙ

Cavatelli con ragù di funghi e sommacco

Serves: 4

Preparation time: 40 minutes, plus 30 minutes resting

Cooking time: 30 minutes

For the Dough:

* 400g/14oz/3 cups semola
* 200ml/7fl oz/scant 1 cup lukewarm water, plus more if needed

For the Mushroom Ragù:

* 3 tbsp extra virgin olive oil
* 1 onion, finely diced
* 1 bay leaf
* 1 garlic clove, unpeeled, lightly crushed (*in camicia*)
* 1 small celery stalk, finely diced
* 1 small carrot, finely diced
* 300g/10½oz/3½ cups mixed mushrooms (such as porcini, portobello, button and chestnut/cremini), finely chopped
* 1 tsp sumac
* ½ tsp dried chilli/hot pepper flakes, or to taste
* 1 tbsp double concentrate tomato purée/paste
* A splash of red wine
* 5–6 fresh basil leaves, torn
* 120ml/4fl oz/½ cup milk or water
* Salt and pepper, to taste

To Garnish:

* Grated ricotta salata (store-bought or make your own – page 270)
* A sprinkle of extra sumac
* Chilli Oil (optional – page 268)

Sumac, or *sommacco* as it's known in Sicily, is a spice with roots deep in Middle Eastern and Mediterranean food heritage. Though often associated with Levantine and North African cooking, sumac made its way into Sicily centuries ago, carried by traders and settlers who left a lasting mark on the island's culture. In Sicily, *sommacco* has become a beloved ingredient. It adds a subtle citrus note to this rich mushroom ragù, bringing a bright, Mediterranean twist to a deeply savoury dish.

In this recipe, homemade cavatelli are paired with a mushroom ragù and a touch of sumac, lending a gentle acidity that lifts the earthiness of the mushrooms. It's a celebration of Sicily's openness to new flavours and the beautiful fusion of ingredients that have come to define its cuisine.

Make the Dough: On a clean work surface, make a mound with the semola and create a well in the centre. Gradually add the water, mixing with your fingers or a fork until a rough dough forms. Knead for 5–7 minutes until smooth and elastic. Cover with a dish towel and let rest for 30 minutes.

Prepare the Mushroom Ragù: In a large frying pan or sauté pan, heat the olive oil over a medium heat. Add the onion, bay leaf, garlic, celery and carrot. Cook for 5–6 minutes until softened. Add the mushrooms and sauté until they release their moisture, about 5 minutes. Stir in the sumac, dried chilli/hot pepper flakes, tomato purée/paste and some salt and pepper and cook for 2–3 minutes. Deglaze with a splash of red wine and let the alcohol evaporate over a high heat for 30 seconds, then reduce to a simmer. Stir in the basil and the milk. Simmer gently for 10–15 minutes until thickened. Adjust the seasoning as needed.

Shape the Cavatelli: Lightly dust a tray and work surface with semola. Divide the rested dough into 4 pieces. Roll one portion into a long rope about 1cm/⅓in thick, using light pressure with the palms of your hands. Cut the rope into small pieces, each roughly 1–2cm/½in long.

Take one piece at a time and, using a gnocchi paddle, press the dough with your thumb and drag it gently against the board away from you to create a slight curl with a hollow centre. The pressure should be firm enough to leave an indent but not so strong that it flattens the dough. You can also roll each piece over the back of a fork for texture, which helps the sauce cling to the pasta. Transfer the cavatelli to the tray, spacing them out so they don't stick together, and keep covered as you work. Repeat with the remaining dough.

Cook the Cavatelli: Bring a large pot of salted water to the boil. Add the cavatelli and cook for about 2–3 minutes, or until they float and the texture is al dente.

Combine and Serve: Before you combine the pasta and sauce, remove the bay leaf from the sauce. Then, using a slotted spoon, lift the pasta directly into the pan with the mushroom ragù, tossing gently to combine and add a splash of pasta water if needed to help the sauce cling evenly. Plate the cavatelli, then garnish with grated ricotta salata and a sprinkle of sumac. Drizzle with a little chilli oil, if using.

RAVIOLI WITH WHIPPED FETA, RICOTTA & BROAD/FAVA BEANS

Ravioli feta e ricotta con fave e menta

Ricotta and broad/fava beans are a match made in heaven in Sicilian cooking: creamy, sweet and full of spring. This version adds a twist with whipped feta, bringing a salty edge. Traditionally, in Sicily, ravioli would be filled with sheep's ricotta. To honour that tradition, the feta recreates the sharp, tangy flavour of sheep's milk. The result is a delightful balance of rich and creamy with a hint of salty, Mediterranean flair.

These plump, handmade ravioli are tossed in a delicate mix of caramelized onions, garden peas and broad beans: fresh ingredients found throughout the Mediterranean. A final touch of mint and Pecorino ties together the simple yet bold flavours, embodying the spirit of shared tables and the communal joy that defines Mediterranean dining. This recipe is my homage to the sun-drenched flavours of the region, a celebration of both tradition and the bounty of the land.

Serves: 4

Preparation time: 30 minutes, plus 30 minutes resting

Cooking time: 15 minutes

For the Dough:

* 400g/14oz/3 cups semola
* 4 eggs

For the Filling:

* 350g/12½oz/1⅓ cups ricotta, well drained
* 100g/3½oz/½ cup feta
* 1 tbsp finely chopped fresh mint
* Salt and pepper, to taste

For the Sauce:

* 2 tbsp extra virgin olive oil
* 1 small onion, finely diced
* 100g/3½oz/½ cup broad/fava beans, shelled and blanched
* 100g/3½oz/⅔ cup garden peas, fresh or frozen
* Salt and pepper, to taste
* Fresh mint leaves, to garnish
* Finely grated Pecorino, to serve

Make the Dough: On a clean work surface, make a mound with the semola and create a well in the centre. Crack in the eggs and gently whisk with a fork, gradually incorporating the semola. Knead for 5–7 minutes until smooth and elastic. Cover with a dish towel and let rest for 30 minutes.

Prepare the Filling: In a large bowl, whisk together the drained ricotta and the feta until creamy and smooth. Add the chopped mint and some salt and pepper to taste. Mix well and set aside in the refrigerator while you roll the ravioli.

Roll and Fill the Ravioli: Lightly dust a tray or cloth and a work surface with semola. Divide the rested dough into 4–6 portions. Roll each piece into a thin sheet, about 1mm thick (setting 5 on a Marcato). Spoon small amounts of the whipped ricotta filling onto one sheet, spaced about 5cm/2in apart. Using the sides of both hands, gently press the dough around each mound of ricotta to seal and space them out. This helps remove any air and ensures the ravioli hold together when cooked. Use a ravioli stamp to cut out each ravioli. If you don't have a stamp, a glass, cookie cutter, pastry wheel or even a small knife will do the job just fine. Set on the tray and keep covered as you work.

Prepare the Sauce: In a frying pan, heat the olive oil over a medium heat. Add the onion and sauté until caramelized and golden, about 5–7 minutes. Add the blanched broad/fava beans and the peas, seasoning with salt and pepper to taste. Cook for another 2–3 minutes until the beans and peas are tender. Remove from the heat and set aside.

Cook the Ravioli: Bring a large pot of salted water to the boil. Cook the ravioli for 3–4 minutes, until they are al dente and float to the surface.

Combine and Serve: Using a slotted spoon, lift the ravioli directly into the pan with the caramelized onions, beans and peas. Toss the cooked ravioli with the sauce. Add a little more olive oil if needed. Plate the ravioli and top with fresh mint leaves and grated Pecorino. Serve immediately.

Notes:

* Fresh broad/fava beans are ideal for this dish, but frozen ones work well too.
* For a light lemon flavour, you can add a little lemon juice to the sauce.
* This ravioli is best served fresh, but you can freeze the uncooked ravioli on a tray, then transfer to a ziplock bag for 2–3 months. Cook from frozen for an additional 1–2 minutes.

FIDEUÀ WITH PEPPERS, ONIONS & SAFFRON

Fideuà di verdure con zafferano

A Mediterranean pantry dish inspired by the Valencian coast, where toasted pasta takes the place of rice and saffron brings everything to life. *Fideuà* is a dish born of improvisation: a fisherman's answer to paella when rice was scarce. In this vegetarian version, fine pasta is toasted and simmered with slow-cooked onions, colourful peppers and a broth infused with saffron and smoked paprika. It's a one-pan meal with big personality and very little fuss. I first tasted a version of this dish on a trip to Catalonia, but it felt instantly familiar, comforting, simple and full of the same spirit of coastal cooking I grew up with in Sicily.

Serves: 4

Preparation time: 15 minutes

Cooking time: 35 minutes

Ingredients:

* 1 red onion
* 1 yellow pepper
* 1 red pepper
* 2 garlic cloves
* 3 tbsp extra virgin olive oil (divided)
* 250g/9oz/2 cups *fideuà* pasta or thin short-cut spaghetti, broken into 3–4cm/1½in pieces
* 1 tsp smoked paprika
* Pinch of saffron threads, infused in 2 tbsp hot water for a few minutes
* 1 tbsp tomato purée/paste or 2 tbsp tomato passata
* 750ml/26fl oz/3¼ cups hot vegetable stock
* Salt, to taste
* Flat-leaf parsley, chopped, to garnish
* Lemon wedges, to serve
* Grilled halloumi slices (for protein), to serve (optional)

Prepare the Vegetables: Thinly slice the onion and the deseeded yellow and red peppers. Mince the garlic and set everything aside.

Toast the Pasta: In a large frying pan or shallow casserole (a paella pan is even better), heat 1 tablespoon of the olive oil. Add the *fideuà* pasta and toast for 3–5 minutes over a medium heat, stirring often, until golden. Transfer to a plate and set aside.

Cook the Vegetables: In the same pan, heat the remaining olive oil. Add the sliced onion and peppers with a pinch of salt and cook gently for 10–12 minutes until soft and caramelized. Stir in the garlic and cook for another minute until fragrant. Add the smoked paprika, saffron threads with their water and tomato purée/paste and cook for 1–2 minutes more.

Simmer the Fideuà: Return the toasted pasta to the pan and pour over the hot stock. Stir once to distribute everything, then leave to cook over a medium heat, uncovered, without stirring, for 10–12 minutes or until the pasta is tender and the liquid mostly absorbed. You should hear a gentle sizzle toward the end, which means a crust is forming on the bottom.

Serve: Remove from the heat and let rest for a few minutes. Scatter over some chopped parsley and serve with lemon wedges for squeezing. For extra texture, finish the pan under a hot grill/broiler for 2–3 minutes to crisp the top. Optionally, add some grilled halloumi for extra protein.

RIGATONI WITH CAPERBERRY & OLIVE RAGÙ

Rigatoni con ragù di cucunci e olive

Serves: 4

Preparation time: 1 hour, plus 30 minutes resting

Cooking time: 35 minutes

For the Dough:

* 400g/14oz/3 cups semola
* 200ml/7fl oz/scant 1 cup lukewarm water

For the Ragù:

* 3 tbsp extra virgin olive oil, plus extra to serve
* 1 red onion, finely sliced
* 1 tbsp double concentrate tomato purée/paste
* 2 tbsp white wine or dry vermouth
* 6–8 caperberries, drained and finely chopped
* 10–12 pitted black or green olives (such as Gordal, Manzanilla or Nocellara), finely chopped
* 400g/14oz/2 cups tomato passata or polpa di pomodoro
* 1 tsp sugar (optional)
* Salt and pepper, to taste

To Serve:

* Caper Powder (optional – page 266)
* Finely grated Pecorino (optional)

A pantry ragù with real personality, born from bold flavours and the Mediterranean instinct to make something special from very little. It's not a ragù in the traditional sense – it's more a chunky sauce without meat – but it has all the depth you'd expect from one. I used caperberries: the fruit of the caper plant, milder in flavour than capers. Mine come from Pantelleria, an island off the coast of Sicily. The name *Pantelleria* is thought to derive from the Arabic *Bint al-Riyāh*, meaning "daughter of the winds", which beautifully captures the island's wild, windswept character.

Olives marry with capers perfectly because they echo the same bold, briny profile but with their own soft richness. Together, they create a sauce that feels both familiar and a little unexpected. I serve it with handmade rigatoni, shaped one by one on a gnocchi paddle. It's slow work, but exactly the kind I find most comforting.

Make the Dough: On a clean work surface, make a mound with the semola and create a well in the centre. Gradually add the water, mixing with your fingers or a fork until a rough dough forms. Knead for 5–7 minutes until smooth and elastic. Cover with a dish towel and let rest for 30 minutes.

Make the Ragù: Heat the olive oil in a wide pan over a medium heat. Add the onion and cook for 10 minutes until soft and caramelized. Stir in the tomato purée/paste and cook for 1–2 minutes until it darkens slightly. Deglaze with the white wine and let it bubble for a minute to evaporate. Add the chopped caperberries and olives, then stir in the passata. Season with salt and pepper, reduce the heat to medium-low and let simmer for 15–20 minutes, stirring occasionally. Add a splash of water if it begins to dry out. Taste and adjust with the sugar if needed.

Shape the Rigatoni: Lightly dust a tray and work surface with semola. Divide the rested dough into 2–4 pieces. Roll each piece into a thin sheet, about 1mm thick (setting 5 on a Marcato). Keep the other portions covered as you work.

Cut the sheet into rectangles about 4cm/1½in wide and 5cm/2in long, or big enough to form a small tube. Place one rectangle diagonally on a gnocchi paddle, positioning a thin wooden stick (a tool that usually comes with the gnocchi paddle, about the thickness of a pencil) across one corner. Roll the pasta over the stick and across the paddle, pressing gently so that the ridges imprint and the edge seals as the tube forms. Slide the rolled rigatoni off the stick and set aside on the tray.

If the dough sticks, dust the paddle, stick and/or your fingers lightly with semola. Repeat with the remaining dough, spacing the rigatoni apart to prevent sticking.

Cook the Rigatoni: Bring a large pot of salted water to the boil. Cook the rigatoni for about 2–3 minutes, or until they float and the texture is al dente.

Combine and Serve: Using a slotted spoon, lift the pasta directly into the pan with the ragù. Toss gently to coat, adding a splash of cooking water if needed to help the sauce cling evenly. Serve with a drizzle of olive oil and a sprinkle of caper powder if you like a bit of saltiness. Optionally, add some grated Pecorino.

SPINACH SPÄTZLE, BROWNED BUTTER, SAGE, HAZELNUT & ALPINE CHEESE

Spätzle agli spinaci, burro, salvia, nocciole e formaggio di montagna

Spätzle has no neat edges. It's dropped, scraped, shaped by gravity. The dough isn't rolled or filled, just pressed through holes into boiling water where it firms up in seconds. I like that about it. It resists being made perfect.

This dish belongs to many places: northern Italy, southern Germany, Austria. Recipes change from valley to valley, but the method stays the same: soft batter, hot water, a bit of care. Traditionally, it's made using a spätzle maker, which looks a bit like a flat cheese grater or potato ricer. But a colander with large holes or a slotted spoon will do the job just as well.

I've included it here because it speaks to what this chapter is about: food that moves across borders, shaped by the people who carry it. Here, spinach goes into the dough, and the rest stays simple: browned butter, toasted hazelnuts, sage and a sharp mountain cheese. It's what I make when I want something unassuming but generous.

Serves: 4

Preparation time: 30 minutes, plus 10–15 minutes resting

Cooking time: 15 minutes

For the Dough:
* 250g/9oz/5 cups spinach
* 3 small eggs
* 100ml/3½fl oz/scant ½ cup water
* Pinch of grated nutmeg
* 250g/9oz/scant 2 cups 00 flour

For the Sauce:
* 60g/2oz/4 tbsp unsalted butter
* 8–10 fresh sage leaves
* 50g/1¾oz/½ cup hazelnuts, toasted and roughly chopped, plus extra to garnish (optional)
* 80g/3oz/1 cup Alpine cheese (e.g. Fontina, Gruyère or Bergkäse), grated, plus extra to serve (optional)

Prepare the Spinach: Blanch the spinach in boiling water for 30 seconds, then drain and transfer immediately to a bowl of iced water. Squeeze out as much moisture as possible, then finely chop or blitz in a food processor until smooth.

Make the Spätzle Batter: In a large bowl, whisk together the chopped spinach, eggs, water and nutmeg. Gradually add the flour, stirring to form a thick but pourable batter. Let rest for 10–15 minutes.

Make the Sauce: In a wide frying pan, melt the butter over a medium-low heat for 3–5 minutes until it begins to foam and brown slightly. Keep swirling the pan to prevent burning. A nutty aroma signals that it's ready. Add the sage leaves and cook for 1–2 minutes until crisp. Add the hazelnuts and stir to coat. Remove from the heat.

Shape and Cook the Spätzle: Bring a large pot of salted water to the boil. Place a *spätzle* maker (hopper) over the pot and pour in some of the batter. Slide the hopper back and forth to press the dough through the holes into the water where it will drop in small, irregular shapes. Work in batches to avoid overcrowding the pot.

If you don't have a *spätzle* maker, you can use a colander with large round holes: place the batter inside and press it through with the back of a ladle or a sturdy spoon. Other alternatives are a flat coarse cheese grater or a wide slotted spoon: simply use a spatula or scraper to push the batter through.

Serve the Spätzle: As soon as the *spätzle* float to the surface (which should take between 30–60 seconds), cook for another minute, then lift them out with a slotted spoon and transfer to the frying pan with the butter, sage and hazelnuts. Toss well. Remove from the heat, add the grated Alpine cheese and stir until just melted. Serve immediately, with extra hazelnuts and cheese on top, if desired.

MALLOREDDUS, CARAMELIZED ONIONS, SAFFRON CREAM & BREADCRUMBS

A Sardinian classic, handmade and humble, soaking up a sweet and golden sauce that tastes like a slow afternoon. Malloreddus, also known as *gnocchetti sardi* (Sardinian gnocchi), are a traditional pasta from Sardinia. Made with semola and water, they are shaped by hand and pressed against a ridged surface like a basket or a gnocchi board. Though they resemble cavatelli, a shape also made in parts of southern Italy including Sicily, malloreddus are typically smaller, firmer and more deeply grooved. These features reflect Sardinia's own culinary identity and its long tradition of durum wheat cultivation.

This comforting dish pairs the ridged pasta with a golden saffron-infused cream sauce, deeply caramelized onions and a topping of crisp breadcrumbs. The flavours are warm, layered and distinctly Mediterranean.

Serves: 4

Preparation time: 30 minutes, plus 30 minutes resting

Cooking time: 40 minutes

For the Dough:

* 400g/14oz/3 cups semola
* 200ml/7fl oz/scant 1 cup lukewarm water

For the Sauce:

* 2 tbsp extra virgin olive oil
* 2 large white onions, thinly sliced
* ½ tsp sugar
* 100ml/3½fl oz/scant ½ cup single/light cream
* Pinch of saffron threads, infused in 1 tbsp hot water
* Salt and pepper, to taste

To Serve:

* 3 tbsp extra virgin olive oil
* 4 tbsp fine breadcrumbs

Make the Dough: On a clean work surface, make a mound with the semola and create a well in the centre. Gradually add the water, mixing with your fingers or a fork to incorporate the semola until a rough dough forms. Knead for 5–7 minutes until smooth and elastic. Cover with a dish towel and let rest for 30 minutes.

Caramelize the Onions: Heat the olive oil in a wide pan over a medium-low heat. Add the sliced onions and a pinch of salt. Cook slowly, stirring occasionally, for 25–30 minutes until soft and golden brown. Add the sugar about halfway through cooking to help the caramelization. Lower the heat if they begin to catch.

Shape the Malloreddus: Lightly dust a tray and work surface with semola. Divide the rested dough into 4 pieces. Roll each into long ropes about 1cm/⅓in thick. Cut into small pieces about 1cm/⅓in long. Press each piece against a *gnocchi* paddle or over the holes of a coarse cheese grater, rolling gently to create ridges and a slight curve. Set aside on the tray while you finish the sauce and keep covered as you work.

Prepare the Sauce: Stir the cream and the saffron threads with their water into the caramelized onions. Simmer for 2–3 minutes until slightly thickened. Season with salt and pepper. Turn off the heat and keep warm.

Toast the Breadcrumbs: In a small frying pan, heat the olive oil over a medium heat. Add the breadcrumbs and cook, stirring often, for 3–4 minutes until golden and crisp. Remove from the heat and set aside.

Cook the Malloreddus: Bring a large pot of salted water to the boil. Cook the malloreddus for 3–4 minutes, or until they are al dente and float to the surface.

Combine and Serve: Using a slotted spoon, lift the malloreddus directly into the pan with the saffron-onion sauce and toss gently, adding a splash of cooking water if needed to help the sauce cling evenly. Plate and top with the toasted breadcrumbs. Serve immediately.

CASARECCE WITH BURNT AUBERGINE/EGGPLANT & TAHINI

Casarecce con crema di melanzane arrostite e tahina

A smoky, cross-cultural pasta that doesn't follow the rules but knows exactly where it's going. You could call this pasta a remix. The flavours are familiar: burnt aubergine/eggplant, tahini, lemon. But they land differently here. Not as a dip or a side, but as a sauce made to cling to the gentle curves of handmade casarecce. This short pasta hails from Sicily, its curled scroll-like shape perfect for catching sauce. The aubergine is charred until the flesh collapses, smoky and tender. The tahini is mellow, not dominant, just enough to leave a trace of sesame warmth. The lemon sharpens, but without taking over. It lives comfortably in its own space, rooted in the same spirit of simplicity and boldness. A dish for when you're in the mood to go off-script but stay grounded in the kind of cooking that feels honest and satisfying. It's best eaten cold or at room temperature.

Serves: 4

Preparation time: 1 hour, plus 30 minutes resting

Cooking time: 25 minutes

For the Dough:

* 400g/14oz/3 cups semola
* 200ml/7fl oz/scant 1 cup lukewarm water

For the Sauce:

* 2 large aubergines/eggplants
* 2 tbsp extra virgin olive oil
* 1 garlic clove, finely grated (optional)
* 2 tbsp tahini
* Zest and juice of ½ unwaxed lemon, or to taste
* ½ tsp dried chilli/hot pepper flakes
* Salt, to taste

To Serve:

* A sprinkle of sumac
* Extra virgin olive oil, for drizzling
* Fresh parsley or mint, chopped
* Pangrattato, to serve (page 248)

Make the Dough: On a clean work surface, make a mound with the semola and create a well in the centre. Gradually add the water, mixing with your fingers or a fork to incorporate the semola until a rough dough forms. Knead for 5–7 minutes until smooth and elastic. Cover with a dish towel and let rest for 30 minutes.

Char the Aubergines/Eggplants: Place the aubergines directly over a gas flame or under a hot grill/broiler. Char until the skins are blackened and the insides are soft and collapsed, turning regularly. This will take about 15–20 minutes. Leave to cool slightly, then peel off the skins and discard. Scoop the flesh into a bowl and mash with a fork.

Make the Sauce: In a large bowl, combine the mashed aubergine flesh with the olive oil, garlic, if using, tahini, lemon zest and juice, dried chilli/hot pepper flakes and some salt, adjusting the seasoning to taste. The sauce should be silky, with a smoky base and a gentle citrus lift. Set aside.

Shape the Casarecce: Lightly dust a tray and work surface with semola. Divide the rested dough into 4 portions. Roll each piece into a rope about 5mm/¼in thick. Cut into 4–5cm/2in segments. Press each piece lengthways along a *ferretto* or a thin metal or wooden rod about 3–4mm/⅛in thick, while rolling gently to create a groove. Pick it up and, using your fingertips, ever so slightly twist the ends in opposite directions, forming the signature casarecce shape. Place on the tray and keep covered as you work. Repeat with the rest.

Cook the Casarecce: Bring a large pot of salted water to the boil. Cook the casarecce for 2–3 minutes, or until they float and the texture is al dente.

Combine and Serve: Using a slotted spoon, lift the pasta directly into the bowl with the aubergine sauce. Toss gently to coat, adding a splash of cooking water if needed to help the sauce cling evenly. Serve sprinkled with sumac and pangrattato, drizzled with extra olive oil and with a sprinkling of herbs.

PISAREI, SMOKY ROASTED RED PEPPER & SPICE-INFUSED PESTO

Pisarei con pesto di peperoni speziati

A robust pasta dish where smoky depth and gentle heat steal the show. I first tasted pisarei, a type of small, hand-rolled pasta dumpling, in a rustic trattoria while road-tripping through northern Italy. Native to the province of Piacenza in Emilia-Romagna, pisarei are traditionally made by hand and served with a hearty bean sauce in the classic dish *pisarei e faso*. I loved their texture: slightly chewy, compact and perfect for holding bold flavours.

This version is an experiment, a way of pairing that traditional shape with something different. The smoky, spiced pesto draws from ingredients I fell in love with during my travels across Spain and Morocco: sweet roasted peppers, cayenne, cumin and smoked paprika.

The idea came one afternoon when I was playing with leftover peppers and pine nuts from a mezze spread and found myself reaching for the paprika. What started as a quick sauce became something worth preserving: a rich, spiced condiment that lives on in this dish. It's earthy, intense and completely satisfying. This dish may look unassuming, but it's one of my favourite pastas in this book.

Serves: 4

Preparation time: 30 minutes, plus 30 minutes resting

Cooking time: 5 minutes

For the Dough:

* 400g/14oz/3 cups semola
* 200ml/7fl oz/scant 1 cup lukewarm water

For the Pesto:

* 2 large red peppers, charred, peeled and deseeded
* 60g/2oz/½ cup pine nuts, toasted
* 1 garlic clove
* 1½ tsp smoked paprika
* ½ tsp ground cumin
* ¼ tsp cayenne pepper
* 50g/1¾oz/½ cup Pecorino, finely grated
* 60ml/2fl oz/¼ cup extra virgin olive oil
* Salt and pepper, to taste

For Garnish:

* Toasted pine nuts
* Pinch of smoked paprika, for sprinkling

Make the Dough: On a clean work surface, make a mound with the semola and create a well in the centre. Gradually add the water, mixing with your fingers or a fork to incorporate the semola until a rough dough forms. Knead for 5–7 minutes until smooth and elastic. Cover with a dish towel and let it rest for about 30 minutes.

Prepare the Pesto: In a food processor, combine the charred red peppers, toasted pine nuts, garlic, smoked paprika, cumin, cayenne and Pecorino. Pulse until coarsely chopped. With the motor running, slowly drizzle in the olive oil until the pesto becomes smooth but still slightly chunky. Taste and season with salt and pepper as needed, adjusting the spices if you prefer more heat or smokiness. Set aside.

Shape the Pisarei: Lightly dust a tray and work surface with semola. Divide the rested dough into 4 portions. Roll each portion into a long rope about 1cm/⅓in in diameter, then cut into 2cm/¾in pieces. To shape the pisarei, gently press the centre of each piece with your thumb or the back of a chopstick to form a small indentation. This creates their signature hollow, helping them catch more sauce. Place the shaped pisarei on the tray and keep covered as you shape the rest of the dough.

Cook the Pisarei: Bring a large pot of salted water to the boil. Cook the pisarei for 2–3 minutes, until they float to the surface. Continue cooking for another 1–2 minutes, until tender.

Combine and Serve: Using a slotted spoon, lift the pisarei directly into a large bowl. Toss with the pesto, adding a splash of pasta water if needed to help the sauce cling evenly. Serve the pisarei garnished with extra toasted pine nuts and a light dusting of smoked paprika for added flavour and colour.

MAFALDINE WITH HARISSA, TOMATO & MIXED COURGETTES/ZUCCHINI

Mafaldine con harissa, pomodoro e zucchine miste

A summery tangle of heat, silk and squash, with one foot in Sicily and the other wherever the flavour takes you. This isn't a dish that cares much for borders. You start with good tomatoes, the kind that cook down into something deep and generous. Stir in a spoonful of harissa for warmth and fire. Add courgettes/zucchini of every shade, sautéed just enough to soften but not lose their nerve. What comes out isn't strictly Italian or Tunisian or anything else. It just makes sense.

The mafaldine are made by hand, of course. Long, ribboned strands with ruffled edges that were clearly designed by someone who understood the joy of pleasing the eye. It's not complicated, but it's full of character. And it belongs in this chapter because the Mediterranean has never stood still. It's always been about movement, exchange and flavour passed from hand to hand. This dish gets that.

Serves: 4

Preparation time: 30 minutes, plus 30 minutes resting

Cooking time: 35 minutes

For the Dough:

* 400g/14oz/3 cups 00 flour
* 4 large eggs

For the Sauce:

* 2 tbsp extra virgin olive oil
* 1 garlic clove, minced
* 2–3 tsp harissa paste, to taste
* 400g/14oz/2 cups canned chopped tomatoes or passata
* Salt and pepper, to taste

For the Courgette/Zucchini:

* 1 small yellow courgette/ zucchini
* 1 small light green courgette/ zucchini
* 1 small dark green courgette/ zucchini
* Extra virgin olive oil (approx. 3 tbsp), for sautéing, plus extra to serve (optional)
* Salt, to taste

Make the Dough: On a clean work surface, make a mound with the flour and create a well in the centre. Crack in the eggs and gently whisk with a fork, gradually incorporating the flour until a rough dough forms. Knead for 5–7 minutes until smooth and elastic. Cover with a dish towel and let rest for 30 minutes.

Make the Sauce: Heat the olive oil in a wide pan over a medium heat. Add the garlic and harissa and let them bloom for 30 seconds until fragrant. Add the chopped tomatoes, season with salt and pepper, then simmer, uncovered, for 20–25 minutes until thickened and flavourful.

Roll and Cut the Mafaldine: Lightly dust a tray and work surface with flour. Divide the rested dough into 4 portions. Roll each piece into a thin sheet, about 1mm thick (setting 5 on a Marcato). Cut into long ribbons using a fluted pasta cutter to form mafaldine or use the dedicated mafaldine attachment if your machine has one. Dust lightly with flour and set aside on the tray, and keep covered as you work.

Cook the Courgettes/Zucchini: Slice each courgette/zucchini into small dice, thin rounds or ribbons. In another pan, sauté the courgettes in olive oil with a pinch of salt over a medium-high heat for 5 minutes, or until just tender and slightly caramelized. Set aside.

Cook the Mafaldine: Bring a large pot of salted water to the boil. Cook the mafaldine for 2–3 minutes, or until al dente.

Combine and Serve: Using tongs, lift the pasta directly into the pan with the harissa tomato sauce. Toss gently to coat, adding a splash of cooking water if needed to help the sauce cling evenly. Serve twirled onto plates, topped with the sautéed courgette and an optional extra drizzle of olive oil. Offer extra harissa at the table for anyone who likes more heat.

COUSCOUS ARANCINI WITH CAPONATA & SMOKED SCAMORZA

Arancini di couscous con caponata e scamorza affumicata

Serves: 4

Preparation time: 45 minutes, plus cooling and chilling

Cooking time: 1 hour 10 minutes

For the Caponata:

* 4 tbsp extra virgin olive oil
* 1 onion, finely sliced
* 1 aubergine/eggplant, cubed
* 2 peppers (1 yellow and 1 red), deseeded and chopped
* 1 celery stalk, finely chopped
* 250ml/9fl oz/1 cup tomato passata or polpa di pomodoro
* 1 tbsp capers, rinsed
* 2 tbsp raisins
* A handful of pitted green olives, chopped
* ½ tsp chilli powder
* 1 tsp ras el hanout (optional)
* 80ml/2¾fl oz/⅓ cup apple cider vinegar, to taste
* 1 tbsp muscovado/brown sugar
* A handful of chopped parsley
* Salt, to taste

For the Couscous:

* 300g/10½oz/2 cups couscous
* 400ml/14fl oz/1⅔ cups vegetable stock
* 2 tbsp extra virgin olive oil
* 2–3 tbsp tomato passata

To Assemble and Fry:

* 150g/5¼oz/1¼ cups plain/all-purpose flour
* 500g/17½oz/5 cups breadcrumbs
* 3 large eggs, beaten
* 100g/3½oz/⅔ cup smoked scamorza, cut into small cubes
* 1l/35fl oz/4¼ cups groundnut/peanut or sunflower oil, for deep-frying
* Salt, to taste

A meeting of worlds in one crisp, golden bite. Couscous isn't native to Sicily, but it's been at home here for centuries. A gift from our North African neighbours, it's still prepared with fish for Sicilian feast days and seaside celebrations. These arancini are a tribute to that cultural exchange, rolling three beloved Sicilian elements into one: couscous, caponata and the joy of frying something stuffed and delicious.

This caponata is a lighter, simplified version, with a non-traditional spice blend: *ras el hanout*. No deep-frying of each vegetable; just a gentle sauté, enough to bring the ingredients together while keeping things fresh. The smoked scamorza adds a savoury pull in the centre, and the couscous forms a soft, nutty shell around it all.

Prepare the Caponata: Heat the olive oil in a non-stick frying pan. Add the onion and cook over a low heat for 10 minutes until softened. Add the aubergine/eggplant, peppers and celery. Stir and cook for 5 minutes, then stir in the passata, capers, raisins, olives, chilli powder and ras el hanout, if using. Season with salt and simmer for 15 minutes, or until the vegetables are tender. Add the vinegar and sugar, then raise the heat briefly to let the vinegar evaporate. Remove from the heat, cool to room temperature and stir in the chopped parsley.

Prepare the Couscous: Traditional method: Steam the couscous over the simmering vegetable stock in a couscoussier or a large sieve/fine-mesh strainer set over a pot, covered with foil and a lid. Steam for 15–20 minutes, fluffing halfway through. Toss with the olive oil, allow to cool, then stir in the passata. Chill for at least 1 hour.

Quick method: Place the couscous in a large bowl. Add the olive oil and rub it through the grains with your hands. Bring the stock to the boil and pour over the couscous. Cover and let sit for 10 minutes. Fluff with a fork, cool then stir in the passata and chill for at least 1 hour.

Shape the Arancini: Place the flour, breadcrumbs and beaten eggs in three separate shallow bowls. Season the breadcrumbs with a pinch of salt. Wet your hands slightly. Scoop a heaped tablespoon of couscous into your palm and flatten it. Press your thumb into the centre and add a spoonful of caponata and a couple of cubes of scamorza. Cover with a little more couscous and shape into a firm ball. Roll the ball first in the flour, then in the beaten egg and finally in the breadcrumbs, making sure it is evenly coated. Repeat with the remaining mixture.

Option 1: Fry the Arancini: Heat the groundnut/peanut or sunflower oil in a deep pan until a small piece of bread dropped in sizzles and turns golden in 30–45 seconds (around 170°C/340°F). Deep-fry the arancini in batches for 3–4 minutes per batch until golden and crisp. Drain on paper towels and serve hot or warm.

Option 2: Bake the Arancini: Preheat the oven to 200°C/400°F/Gas Mark 6. Place the shaped arancini on a baking sheet lined with baking parchment. Drizzle lightly with oil or use olive oil spray. Bake for 18–22 minutes, turning once, until golden and crisp.

OLIVE LEAF PASTA WITH BLACK OLIVES & SUN-DRIED TOMATOES

Foglie d'ulivo con olive nere e pomodori secchi

Foglie d'ulivo (literally "olive leaves") is a hand-shaped pasta from southern Italy, particularly associated with Puglia. Its name comes from its narrow, pointed shape, which resembles the leaves of the olive tree. Related to orecchiette in how it's formed, it is distinct in look and feel. Oval, tapered and slightly ridged, it's the kind of shape that naturally works with simple Mediterranean ingredients like fresh tomatoes, ricotta, olive oil and basil.

The dough is traditionally made with semola and water, but in this version, spinach is added to give it a green hue: a visual hint to the leaves themselves. Here, I've paired it with black olives and sun-dried tomatoes, a combination that feels at home anywhere around the olive belt. A shape rooted in tradition, with flavours that speak across regions . . . which is exactly why it belongs in this chapter.

Serves: 4

Preparation time: 30 minutes, plus 30 minutes resting

Cooking time: 5 minutes

For the Spinach Dough:

* 400g/14oz/3 cups semola
* 100g/3½oz/⅔ cup cooked spinach, squeezed dry and finely chopped or puréed
* 150ml/5fl oz/⅔ cup lukewarm water, or as needed

For the Sauce:

* 3 tbsp extra virgin olive oil, plus extra to serve
* 1 garlic clove, finely chopped
* 80g/3oz/⅓ cup pitted black olives, whole or roughly chopped
* 80g/3oz/½ cup sun-dried tomatoes in oil, drained and chopped
* Zest of ½ unwaxed lemon
* A few fresh basil leaves, roughly chopped or torn
* Salt and pepper, to taste

Make the Dough: On a clean work surface, make a mound with the semola and create a well in the centre. Add the spinach, then add the water gradually, mixing with your fingers or a fork to incorporate the semola until a rough dough forms. Knead for 5–7 minutes until smooth and elastic. Cover with a dish towel and rest for 30 minutes.

Prepare the Sauce: In a wide pan, heat the olive oil over a medium heat. Add the garlic and let it sizzle for 30 seconds until fragrant. Stir in the olives and sun-dried tomatoes and sauté for 2–3 minutes until softened. Season with salt and pepper and set aside.

Shape the Foglie d'Ulivo: Lightly dust a tray and a wooden board or work surface with semola. Divide the rested dough into 4–6 portions and cut into oval, walnut-size pieces about 3cm/1¼in long and 1cm/⅓in wide. Anchor one long edge of a dough piece with your thumb. Press the flat, blunt side of a butter knife onto the longer edge and drag the blade sideways to create a curved shape resembling an olive leaf. Pinch the ends slightly to make them pointy. Lightly dust with semola and set aside on the tray, and keep covered as you work.

For a quicker method (though less defined in texture), roll the dough into ropes about 1cm/⅓in thick. Cut into 3cm/1¼in segments, then flatten each one into an oval with your thumb or the heel of your palm. Pinch the ends and curve them slightly to echo the shape of a leaf.

Cook the Foglie d'Ulivo: Bring a large pot of salted water to the boil. Cook the foglie d'ulivo for 2–3 minutes, or until they float and the texture is al dente.

Combine and Serve: Using a slotted spoon, lift the pasta directly into a large serving bowl. Add the lemon zest, basil and the olive and sun-dried tomato sauce. Toss gently to coat, adding a splash of cooking water if needed to help the sauce cling evenly. Serve warm, with an extra drizzle of olive oil.

PUMPKIN GNOCCHI WITH MUM'S SAGE PESTO

Gnocchi di zucca con pesto di salvia e noci

Serves: 4

Preparation time: 45 minutes, plus 30 minutes cooling and 15 minutes resting

Cooking time: 35 minutes

For the Dough:

* 1kg/2¼lb/6½ cups pumpkin, peeled, deseeded and cubed
* 400g/14oz/3 cups 00 flour
* 200g/7oz/1⅔ cups potato starch
* 1 tsp salt, plus extra for the blanched pumpkin

For the Pesto:

* 35g/1¼oz/1 cup packed fresh sage leaves
* 10 walnut halves, plus extra crushed walnuts to serve
* A small bunch of fresh parsley
* 100ml/3½fl oz/scant ½ cup (divided) extra virgin olive oil, plus more as needed and to serve
* Salt and pepper, to taste

I didn't grow up with this dish. It wasn't passed down or scribbled in a notebook. My mum just tried it once, loved it and sent me a voice note with the rough idea. That was enough.

Sage wasn't a herb I ever imagined turning into pesto. Too bold, too velvety, too rarely eaten raw. But paired with parsley, it works. The sharpness softens, the edges round out. It becomes something delicate but distinctive. Unexpected in the best way. The pumpkin *gnocchi* are sweet and light, a perfect match with sage. I made it with caution the first time, curiosity the second and affection ever since.

Ultimately, it reminds me of my mum. She was rarely adventurous with food, which makes this discovery even more special. It fits into this chapter because it's a gentle blend of broader flavours: autumnal, herbaceous, a little unorthodox. A reminder that even familiar ingredients can travel in new directions.

Roast the Pumpkin: Preheat the oven to 180°C/350°F/Gas Mark 4. Bring a large pot of water to the boil. Add the pumpkin cubes and blanch for 5–6 minutes, just until the outside begins to soften but the inside remains firm. Drain, season lightly with the salt and transfer to a baking sheet lined with baking parchment. Roast in the hot oven for 30 minutes until tender and dry. Mash thoroughly until smooth. Leave to cool to room temperature.

Make the Dough: On a clean work surface, combine the mashed pumpkin, flour, potato starch and measured salt. Mix and knead gently for 5–7 minutes until you have a soft, slightly sticky dough that pulls away from the counter. Add a little extra flour only if needed. Cover with a dish towel and let rest for 15 minutes.

Shape the Gnocchi: Lightly dust a tray and work surface with flour. Divide the rested dough into 4–6 portions and roll each into a rope about 2cm/¾in thick. Cut into small, even pieces. You can leave them as is or gently press with the tines of a fork for ridges. Dust lightly with flour and set aside on the tray, and keep covered as you work.

Make the Pesto: In a blender or food processor, combine the sage, walnuts, parsley and some salt and pepper and blitz until chunky. With the motor running, slowly drizzle in the olive oil until the pesto is smooth but still textured or until you reach your desired consistency. Set aside.

Cook the Gnocchi: Bring a large pot of salted water to the boil. Add the gnocchi in batches and cook for 1 minute, until they float to the surface.

Combine and Serve: Using a slotted spoon, lift the gnocchi directly into a large bowl. Add the pesto and a splash of cooking water if needed to help the sauce cling evenly. Stir gently and then serve immediately, with extra olive oil and crushed walnuts, if you like.

HALF MOONS WITH ORANGE ZEST, ROOT GINGER & PISTACHIOS

Mezzelune con zeste d'arancia, zenzero e pistacchi

This flavour combination brings together my love for the Mediterranean and the fragrant ingredients of Eastern kitchens. *Mezzelune*, meaning "half-moons" in Italian, are filled with a gently aromatic mix of orange zest, fresh root ginger and finely chopped pistachios. The filling is both unexpected and familiar, just enough sweetness to intrigue, just enough spice to lift.

The saffron cream sauce lends complexity rather than dominance. It's delicate, not bold and lets the flavours of the filling come through in every bite. What I enjoy most about this dish is the surprise it holds: you think you know what to expect, and then it shifts, just slightly, into something more layered. It's a kind of celebration of cross-cultural flavour, where no single element steals the show.

Serves: 4

Preparation time: 40 minutes, plus 30 minutes resting

Cooking time: 10 minutes

For the Dough:

* 400g/14oz/3 cups 00 flour
* 4 eggs

For the Filling:

* 500g/17½oz/2 cups ricotta, well drained
* Zest of 1 large orange
* 1 tbsp finely grated root ginger
* 40g/1½oz/⅓ cup pistachios, finely chopped
* 3 tbsp finely grated Parmigiano Reggiano
* Salt and pepper, to taste

For the Sauce:

* 4 tbsp extra virgin olive oil
* 2 tbsp unsalted butter
* 1 small garlic clove, lightly crushed
* 10–12 saffron threads, infused in 2 tbsp hot water
* Juice of ½ orange
* Salt, to taste

For Garnish:

* Chopped pistachios
* Fresh parsley, chopped
* Orange zest

Make the Dough: On a clean work surface, make a mound with the flour and create a well in the centre. Crack in the eggs and whisk gently, gradually incorporating the flour until a rough dough forms. Knead for 5–7 minutes until smooth and elastic. Cover with a dish towel and let rest for 30 minutes.

Prepare the Filling: In a bowl, mix the ricotta with the orange zest, root ginger, pistachios, Parmigiano and a pinch of salt. Taste and adjust the seasoning. Keep chilled until needed.

Shape the Mezzelune: Lightly dust a tray and work surface with flour. Divide the rested dough into 4–6 portions. Roll each piece into a thin sheet, about 1mm thick (setting 5 on a Marcato). Use a round cookie cutter or a glass (about 8cm/3¼in diameter) to cut out circles. Place a small spoonful of the filling mixture in the centre of each circle, fold in half into a half-moon shape and press the edges firmly to seal, ensuring there are no air pockets. Transfer to the floured tray and keep covered as you work.

Make the Sauce: In a small saucepan, heat the olive oil and butter over a low heat. Add the crushed garlic and let it infuse gently for 1 minute without colouring. Add the saffron threads with their water, the orange juice and a pinch of salt. Let everything warm through and reduce for another 2 minutes to allow the flavours to meld. Remove from the heat.

Cook the Mezzelune: Bring a large pot of salted water to the boil. Add the mezzelune and cook for 2–3 minutes, until they float and the texture is al dente.

Combine and Serve: Using a slotted spoon, lift the mezzelune directly into the saucepan with the saffron sauce. Toss gently to coat. Divide the mezzelune among plates, spooning any remaining sauce over the top. Garnish with extra chopped pistachios, chopped parsley and a sprinkle of fresh orange zest for an added burst of flavour. Serve immediately.

FARRO SALAD WITH GRILLED COURGETTE/ ZUCCHINI, OLIVES & RED ONION

Insalata di farro, zucchine grigliate, olive e cipolla

A warm-weather dish with ancient roots and fresh intentions. Farro has been cultivated in Sicily since ancient times, brought by the Greeks and prized by the Romans. It's one of the island's oldest grains, a kind of ancestral wheat with a nutty flavour and resilient bite. Though less commonly used today, *farro* still holds symbolic importance, especially during the Feast of Santa Lucia on 13 December.

In Sicilian households, Santa Lucia is not just a saint's day. It's a day of remembrance. According to tradition, a famine once swept Palermo in the 1600s. The people had nothing, not even flour to make bread. On that day, a ship miraculously arrived in port, carrying wheat. Rather than grind it into flour, the starving people boiled the grain and ate it as it was. That act of necessity became a ritual of gratitude. No bread, no pasta, only boiled farro made into *cuccìa*, either savoury – usually with chickpeas/garbanzo beans and a few simple spices – or sweetened with ricotta, honey or chocolate.

This salad doesn't belong to that tradition exactly, but it shares its spirit. It's about making something special from simple things. Here, farro is paired with smoky grilled courgette/zucchini, sweet red onion, olives, capers and herbs to create a dish that speaks of tradition, remembrance and the Mediterranean in every forkful.

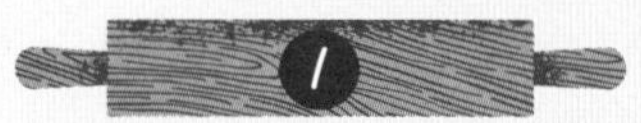

Serves: 4

Preparation time: 15 minutes, plus overnight soaking

Cooking time: 30 minutes

Ingredients:

* 200g/7oz/1 cup farro
* Juice of 1 lemon (divided)
* 2 courgettes/zucchini, cut into thick batons or large chunks
* 3 tbsp extra virgin olive oil (divided)
* 1 large red onion, thinly sliced
* 15g/½oz/½ cup fresh mint leaves, chopped, plus extra to garnish
* 15g/½oz/½ cup fresh basil leaves, chopped, plus extra sprigs to garnish (optional)
* 50g/1¾oz/⅓ cup pitted black olives, halved
* 1 tbsp capers, rinsed
* 30g/1oz/4 tbsp pine nuts, toasted (optional)
* 2 tbsp raisins (optional)
* Salt and pepper, to taste

Soak the Farro: The night before, rinse the *farro* and place it in a bowl. Add the juice of half a lemon and the squeezed lemon half. Cover with cold water and soak overnight.

Cook the Farro: The following day, drain the soaked *farro* and discard the lemon half. Place it in a saucepan with fresh water and a pinch of salt. Bring to the boil and cook for 5–10 minutes, until tender but still pleasantly chewy. Drain and set aside to cool.

Grill/Broil the Courgettes/Zucchini: Preheat a griddle/grill pan over a medium-high heat. Brush the courgettes with 1 tablespoon of the olive oil and season with salt and pepper. Grill for 2–3 minutes on each side until tender and lightly charred. Set aside.

Sauté the Onion: In a separate pan, heat another tablespoon of the olive oil over a medium heat. Add the red onion and cook gently for 10 minutes until soft and caramelized. Set aside.

Assemble the Salad: In a large bowl, combine the cooked farro, grilled courgette and caramelized onion. Add the chopped mint and basil, the olives, capers and the pine nuts and raisins, if using.

Dress and Serve: Drizzle the remaining tablespoon of olive oil over the salad and add the juice of the remaining lemon half. Season with salt and pepper and toss gently to combine. Serve at room temperature or lightly chilled, garnished with extra mint and/or basil sprigs, if desired.

Ch. 5

THE SPICE of Life

Spices have always held a special place in my kitchen, not just for their ability to transform a dish, but for the stories they carry: stories of travel, exchange and culture. Growing up in Sicily, I was surrounded by the aromas of fennel, cinnamon, oregano and saffron. But as I moved through life, my relationship with spices deepened and evolved.

In 2009, I left Italy for Singapore, a city that would unexpectedly become home for the next ten years after I met my soulmate, Akshay, who had landed from his native India the same day I did. Call it destiny. We got engaged two months after meeting and married five months later.

Together, we travelled across Southeast and East Asia, always eating, always exploring. Singapore was the perfect backdrop: a place where Chinese, Malay, Tamilian and international cuisines coexist in delicious harmony. We followed food trails in Bali and Bangkok, tasting the bright tang of lemongrass and lime leaf, the herbal lift of Thai basil and the crunch of fresh green peppercorns. We discovered the fragrant complexity of Indonesian sambals, the numbing tingle of Sichuan peppercorns and the deep umami of Japanese miso.

That decade shaped the way I cook more than any other. Italian ingredients were hard to find, so I began adapting Italian dishes with local produce and spices. My pantry expanded, my curiosity deepened and my understanding of flavour changed. The blend of Mediterranean and Asian influences now defines how I cook. It's not a deliberate fusion, but something that emerged naturally from a life lived between cultures.

When people ask me what kind of book this is, they expect a collection of Sicilian or Italian recipes. And while those roots run deep, this chapter is the one that represents me most truthfully. It reflects the life I've lived, the places I've called home and the flavours I've embraced along the way. It's about bringing together what I've seen, tasted and loved into dishes that feel instinctively right to me, while honouring where those ingredients come from and the people who taught me how to use them. Every dish carries a story: a market stall in Chiang Mai, a seaside meal in Langkawi, a street corner in Tokyo.

RADICCHIO & RED ONION LASAGNA WITH CARAWAY-SPICED BÉCHAMEL

Serves: 4

Preparation time: 45 minutes, plus 30 minutes resting

Cooking time: 1 hour 10 minutes

For the Dough:

* 400g/14oz/3 cups 00 flour
* 4 large eggs

For the Filling:

* 3 tbsp extra virgin olive oil
* 2 red onions, thinly sliced
* 1 head of radicchio, thinly sliced
* Salt and pepper, to taste

For the Caraway-Spiced Béchamel:

* 50g/1¾oz/3½ tbsp unsalted butter
* 50g/1¾oz/¼ cup plain/all-purpose flour
* 500ml/17fl oz/2 cups whole milk
* 1 tsp caraway seeds, lightly toasted and ground in a mortar and pestle or spice grinder
* Salt and pepper, to taste

To Assemble:

* 100g/3½oz/1 cup Parmigiano Reggiano or Pecorino, finely grated
* 100g/3½oz/¾ cup mozzarella, shredded
* Fresh parsley or chives, roughly chopped, to garnish (optional)

A comforting dish that brings together the bittersweet flavours of northern Italy with a gentle, unexpected spice. Radicchio reminds me of the years I spent in the Veneto region during university and my early career. I learned to love radicchio's gentle bitterness, especially when paired with something sweet or creamy. One of the first dinners I cooked with roommates was a radicchio risotto that turned slightly purple. We were all from Italy, and this ingredient felt new and exotic.

I first came across caraway seeds on a trip to Warsaw years ago, in a loaf of warm rye bread. That tiny seed, with its peppery, aromatic bite, stuck with me. Years later, it found its way into my béchamel, almost by instinct. I love adding caraway to my salads, especially one I make often with chicory/endive, radicchio, Parmigiano Reggiano and walnuts.

Make the Dough: On a clean work surface, make a mound with the flour and create a well in the centre. Crack in the eggs and whisk gently with a fork, gradually incorporating the flour until a rough dough forms. Knead for 5–7 minutes until smooth and elastic. Cover with a dish towel and let rest for 30 minutes.

Prepare the Filling: In a large frying pan, heat the olive oil over a medium heat. Add the sliced red onions, season with salt and cook until softened and caramelized, about 10–15 minutes. Add the sliced radicchio to the pan and cook, stirring occasionally, for another 4–5 minutes until it wilts and becomes tender. Season with salt and pepper to taste. Set aside.

Make the Béchamel: In a saucepan, melt the butter over a medium heat. Add the flour and whisk into a smooth paste, then cook for 2–3 minutes until lightly golden. Gradually add the milk, whisking constantly to prevent lumps. Continue simmering until the sauce thickens, about 5–7 minutes. Add the ground caraway and some salt and pepper to taste. Stir well and set aside.

Roll and Cut the Lasagna Sheets: Lightly dust a work surface with flour. Divide the rested dough into 4–6 portions. Roll each portion into a thin sheet, about 1mm thick (setting 5 on a Marcato). Cut the sheets to fit your baking dish, dusting them lightly with flour to prevent sticking.

Layer the Lasagna: Preheat the oven to 180°C/350°F/Gas Mark 5. In your baking dish, spread a thin layer of béchamel on the bottom, then add a layer of lasagna sheets. Top with a portion of the radicchio and onion mixture, a sprinkle of the Parmigiano and mozzarella, then more béchamel.

Repeat Layers: Continue layering until you've used all the ingredients, finishing with a layer of lasagna, then béchamel topped with Parmigiano and mozzarella.

Bake: Cover with foil and bake for 25 minutes. Remove the foil and bake for an additional 10–15 minutes, until the top is golden and bubbling.

Garnish and Serve: Let the lasagna cool for a few minutes before slicing. Serve with fresh parsley or chives, if using, on top.

THAI-STYLE EGG NOODLES WITH THAI BASIL & GREEN PEPPERCORNS

Noodle all'uovo alla tailandese con basilico e pepe verde

A fragrant, fiery stir-fry inspired by my early wanderings in Bangkok and Chiang Mai, the first adventure my husband and I went on. I remember our tuk-tuk driver taking us to the opposite end of the city from where we were meant to be. Tired and a little overwhelmed, we found a tiny outdoor restaurant tucked down a small alley. That meal was a revelation. It was the first time I tasted green curry with jasmine rice: there was lemongrass, kaffir lime, coconut milk and a kind of balance that felt both electrifying and effortless.

Back in Singapore, Thai food became a favourite of ours. We found a little family-run restaurant that made a version of this dish – stir-fried with Thai basil, green peppercorns and spongy fried tofu, all tangled with egg noodles. This dish is my tribute to that flavour memory.

While I make fresh pasta in most of my recipes, for this dish I prefer to use store-bought *bami* noodles from an Asian supermarket, as they capture the authentic texture. If you'd like to make your own, a basic egg pasta dough rolled and cut into thin strips will work beautifully; just expect a more delicate result.

Serves: 4

Preparation time: 10 minutes

Cooking time: 10 minutes

Ingredients:

* 1 large red onion
* 1 red pepper
* 1 green pepper
* 2 tbsp neutral oil (such as sunflower oil)
* 5–6 stems fresh green peppercorns (available at Asian supermarkets), plus extra to garnish (optional)
* 200g/7oz/1⅓ cups deep-fried tofu cubes, vacuum-packed and ready to use (available at Asian supermarkets)
* 400g/14oz/6 cups fresh egg noodles (*bami*), or dried egg noodles, cooked according to package directions, cooled and tossed in a splash of neutral oil
* 2 tbsp light soy sauce
* 1 tsp dark soy sauce or mushroom soy
* 1 tbsp sweet chilli sauce
* 1 tsp sugar or palm sugar
* A handful of fresh Thai basil leaves, plus extra to garnish (optional)

Prepare the Vegetables: Slice the red onion into wide strips, then deseed and cut the peppers into slices.

Stir-fry the Aromatics and Vegetables: Heat the oil in a large wok or deep frying pan over a medium-high heat. Add the red onion strips and stir-fry for 1–2 minutes until they begin to soften but still retain some crunch. Add the sliced red and green peppers and continue stir-frying for another minute.

Add the Peppercorns and Tofu: Add the green peppercorn stems and tofu cubes. Toss everything together gently and sauté for 5 minutes, allowing the tofu to warm through and absorb the flavours.

Season the Noodles: Add the fresh (or cooked dried) noodles to the wok. Pour in the light soy sauce, dark soy, sweet chilli sauce and sugar. Increase the heat to high for a few seconds, then lower back to medium. Toss well to combine and coat the noodles evenly in the glaze. If the mixture seems too dry, add a splash of water to help loosen and coat the noodles.

Finish and Serve: Turn off the heat and add the Thai basil. Toss just until the leaves are wilted and fragrant. Divide the noodle mixture between bowls and serve immediately, with extra basil and/or green peppercorns for garnish, if you like.

FILEJA WITH CHARRED CHERRY TOMATO, MISO & MINT PESTO

Fileja con pesto di pomodorini arrosto, miso e menta

Serves: 4

Preparation time: 40 minutes, plus 30 minutes resting

Cooking time: 10 minutes

For the Dough:

* 400g/14oz/3 cups semola
* ½ tsp chilli powder (optional)
* 200ml/7fl oz/scant 1 cup lukewarm water

For the Charred Cherry Tomato, Miso & Mint Pesto:

* 400g/14oz/2½ cups cherry tomatoes
* 2 tsp white miso paste
* 50g/1¾oz/½ cup Parmigiano Reggiano, finely grated
* 10g/⅓oz/½ cup packed fresh mint leaves
* 10g/⅓oz/½ cup packed fresh basil leaves
* 60ml/2fl oz/¼ cup extra virgin olive oil
* Salt, to taste

To Serve:

* 200g/7oz/1 cup ricotta
* Fresh mint leaves or finely grated Parmigiano Reggiano (optional)

A southern Italian pasta meets a tomato pesto with unexpected depth. Miso is a fermented paste rich in glutamates, known for creating depth and savouriness. It's used far beyond Japanese soups and broths, often stirred into sauces and stews to add the kind of flavour that usually comes from aged cheese, anchovies or long, slow cooking.

Here, it anchors a pesto made from cherry tomatoes, Parmigiano, mint and olive oil. The tomatoes bring acidity, the mint freshness and the miso ties everything together. What began as a light sauce became something far more layered, simply by adding a spoonful of miso.

I keep miso in the refrigerator the way others keep butter or cheese. Not because I use it in everything, but because every now and then, it solves a problem. A sauce that feels too thin. A flavour that won't land.

The pasta is fileja, a hand-rolled shape from Calabria made by wrapping dough around a thin rod or *ferretto*. You'll find similar shapes across southern Italy: *maccheroni al ferretto* in Campania and Molise, *maccarruna* in Sicily. I mixed a bit of red chilli powder into the dough for its colour and the faint heat it brings against the sweetness of the tomatoes.

Make the Dough: On a clean work surface, mix the semola with the chilli powder, if using. Gradually add the water, mixing with your fingers or a fork to incorporate the semola until a rough dough forms. Knead for 5–7 minutes until smooth and elastic. Cover with a dish towel and let rest for 30 minutes.

Char the Tomatoes: Heat a griddle/grill pan or dry frying pan over a high heat. Add the cherry tomatoes and blister until charred in spots and softened, about 2–3 minutes. Set aside to cool slightly.

Make the Pesto: Reserve half of the charred tomatoes for serving, and add the rest to a food processor with miso, Parmigiano, mint, basil and olive oil. Blitz until smooth but slightly textured. Adjust the miso, mint or oil if needed. Set aside.

Shape the Fileja: Lightly dust a tray and work surface with semola. Divide the rested dough into small portions, roughly the size of a golf ball. Roll each piece into a long rope about 1cm/⅓in in diameter. Cut into 4–5cm/2in lengths. Roll each piece around a *ferretto* or bamboo skewer, then gently press and roll to create the hollow shape. Slide it off and place on the tray, keeping covered as you work. Repeat with the remaining dough.

Cook the Fileja: Bring a large pot of salted water to the boil. Cook the fileja for 2–3 minutes, or until they float and the texture is al dente.

Combine and Serve: Using a slotted spoon, lift the pasta directly into a large bowl. Toss the cooked pasta with the pesto, adding a splash of cooking water if needed to help the sauce cling evenly. Plate and finish with spoonfuls of fresh ricotta and the reserved charred tomatoes. Serve garnished with extra mint or grated Parmigiano, if you like.

CARAMELLE WITH SPICED BUTTERNUT SQUASH & CLOVE CREAM

Caramelle con zucca speziata e crema ai chiodi di garofano

Serves: 4

Preparation time: 1 hour, plus 30 minutes resting (plus time for draining squash)

Cooking time: 25 minutes

For the Butternut Squash Filling:

* 300g/10½oz/1½ cups butternut squash, peeled, deseeded and chopped into 2.5cm/1in cubes
* 50g/1¾oz/½ cup Parmigiano Reggiano, finely grated
* 1 tsp finely grated root ginger
* Salt and pepper, to taste

For the Dough:

* 300g/10½oz/2¼ cups 00 flour
* 3 eggs
* ½ tsp ground turmeric

For the Clove Cream Sauce:

* 2 tbsp unsalted butter
* 240ml/9fl oz/1 cup whole milk
* 50g/1¾oz/½ cup Parmigiano Reggiano, finely grated
* ½ tsp ground cloves, or to taste
* 15g/½oz/½ cup fresh fenugreek leaves or a mix of flat-leaf parsley and a few coriander/cilantro sprigs
* Salt and pepper, to taste

To Garnish:

* Kashmiri red chilli powder (optional)

A gentle interplay of spice and sweetness, for those who crave comfort without heaviness. Clove, root ginger, fenugreek, turmeric: these are all flavours I came to understand more deeply during the years I spent travelling back and forth from India. North India – especially Delhi and Gurgaon for work; south India – Hyderabad and Bangalore to visit family. Spice isn't just about heat, the way we often think of it in the West. It's about balance, aroma and depth: the kind that gives a dish structure without needing to be the most dominating flavour on the plate.

This dish brings that approach into a pasta context. The dough is tinted with turmeric, the filling built around butternut squash, root ginger and cheese, and the sauce finished with clove. A handful of fenugreek (*methi*) leaves adds brightness at the end, but if you can't find any, a mix of flat-leaf parsley and fresh coriander/cilantro leaves will mimic the green bitterness and citrusy lift without overpowering.

Prepare the Butternut Squash Filling: Boil or steam the squash for 15 minutes until soft, then place it in a muslin cloth/cheesecloth, tie securely and hang over a bowl to drain for at least 2 hours or overnight. Reserve the drained liquid for the sauce. Once drained, mash the squash until smooth. Add the Parmigiano, root ginger and some salt and pepper. Mix well and adjust the seasoning to taste. Set aside.

Make the Dough: On a clean work surface, make a mound with the flour and create a well in the centre. Crack in the eggs, add the turmeric and gently whisk with a fork, gradually incorporating the flour until a rough dough forms. Knead for 5–7 minutes until smooth and elastic. Cover with a dish towel and let rest for 30 minutes.

Make the Sauce: In a large pan over a medium-low heat, melt the butter. Add the milk, Parmigiano and reserved drained squash liquid. Stir continuously for 4–5 minutes until the sauce begins to thicken and bubble. Add the ground cloves and some salt and pepper. Let the sauce reduce slightly for another minute until thickened. Stir in the fenugreek leaves and cook just until wilted. Set aside.

Shape the Caramelle: Lightly dust a tray and work surface with flour. Divide the rested dough into 4–6 portions. Roll each piece into a thin sheet, about 1mm thick (setting 5 on a Marcato) and cut into 8 x 8cm/3¼ x 3¼in squares. Place a small amount of the butternut squash filling in the lower third of each square. Fold the dough up over the filling, then fold over again to create a compact, sealed bundle with the seam underneath. Pinch both ends firmly to form the caramelle (candy) shape, making sure they're tightly closed to prevent any filling from escaping. Place on the floured tray as you make them and cover with a dish towel.

Cook the Caramelle: Bring a large pot of salted water to the boil. Cook the caramelle for 3–4 minutes, until they float and the texture is al dente.

Combine and Serve: Using a slotted spoon, lift them directly into the clove cream sauce and warm everything through for a few seconds. Plate and garnish with a light dusting of Kashmiri red chilli powder, if desired. Serve immediately.

UDONG WITH VODKA SAUCE & GOCHUJANG

Udong alla vodka e gochujang

A pantry pasta with a Korean twist. Creamy, spicy and incredibly addictive. I first made this while living in Singapore, years ago, in one of those "what if" moments that turns into a "why not". I had the usual ingredients for a classic vodka sauce – tomato purée/paste, cream, vodka – and a little tub of gochujang in the refrigerator. I stirred it in just to see what would happen, and it worked. So well, in fact, that I never made the original version again. This isn't traditional, and it's not trying to be. It's just very, very good.

I first tasted gochujang in a bowl of bibimbap at a little vegan café in the Bugis area of Singapore called New Green Pastures. I believe the red paste was thinned with soy sauce, sesame oil or vinegar and mixed into hot rice until it coated every grain. That was my introduction: deeply savoury, a little hot, a little sweet; and I've been using it ever since.

The sauce here is as simple as the Italian original: tomato purée/paste, cream, vodka, gochujang and a touch of chilli oil. Traditionally, you'd use penne. I prefer udon (or udong in Korean); thick, chewy wheat noodles that are a little slippery to eat. I use the vacuum-packed udon sold in most Asian supermarkets, both for the texture and because they're ready in minutes. If you prefer to make your own, any fresh pasta rolled slightly thick and cut into wide strips will do. Just make sure it has enough bite.

Serves: 4

Preparation time: 5 minutes

Cooking time: 10 minutes

Ingredients:

* 400g/14oz fresh vacuum-packed Korean udong noodles, or dried/frozen udong noodles, or fresh pasta (made with 00 flour, water and potato starch for chewiness)
* 1 tbsp neutral oil (such as sunflower or vegetable)
* 2 tbsp double concentrate tomato purée/paste
* 1½ tbsp gochujang
* 60ml/2fl oz/¼ cup vodka
* 200ml/7fl oz/scant 1 cup double cream/heavy cream
* 1 tbsp chilli oil, plus extra to serve (optional)
* Salt, to taste
* Fresh parsley, chopped, to garnish (optional)

Prepare the Noodles: If using vacuum-packed udong, place them in boiling water for 1–2 minutes to loosen. Drain and set aside. If using dried or frozen udong, cook according to the package directions. If you prefer using fresh pasta, roll to a medium thickness, about 2.5mm thick (setting 2 on a Marcato) and cut into 2.5mm wide strips. Reserve a ladleful of the cooking water.

Make the Sauce: Heat the oil in a large pan over a medium heat. Add the tomato purée/paste and gochujang and cook for 1–2 minutes, stirring constantly, until the paste darkens slightly and becomes fragrant. Carefully add the vodka and let it bubble for 30 seconds to burn off the alcohol. Stir in the cream and chilli oil. Lower the heat and let the sauce simmer gently for 2–3 minutes until smooth and slightly thickened. Taste and add salt if needed.

Combine and Serve: Add the noodles to the sauce and toss to coat. If the sauce is too thick, add a splash of the noodle cooking water to loosen. Serve immediately, with a garnish of chopped parsley and a drizzle of chilli oil, if you like.

STRASCINATI WITH JACKFRUIT RAGÙ

Strascinati con ragù di jackfruit

Serves: 4

Preparation time: 1 hour, plus 30 minutes resting

Cooking time: 45 minutes

For the Dough:

* 400g/14oz/3 cups semola
* 200ml/7fl oz/scant 1 cup lukewarm water

For the Jackfruit Ragù:

* 2 tbsp extra virgin olive oil, plus extra to serve
* 1 small red onion, finely chopped
* 1 small carrot, finely chopped
* 1 celery stalk, finely chopped
* 1 tsp fennel seeds, lightly crushed
* ½ tsp ground cumin
* ½ tsp smoked paprika
* Pinch of ground cinnamon
* Pinch of dried chilli/hot pepper flakes, or 1 fresh red chilli, finely chopped (optional)
* 400g/14oz/2½ cups canned young jackfruit in brine, drained and shredded
* 2 tbsp tomato purée/paste
* 400ml/14fl oz/1⅔ cups tomato passata
* A handful of torn fresh basil leaves, plus extra to garnish
* Splash of milk, as needed
* Salt and pepper, to taste
* Finely grated Parmigiano Reggiano (or desiccated/dried shredded coconut), to finish (optional)

Another southern pasta shape paired with a rich, meatless ragù inspired by Indian jackfruit dishes. In Indian cuisine, jackfruit is used in dishes like biryani to match the texture of meat and soak up flavour. That was what I had in mind when I first made this sauce: the depth and richness of a slow-cooked pork ragù, without the meat. Jackfruit, with its fibrous texture, does the job beautifully. I use young jackfruit in brine, which is easy to find and quick to prepare. Frozen jackfruit works just as well. Fresh would be ideal, but it's hard to find and fiddly to clean.

The pasta is strascinati, a hand-formed shape from Basilicata and Puglia. The shape is like rustic orecchiette, only flat. It's one of the easiest shapes to make, and one of the most satisfying to eat. This is a dish that borrows freely: Indian jackfruit, Italian ragù, southern pasta. But it feels like its own thing.

Make the Dough: On a clean work surface, make a mound with the semola and create a well in the centre. Gradually add the water, mixing with your fingers or a fork to incorporate the semola until a rough dough forms. Knead for 5–7 minutes until smooth and elastic. Cover with a dish towel and let rest for 30 minutes.

Shape the Strascinati: Lightly dust a tray and work surface with semola. Cut the rested dough into 6 pieces and roll each one into a rope about 1cm/⅓in thick. Slice into 2cm/¾in nuggets. Place one nugget on a wooden board or work surface. Hold a butter knife almost flat, with the blade tilted to about 20–30°, so that the edge, not the flat side, touches the dough. Press down and drag the dough toward you in one firm motion. This will flatten the piece and curl the edges lightly as it slides, giving it a stretched, elongated shape with a slight lip, not a deep hollow like *orecchiette*. Transfer to the tray and keep covered as you work. Repeat with the remaining dough.

Prepare the Ragù: Heat the olive oil in a wide pan over a medium heat. Add the chopped onion, carrot and celery and cook gently for 8–10 minutes, until soft and translucent. Add the fennel seeds, cumin, smoked paprika, cinnamon and dried chilli/hot pepper flakes, if using, and cook for another minute until fragrant.

Add the shredded jackfruit and cook for 2–3 minutes, letting it absorb the spiced oil and begin to colour. Stir in the tomato purée/paste, passata and the torn basil leaves, season with salt and pepper and add a splash of milk.

Simmer over a low heat for 20–25 minutes, stirring occasionally and breaking up the jackfruit pieces further with the back of a spoon. The ragù should be thick, glossy and deeply flavoured. Finish with a swirl of olive oil before serving.

Cook the Strascinati: Bring a large pot of salted water to the boil. Cook the strascinati for 3–4 minutes, or until they are al dente and float to the surface.

Combine and Serve: Using a slotted spoon, lift the strascinati directly into the ragù and toss to combine, adding a little cooking water to help the sauce cling evenly. Serve with fresh basil and Parmigiano, if using.

AJWAIN & TURMERIC GNOCCHI WITH CORIANDER/CILANTRO CHILLI PESTO

Gnocchi di patate e semi di carom con pesto di coriandolo, anacardi e peperoncino verde

Serves: 4

Preparation time: 45 minutes

Cooking time: 15–20 minutes

For the Dough:

* 500g/17½oz/3 cups cooked and mashed/riced starchy potatoes
* 130g/4½oz/1 cup plain/all-purpose flour
* 2 tbsp potato starch
* 1 tsp ajwain seeds

For the Pesto:

* A small bunch of fresh coriander/cilantro, tough stems removed
* 50g/1¾oz/⅓ cup cashews, soaked in hot water for 15–20 minutes, then drained
* 1–2 green chillies, to taste
* 1 tbsp lime juice
* 4 tbsp extra virgin olive oil, plus extra for sautéing
* Salt, to taste

To Serve:

* 130g/4½oz baby corn, sliced into discs
* Fresh coriander/cilantro leaves
* Sliced green chilli (optional)

Inspired by one of my favourite flavour pairings in Indian cooking – potato and ajwain – reimagined in this herb-laced gnocchi dish. In one of my favourite recipe books, *The Science of Spice*, Dr Stuart Farrimond explains how ajwain (or *carom*), a small but intensely aromatic seed, belongs to the same botanical family as parsley and coriander/cilantro. Though tiny, its flavour is bold and unmistakable. It tastes of thyme (thanks to a compound called thymol) but sharper, with a peppery edge. It's the kind of spice that instantly transforms potatoes, which is how I came to love it, folded into aloo paratha, samosa or potato sabzi.

That pairing was the starting point for what became potato gnocchi, spiced with ajwain and served with a fresh green chilli, coriander and cashew pesto. I added baby corn for some crunch and colour, and because it's an ingredient I associate with my favourite Asian cuisines. When shaping the gnocchi, I used a silicone mat with a honeycomb texture. The result looked like miniature corn cobs, which made it all the more fun. You don't need any special equipment for this. It's just a reminder that playfulness has its place in the kitchen. Try something new, use what you have and don't be afraid to make it your own.

Make the Dough: In a large bowl, combine the mashed potatoes with the flour and potato starch. Add the ajwain seeds and knead for 4–5 minutes until a soft, slightly tacky dough forms. Avoid overworking it. Divide the dough into 4 portions and lightly dust a tray and work surface with flour. Roll each into a rope about 1.5cm/½in thick and cut into bite-size pieces. Shape the gnocchi by rolling each piece on a gnocchi board, fork, over the holes of a cheese grater or leave them plain. I used a textured silicone mat with a honeycomb pattern, but you can roll them on any surface with texture. Lightly dust with flour and set aside on the tray, and keep covered as you work.

Make the Pesto: In a blender or food processor, combine the coriander/cilantro, cashews, green chilli, lime juice and extra virgin olive oil. Blend until creamy, adding a splash of hot water if needed to loosen. Taste and adjust the salt or acidity to your liking. Set aside.

Cook the Gnocchi: Bring a large pot of salted water to a gentle boil. Add the gnocchi in batches and cook until they float to the surface, about 2–3 minutes. Let them cook for 30 seconds more, then remove with a slotted spoon and drain well. Reserve some of the cooking water.

Finish and Serve: In a wide pan, sauté the baby corn in a little olive oil over a medium heat for 5–7 minutes until golden. Add the cooked gnocchi and toss gently. Remove the pan from the heat and stir through the pesto, adding a splash of cooking water if needed to help the sauce cling evenly. Serve immediately, with extra coriander, and sliced green chilli, if desired.

GARGANELLI WITH COCONUT SPICE SAUCE (INSPIRED BY RENDANG)

Garganelli con sugo speziato al cocco

Hand-rolled pasta tubes tossed in a fragrant coconut sauce, inspired by the bold, warming spices of Southeast Asian rendang. Years ago in Singapore, I stumbled on a small Italian place near my office serving spaghetti with a rendang-style sauce. I loved it from the get-go: the coconut, the slow-cooked flavours, the heat, the way the sauce coated the pasta. I went home and tried to recreate it using a store-bought rendang paste, available everywhere in Singapore, and it just worked. I've made it ever since.

Rendang originates from West Sumatra, where it's traditionally made with beef slow-cooked in coconut milk and a rich blend of spices until deeply caramelized. Over time, it spread across the rest of Indonesia, as well as to Malaysia, Singapore and Brunei, each place putting its own spin on it.

This dish is fully plant-based, quick to make and loosely inspired by rendang. The sauce is rich and spicy, with vegan minced/ground meat simmered in coconut cream, kaffir lime leaves and lemongrass. I used a ready-made paste for ease, though you could make your own if you're up for it. For the pasta, I chose garganelli: a ridged tube originating in Emilia-Romagna and rolled entirely by hand, one by one. The original dough uses 00 flour and eggs, but I'm using semola and water to keep the recipe vegan. It's easy to shape using a gnocchi paddle and a small stick or skewer and goes well with ragù and thick sauces, so I thought it would be perfect for this.

Serves: 4

Preparation time: 1 hour, plus 30 minutes resting

Cooking time: 40 minutes

For the Dough:

* 400g/14oz/3 cups semola
* 200ml/7fl oz/scant 1 cup lukewarm water

For the Sauce:

* 2 tbsp extra virgin olive oil
* 1 small onion, finely chopped
* 1 small carrot, finely chopped
* 1 celery stalk, finely chopped
* 2 kaffir lime leaves
* 1 stalk lemongrass, bruised
* 2 heaped tbsp rendang paste (store-bought or homemade)
* 250g/9oz/1½ cups plant-based minced/ground meat
* 200ml/7fl oz/scant 1 cup full-fat coconut cream
* Salt, to taste

Make the Dough: On a clean work surface, make a mound with the semola and create a well in the centre. Gradually add the water, mixing with your fingers or a fork to incorporate the semola until a rough dough forms. Knead for 5–7 minutes until smooth and elastic. Cover with a dish towel and let rest for 30 minutes.

Prepare the Sauce: In a wide pan, heat the olive oil over a medium heat. Add the onion, carrot and celery and cook for 8–10 minutes until soft. Stir in the kaffir lime leaves, bruised lemongrass and rendang paste. Cook for 2 minutes to release the aromas and until the oil separates.

Add the plant-based minced/ground meat and cook, stirring, for 2–3 minutes to coat in the spices. Pour in the coconut cream, reduce the heat slightly and let simmer for 15–20 minutes, stirring occasionally, until the sauce thickens and coats the plant-based minced meat. Season with salt to taste. Remove the lemongrass and lime leaves before serving.

Shape the Garganelli: Lightly dust a tray and work surface with semola. Divide the rested dough into 4 portions. Roll each piece into a thin sheet, about 1mm thick (setting 5 on a Marcato). Cut into squares, about 4 x 4cm/1½ x 1½in each. Place a square diagonally on a gnocchi paddle or ridged board. Using a small wooden stick (a tool that usually comes with the gnocchi paddle, about the thickness of a pencil), roll the square diagonally into a tube, pressing lightly to form ridges. Seal the edge with your finger. Set it on the tray and keep covered as you work. Repeat with the remaining dough.

Cook the Garganelli: Bring a large pot of salted water to the boil. Cook the garganelli for 2–3 minutes, until al dente.

Combine and Serve: Using a slotted spoon, lift the pasta directly into the pan with the sauce. Toss gently to coat, adding a splash of cooking water if needed to help the sauce cling evenly. Serve immediately.

10-MINUTE FUSILLI WITH SPICY PEANUT SAUCE

Fusilli con salsa di arachidi

A quick no-cook sauce that tastes even better at room temperature. I may well lose my Italian passport over this but so be it! This is one of my favourite pastas in the world. I've made it countless times since first throwing it together in Singapore as a lazy weeknight dinner. It's fast, always reliable and it hits every craving when you want something punchy and comforting. The sauce is completely uncooked and comes together in less than a minute: just shake everything in a jar and the whole dish is done by the time the pasta's boiled.

I like to use store-bought pasta here – fusilli, penne, farfalle are my usual choices, but spaghetti works well too – and while it's great on its own, I usually throw in some broccoli florets to cook with the pasta in the same pot. It makes it feel more like a proper meal and gives you one of your five a day.

It's delicious hot, but somehow even better once it's cooled a little, which makes it ideal for a packed lunch or picnic. And it's endlessly adaptable: keep it mild or add chilli, add garlic, swap in another green. Whatever works.

Serves: 4

Preparation time: 10 minutes

Cooking time: According to package directions

Ingredients:

* 400g/14oz/4 cups fusilli
* 1 head of broccoli, broken into small florets
* 3 heaped tbsp peanut butter (smooth or crunchy)
* Juice of 1 lemon
* 2 tbsp light soy sauce
* 1 tbsp sesame oil
* 1 small garlic clove, grated (optional)
* Dried chilli/hot pepper flakes, or a few drops of chilli oil (optional)

Cook the Pasta and Broccoli: Bring a large pot of salted water to the boil. Add the fusilli and cook according to the package directions. In the last 3–4 minutes of cooking, add the broccoli florets to the same pot. Reserve a ladleful of the cooking water, then drain.

Make the Sauce: While the pasta is cooking, place the peanut butter, lemon juice, soy sauce, sesame oil and any optional garlic or chilli in a jar. Shake until smooth and emulsified.

Combine: Drain the pasta and broccoli, return to the pan or a large bowl, and immediately toss with the sauce. Add a splash of the cooking water to help the sauce coat the pasta evenly. Mix well.

Serve: Serve warm, at room temperature, or cold . . . whatever you prefer. Keeps well in the refrigerator for 2–3 days for packed lunches.

MEE GORENG
Mi goreng

Serves: 4

Preparation time: 5 minutes

Cooking time: 15 minutes

For the Noodles:

* 500g/17½oz/4 cups fresh yellow noodles

For the Stir-Fry:

* 2 tbsp vegetable oil
* 200g/7oz/1⅓ cups tempeh, sliced into thin batons
* 2 garlic cloves, minced
* 4 eggs (optional)
* 90g/3¼oz/¾ cup bean sprouts
* 2 red peppers, deseeded, sliced
* 150g/5¼oz/2 cups choy sum or Asian greens, roughly chopped
* 2 spring onions/scallions, sliced, to serve

For the Sauce:

* 2 tbsp kecap manis (available at Asian supermarkets)
* 1 tbsp light soy sauce
* 1 tbsp sweet chilli sauce
* 2 tsp chilli paste or sambal oelek

A nostalgic hawker-style noodle dish from Singapore, sweet, spicy, the ultimate comfort food. I love mee goreng because it reminds me of my mum's Frittata Di Pasta (page 254), the kind she would make by frying leftover tomato spaghetti with scrambled eggs. That simple, satisfying dish lives on in this fiery Southeast Asian version, which for years was my go-to lunch at a hawker stall in Singapore.

Mee goreng (literally "fried noodles") is a beloved Southeast Asian dish with regional variations across Malaysia, Indonesia and Singapore. It's the kind of dish that changes hands and flavours as it travels, and it never disappoints. This version is based on the slightly sweet, tomato-rich style common in Singapore, a memory of breakfast hawker meals and plastic forks digging into Styrofoam boxes. It has all the punch of the classic: chilli, soy, garlic, tomato and that unmistakable sweetness from kecap manis (sweet and syrupy soy sauce).

I use store-bought fresh yellow noodles here for ease and authenticity. They're quick to cook and have the springy, chewy bite that's essential to mee goreng. Tempeh replaces meat with a nutty flavour and satisfying texture, while choy sum or any other leafy green adds balance. You can adjust the heat as you like, but the sauce should always be sticky, glossy and intense.

Stir-fry the Tempeh: Heat 1 tablespoon of the vegetable oil in a wok or large frying pan over a medium-high heat. Add the tempeh and stir-fry for 5–6 minutes until golden on all sides. Remove and set aside.

Prepare the Sauce: In a small bowl, mix the kecap manis, soy sauce, sweet chilli sauce and chilli paste. Set aside.

Stir-fry the Noodles: In the same wok or frying pan, add the remaining tablespoon of oil over a medium-high heat. Stir-fry the garlic for 2–3 minutes until fragrant. If using eggs, push the garlic to one side and fry the eggs briefly, then scoop them out and set them aside. Add the yellow noodles and the prepared sauce to the garlic in the wok, tossing quickly to coat. If the noodles seem dry, add a splash of water.

Add the Tempeh and Greens: Return the fried tempeh to the wok, along with the bean sprouts, red peppers and choy sum. Stir-fry for another 2–3 minutes until the greens are wilted and everything is glossy and coated.

Serve: Divide between bowls and top with the sliced spring onions/scallions and a fried egg, if using. Eat immediately.

PALAK PANEER TORTELLACCI

Tortellacci al palak paneer

Serves: 4

Preparation time: 45 minutes, plus 30 minutes resting

Cooking time: 15 minutes

For the Dough:

* 400g/14oz/3 cups 00 flour
* 4 eggs

For the Filling:

* 1 block of paneer (200g/7oz), grated
* 250g/9oz/1 cup ricotta, well drained
* 50g/1¾oz/½ cup Parmigiano Reggiano, finely grated
* ½ tsp ground cumin
* ½ tsp garam masala
* Salt and pepper, to taste

For the Palak Curry Sauce:

* 2 tbsp neutral oil (such as sunflower)
* 1 tsp cumin seeds
* ½ tsp ground turmeric
* 1 tsp root ginger-garlic paste (store-bought or homemade, see Note)
* 1–2 green chillies, slit, to taste
* 2 shallots, finely chopped
* 1 tbsp tomato purée/paste
* ½ tsp Kashmiri red chilli powder
* ½ tsp ground coriander
* ½ tsp ground cumin
* ½ tsp dried mango powder (*amchur*) (optional)
* ½ tsp garam masala
* 200g/7oz/4 cups packed baby spinach
* 100ml/3½fl oz/scant ½ cup double cream/heavy cream
* A drizzle of chilli oil, to garnish (optional)
* Sliced ginger, to garnish (optional)

A cross-cultural comfort dish filled with love, spinach and a little misadventure. The first time I made palak paneer, I wanted to surprise my then-boyfriend (now husband) by cooking him something from his home: India. I had never made Indian food before, so I threw myself into YouTube videos and recipe blogs, then headed to the chaotic, glorious Mustafa Centre in Little India to buy all the ingredients.

I've turned the classic dish into giant tortellacci, stuffed with a creamy mixture of paneer, ricotta and Parmigiano, and served with a palak (spinach) curry. It's still palak paneer. Just wrapped in a little pasta.

Make the Dough: On a clean work surface, make a mound with the flour and create a well in the centre. Crack in the eggs and whisk gently with a fork, gradually incorporating the flour until a rough dough forms. Knead for 5–7 minutes until smooth and elastic. Cover with a dish towel and let rest for 30 minutes.

Make the Filling: In a bowl, mix the grated paneer, ricotta, Parmigiano, cumin, garam masala and some salt and pepper until well combined. Set aside in the refrigerator while you roll the dough.

Roll and Fill the Tortellacci: Lightly dust a tray and work surface with flour. Divide the rested dough into 4–6 portions. Roll each piece into a thin sheet, about 1mm thick (setting 5 on a Marcato). Cut into large squares (about 8 x 8cm/3¼ x 3¼in). Place a spoonful of cheese filling in the centre of a square. Fold in half diagonally to form a triangle, pressing out any air pockets and sealing the edges. Bring the two opposite corners of the long edge together and press to seal, forming the tortellacci shape. Place on the floured tray and keep covered as you make the rest.

Make the Palak Curry Sauce: Heat the oil in a large pan. Add the cumin seeds and let them sizzle for a few seconds, until fragrant. Stir in the turmeric and root ginger-garlic paste, then the slit green chillies and the shallots. Cook for 2–3 minutes until softened. Add the tomato purée/paste, Kashmiri chilli powder, coriander, cumin, dried mango powder, if using, and garam masala. Stir well and cook for 2–3 minutes until aromatic.

Add the spinach and cook for 3–4 minutes until wilted. Transfer everything to a blender and blend to a smooth sauce. Return the sauce to the pan, stir in the cream and let it bubble gently for a few seconds.

Cook the Tortellacci: Bring a large pot of salted water to the boil. Cook the tortellacci for 2–3 minutes, until they float and the texture is al dente.

Combine and Serve: Serve the sauce into bowls and use a slotted spoon to lift the tortellacci directly on top, before drizzling with a little chilli oil and adding sliced ginger to garnish, if desired.

Note: To make the root ginger-garlic paste at home, blend equal parts of fresh root ginger and garlic cloves with a little water or neutral oil to form a paste. Store in a clean, airtight container in the refrigerator for up to 1 week or freeze in small portions for up to 1 month (no need to thaw or defrost).

RED LENTIL CASARECCE WITH CURRIED COCONUT SAUCE

Casarecce di lenticchie rosse alla salsa al cocco

Serves: 4

Preparation time: 45 minutes, plus 30 minutes resting

Cooking time: 15 minutes

For the Dough:

* 250g/9oz/scant 2 cups plain/all-purpose flour
* 150g/5¼oz/1¼ cups red lentil flour
* 180ml/6fl oz/¾ cup water, more if needed

For the Sauce:

* 1 tbsp coconut or neutral oil (such as sunflower oil)
* 1 small onion, finely chopped
* 1 garlic clove, grated
* 1½–2cm/¾in piece of root ginger, grated (about 1 tsp grated)
* 1 tsp curry powder
* ½ tsp ground turmeric
* 200ml/7fl oz/scant 1 cup full-fat coconut milk
* Juice of ½ lime, plus lime zest to garnish
* Salt, to taste
* Fresh coriander/cilantro, chopped, to garnish
* Toasted desiccated/dried shredded coconut or a pinch of chilli powder, to garnish (optional)

A pasta that doesn't apologize for being different. Creamy, spiced and powered by pulse flour. This is one of those dishes that doesn't pretend to be Italian. It's not fusion for the sake of it. It's just what I want to eat when I need something grounding and bright at the same time. The red lentil casarecce holds up to the richness of the coconut milk and the heat of the curry. It doesn't go limp, it doesn't disappear.

This isn't a sauce that simmers for hours. It's quick. A few spices, good coconut milk and something sharp to finish it off: lime, coriander/cilantro, maybe some toasted coconut if you feel like it. It belongs in this chapter because it uses spice the way I've come to understand it: not just to add flavour, but to *wake up* food. To make a bowl of pasta feel alive.

Make the Dough: In a large bowl, mix the plain/all-purpose flour and red lentil flour. Add the water gradually, mixing with your fingers until a rough dough forms. Transfer to a clean work surface and knead for 5–7 minutes until smooth and elastic. Cover with a dish towel and let rest for 30 minutes.

Make the Sauce: In a large frying pan, heat the oil over a medium heat. Add the onion and cook for 3–4 minutes until soft. Stir in the garlic, root ginger, curry powder and turmeric. Cook for another minute until fragrant. Pour in the coconut milk and season with salt. Let it simmer gently for 4–5 minutes until slightly thickened. Add the lime juice and adjust the seasoning as needed. Set aside and keep warm.

Shape the Casarecce: Lightly dust a tray and work surface with flour. Divide the rested dough into 4 pieces. Roll one piece at a time into a rope about 5mm/¼in thick. Cut into 4–5cm/2in segments. Press each piece lengthways along a *ferretto* or a thin metal or wooden rod about 3–4mm/⅛in thick (similar to a knitting needle) to form an indentation, while rolling back and forth to create a groove. Lentil dough tends to be crumblier than traditional dough, so there is no need to twist the ends in opposite directions to form the signature casarecce shape. Instead place on the floured tray and keep covered as you work. Repeat with the remaining dough.

Cook the Casarecce: Bring a large pot of salted water to the boil. Cook the casarecce for 2–3 minutes, or until they float and the texture is al dente.

Combine and Serve: Using a slotted spoon, lift the pasta directly into the pan with the sauce. Toss gently to coat, adding a splash of cooking water if needed to help the sauce cling evenly. Serve topped with fresh coriander/cilantro, lime zest, and toasted desiccated/dried shredded coconut or chilli powder, if using.

Ch. 6

MINDFUL Preparation

In Sicily, the kitchen is a place of patience, where the slow rhythm of preparing food mirrors the unhurried pace of life. I've carried that mindfulness with me everywhere I've lived. It's not about rushing to get dinner on the table, but about taking your time, letting your hands move with intention and appreciating the journey. When my mind races, I focus on the soft sound of tomato sauce bubbling on the hob/stovetop, the sizzle of garlic hitting hot oil or the rhythmic chopping of vegetables: each sound, each movement, is an invitation to be present.

This chapter is about those dishes that require more time, but in a way that nurtures rather than demands. Recipes that allow you to lose yourself in the moment: forming delicate ravioli by hand, rolling out tiny shapes one-by-one or carefully folding intricate shapes of pasta (which is why you'll find the preparation times a little longer in this chapter). These actions bring you fully into the here and now, creating a space where the outside world can fall away. Each dish is a reminder that cooking can be an act of meditation, a way to escape the noise and focus on the rituals that nourish us.

My journey with cooking has taught me that meaningful meals are often the ones where the process itself becomes part of the therapy. There's something soothing about working with dough: the tactile pleasure of kneading it, feeling it change beneath your hands, knowing that you're creating something from just flour and water. It reminds me that good things take time, that there's value in slowing down Stirring a sauce to the right consistency, waiting for flavours to develop or letting a dish simmer on the hob/stovetop: these are the moments that ground us, offering a sense of peace in a chaotic world.

For me, the kitchen is a refuge, a place where I can reconnect with myself. I hope this chapter invites you to do the same. Mindful Preparation isn't just about the final meal; it's about the journey you take to get there. It's about finding joy in the process, in the overlooked moments that make cooking an act of self-care and reflection. Let these recipes be a guide for slowing down, for being present and for discovering the joy that comes from creating something with intention and care.

CASUNZIEI WITH BUTTER & POPPY SEEDS

Casunziei all'ampezzana

Serves: 4

Preparation time: 45 minutes, plus 30 minutes resting

Cooking time: 5 minutes

For the Dough:

* 400g/14oz/3 cups 00 flour
* 4 eggs

For the Filling:

* 250g/9oz cooked and peeled beetroot/beets (2–3 medium or 1–2 large)
* 250g/9oz/1 cup ricotta, drained well
* 30g/1oz/¼ cup Parmigiano Reggiano, finely grated
* 2 tbsp breadcrumbs
* Salt and pepper, to taste

For the Sauce:

* 100g/3½oz/½ cup unsalted butter
* 1 tsp poppy seeds, plus extra to garnish (optional)
* Salt, to taste

Bright pink beetroot/beet-filled ravioli from the Veneto region, served with a simple sauce of butter, poppy seeds and beetroot juice. Veneto holds a special place in my heart, as I spent a decade of my life living in Venice and Padova during my university years and early career. It's one of my favourite regions in Italy, and its cuisine never fails to draw me back. Casunziei all'Ampezzana is a dish from the Dolomites, known for its striking pink colour and delicate, comforting flavour. These beetroot-filled ravioli, with their poppy-seed butter sauce, are a celebration of the simplicity and elegance that Veneto's cuisine embodies. The gentle sweetness of the beetroots, the creaminess of ricotta and the nuttiness of the poppy seeds come together in perfect harmony. It's a dish that's both visually and tastefully unforgettable.

Make the Dough: On a clean work surface, make a mound with the flour and create a well in the centre. Crack in the eggs and whisk gently with a fork, gradually incorporating the flour until a rough dough forms. Knead for 5–7 minutes until smooth and elastic. Cover with a dish towel and let rest for 30 minutes.

Prepare the Filling: Grate the beetroot/beets and place it in a muslin cloth/cheesecloth in a large bowl. Set a weight on top and let it drain for at least 15 minutes to release its juice. Reserve 2 tablespoons of the juice for the sauce. In a bowl, combine the drained beetroot with the ricotta, Parmigiano and breadcrumbs. Season with salt and pepper. The filling should be smooth but firm enough to hold its shape.

Roll out the Dough: Lightly dust a tray and work surface with flour. Divide the rested dough into 4 pieces and keep them covered. Roll each piece into a thin sheet, about 1mm thick (setting 5 on a Marcato). Lightly dust with flour as needed to prevent sticking. Cut into circles using a pastry cutter or glass, about 8–9cm/3½in in diameter. Set aside on the floured tray and cover with a dish towel while you roll and cut the rest.

Roll and Fill the Casunziei: Place a teaspoon of filling in the centre of each circle. Fold over into a half-moon and press firmly to seal. If needed, use a little water around the edge. Lay them on the floured tray while you shape the rest. You can do this step by hand or use a dumpling or gyoza mould like I did, for a prettier result.

Cook the Casunziei: Bring a large pot of salted water to the boil. Cook the casunziei for 3–4 minutes, or until they float and the texture is al dente.

Make the Sauce: While the pasta cooks, melt the butter in a wide pan over a low heat. Stir in the poppy seeds and reserved beetroot juice and season with salt. Keep warm.

Combine and Serve: Using a slotted spoon, lift the casunziei directly into the pan with the sauce. Toss gently to coat, adding a splash of cooking water if needed to help the sauce cling evenly. Serve immediately, with a sprinkle of extra poppy seeds on top, if you like.

CASARECCE WITH COURGETTE/ ZUCCHINI & CONFIT CHERRY TOMATOES

Casarecce con zucchine e pomodorini confit

A summer pasta that draws flavour from simple ingredients. Courgettes/zucchini and tomatoes were everyday staples that made their way into countless family meals, especially in the warmer months. This dish brings them together in a way that's comforting and satisfying. It doesn't ask for much, just attention. The ingredients are few, but each one is treated with care to draw out lots of flavour.

The cherry tomatoes are slow-cooked until they collapse, releasing their juices and becoming rich and jammy. The juice is used to cook slices of courgette, softened just enough to keep their bite. Whole garlic cloves, roasted alongside the tomatoes, are squeezed into the pan until they melt into the sauce.

The pasta is rustic Sicilian casarecce, shaped one by one with a *ferretto* – a thin metal or wooden rod, usually about 3–4mm/⅛in thick (similar to a knitting needle). It's a relaxing, repetitive process that I find grounding. This recipe invites you to slow down.

Serves: 4

Preparation time: 1 hour, plus 30 minutes resting

Cooking time: 15 minutes (plus time for the confit tomatoes if you aren't making them in advance)

For the Dough:

* 400g/14oz/3 cups semola
* 200ml/7fl oz/scant 1 cup water

For the Sauce:

* 2 courgettes/zucchini
* 2 tbsp extra virgin olive oil
* 200g confit cherry tomatoes, plus 3–4 tbsp of their cooking juices
* 2–4 roasted garlic cloves
* A small bunch of fresh flat-leaf parsley, finely chopped
* 1 tsp chilli oil, plus extra to serve (optional – page 268)
* Salt and pepper, to taste

Make the Dough: On a clean work surface, make a mound with the semola and create a well in the centre. Gradually add the water, mixing with your fingers or a fork to incorporate the semola until a rough dough forms. Knead for 5–7 minutes until smooth and elastic. Cover with a dish towel and let rest for 30 minutes.

Prepare the Confit Cherry Tomatoes: Preheat the oven to 140°C/275°F/Gas Mark 1. Follow the recipe on page 247.

Shape the Casarecce: Lightly dust a tray and work surface with semola. Cut off a small piece of the rested dough and keep the rest covered. Roll the dough into a long rope about 5mm/¼in thick. Cut into short pieces, each about 4–5cm/2in long. Working one piece at a time, press a *ferretto* or a thin metal or wooden rod into the centre of the dough and roll it toward you, flattening and curling it slightly. Gently slide it off and using your fingertips, ever so slightly twist the ends in opposite directions, forming the signature casarecce shape. Set aside on the tray and cover with a dish towel while you continue shaping the rest.

Prepare the Courgettes/Zucchini: Trim the courgettes and slice them thinly (2–3mm/⅛in thick) using a mandoline or sharp knife. Heat the olive oil in a wide pan over a medium heat. Add the courgette slices and a pinch of salt. Cook gently for 3–4 minutes, just until softened. Add the reserved tomato juices and continue to cook for another 2–3 minutes, letting the courgettes absorb the flavour.

Add the Garlic and Tomatoes: Squeeze the roasted garlic cloves to extract the soft insides. Add this garlic paste to the pan and stir to combine. Add the confit cherry tomatoes and let everything warm through over a low heat. Taste and adjust the seasoning with salt and pepper. Stir in most of the chopped parsley (reserving some for garnish) and the chilli oil, if using. Turn off the heat and keep warm.

Cook the Casarecce: Bring a large pot of salted water to the boil. Add the casarecce and cook for 3–4 minutes, or until they float and the texture is al dente.

Combine and Serve: Using a slotted spoon, lift the pasta directly into the pan with the sauce. Toss gently to coat, adding a splash of cooking water if needed to help the sauce cling evenly. Serve immediately, with the reserved parsley and/or a drizzle of chilli oil on top.

CRISPY STUFFED GNOCCHI WITH TOMATO & ONION DIP

Gnocchi ripieni croccanti con dip di pomodoro e cipolla

Crisp on the outside, soft in the middle. Served with a thick, rich tomato and onion sauce and a scatter of chives. In this recipe, each gnocco is shaped by hand, filled with a small frozen ball of tomato and cheese, then sealed. The dough is soft but easy to work with, and once they hit the pan, the outside crisps up while the middle stays molten.

The tomato sauce is cooked slowly until it thickens and deepens in flavour. Onions break down over a low heat, and the tomato takes on a richness that comes only from patience. It's thick enough to serve on the side: something to swipe the gnocchi through, not something that drowns them.

The result is clean, focused and satisfying. A plate of crisp gnocchi, a small bowl of warm sauce and a sprinkle of chives. Nothing complicated. Just a series of small, thoughtful steps that are worth taking.

Serves: 4

Preparation time: 1 hour, plus freezing time

Cooking time: 2 hours

For the Filling:
* 2 tbsp tomato purée/paste
* 80g/2¾oz/¾ cup mozzarella, grated

For the Dough:
* 800g/1¾lb floury potatoes (about 4 medium-large)
* 200g/7oz/1½ cups plain/all-purpose flour, plus more as needed
* 1 egg

For the Sauce:
* 3 tbsp extra virgin olive oil
* 2 large onions, finely sliced
* 1½ tbsp tomato purée/paste
* 200ml/7fl oz/scant 1 cup tomato passata
* 100ml/3½fl oz/scant ½ cup water
* Salt and pepper, to taste

To Finish:
* Olive oil or unsalted butter, for frying
* Fresh chives, finely chopped

Prepare the Filling: Line two baking sheets or plates with baking parchment. Using a piping bag or a tube of tomato purée/paste, portion the tomato purée into small marble-size drops: you'll need around 60. Repeat the process with the grated mozzarella, shaping it into small tight balls using your fingertips. Place both baking sheets in the freezer for at least 1 hour, or until the balls are solid.

Make the Dough: Peel and boil the potatoes whole for 45–50 minutes or longer (depending on size) until completely tender. Drain, then pass them through a potato ricer or mash until smooth. Spread the mashed potatoes out onto a clean baking sheet or plate and leave to cool slightly.

Sprinkle over the flour and crack in the egg. Mix gently with your hands and knead just until a rough dough comes together, soft but not sticky. Avoid overworking.

Shape the Gnocchi: Lightly dust a tray and work surface with flour. Tear off a small piece of dough and roll it into a ball a little smaller than a walnut between your palms. Press your thumb into the centre to make space for the filling. Insert both a frozen tomato ball and frozen mozzarella ball, then pinch the dough closed. Roll again between your hands to seal and smooth. Place on the floured tray and keep covered as you work. Repeat with the remaining dough and filling.

Make the Sauce: Heat the olive oil in a wide pan over a low heat. Add the onions and a pinch of salt. Cook slowly for 25–30 minutes, stirring often, until soft and golden. Stir in the tomato purée/paste, cook for 1–2 minutes until fragrant, then add the tomato passata. Let it cook for 5 more minutes, then add the water gradually. Simmer, uncovered, for 20–25 minutes, until the sauce has thickened. Season to taste with salt and pepper. Keep warm.

Pan-fry the Gnocchi: Heat a large, non-stick pan over a medium heat. Add a thin layer of olive oil. Fry the gnocchi in batches, turning gently every couple of minutes, until golden and crisp on all sides, around 6–8 minutes per batch.

Serve: Spoon the sauce into a small bowl or ramekin. Arrange the crispy gnocchi on a serving plate, sprinkle with chopped chives and serve hot, with the sauce on the side for dipping.

BUCKWHEAT & SWEET POTATO GNOCCHI WITH HAZELNUTS & BLUE CHEESE

Gnocchi al grano saraceno e patata dolce

Serves: 4

Preparation time: 45 minutes

Cooking time: 15 minutes

For the Dough:

* 1 large sweet potato (approx. 400g/14oz)
* 200g/7oz/1½ cups buckwheat flour
* 1 large egg
* 2 tbsp fine breadcrumbs (gluten-free or optional)
* Zest of 1 orange

For the Sauce:

* 50g/1¾oz/3½ tbsp unsalted butter
* 8–10 fresh sage leaves
* 50g/1¾oz/½ cup hazelnuts, roughly chopped, toasted, plus extra to garnish
* 100g/3½oz/½ cup gorgonzola
* Salt, to taste
* Freshly ground black pepper, to taste, plus extra to serve

Nutty gluten-free buckwheat gnocchi with sweet potato, paired with a rich gorgonzola and hazelnut sauce, finished with crispy sage. This recipe is all about balance. The gnocchi have a slightly nutty, almost earthy flavour from the buckwheat, which pairs naturally with the sweetness of the potato. The citrus zest doesn't draw attention to itself but brings everything into focus. Shaping them takes a little rhythm and patience. The dough is soft, so instead of rolling and cutting, you pipe them straight into boiling water, piece by piece.

The sauce is simple and generous. Gorgonzola melts into butter, then toasted hazelnuts are stirred through for texture, and crispy sage leaves finish the dish. It's not a heavy meal, but there's richness in every bite.

There's no need to rush through the steps. Once you've set everything up, the process becomes steady. You make one thing at a time and bring them together at the end, which is what cooking often comes down to.

Cook the Sweet Potato: Peel and dice the sweet potato. Steam or boil it until tender, about 10 minutes. Once cooked, mash it until smooth and set aside to cool slightly.

Make the Dough: In a large bowl, combine the mashed sweet potato, buckwheat flour, egg, breadcrumbs and orange zest. Mix well until a wet dough forms. The dough should be soft but not overly sticky.

Shape the Gnocchi: Transfer the dough to a piping bag fitted with a wide nozzle (about 1cm/⅓in diameter). Bring a large pot of salted water to the boil. Hold the piping bag over the boiling water and squeeze the dough out, using a knife or kitchen scissors to cut the dough into 2cm/¾in pieces directly into the water. Work quickly so they cook evenly.

Make the Sauce: In a large pan, melt the butter over a medium heat. Add the sage leaves and fry until crispy, about 30 seconds, then remove from the pan and set aside. Add the hazelnuts to the pan and toast for 1 minute, then add the gorgonzola, stirring gently until mostly melted and creamy. Season with salt and pepper to taste. Keep the sauce warm over a low heat.

Cook the Gnocchi: Once the gnocchi float to the surface of the water, about 2–3 minutes, let them cook for an additional 30 seconds.

Combine and Serve: Using a slotted spoon, lift the gnocchi directly into the pan with the gorgonzola sauce. Gently toss the cooked gnocchi in the sauce until well coated. Serve topped with the crispy sage leaves, extra toasted hazelnuts and a sprinkle of black pepper. Serve immediately.

SPELT STROZZAPRETI ("PRIEST STRANGLERS") WITH KALE PESTO

Strozzapreti al farro con pesto di cavolo nero

Hearty, rustic strozzapreti made with spelt flour, paired with a kale pesto. The name strozzapreti is steeped in Italian folklore, translating to "priest stranglers". Legend has it that this hand-rolled pasta got its name from priests who enjoyed it so much that they devoured it too quickly, nearly choking in their enthusiasm. Whether the story is true or not, strozzapreti remains a deeply traditional pasta, often made in Italian homes and celebrated for its rustic simplicity.

When made with spelt flour, this pasta takes on a distinctively nutty flavour, adding a layer of depth that pairs beautifully with hearty sauces. In this version, the boldness of cavolo nero (Tuscan kale) is transformed into a vibrant pesto that coats the strozzapreti with a rich, slightly bitter yet comforting sauce. This dish is a celebration of simple, wholesome ingredients that come together in a way that feels both nourishing and comforting. A true expression of rustic therapy in your kitchen.

Serves: 4

Preparation time: 45 minutes, plus 30 minutes resting

Cooking time: 5 minutes

For the Dough:

* 250g/9oz/scant 2 cups spelt flour
* 150g/5¼oz/1¼ cups 00 flour
* 200ml/7fl oz/scant 1 cup lukewarm water

For the Kale Pesto:

* 150g/5¼oz/3 cups packed cavolo nero (Tuscan kale), tough stems removed
* 50g/1¾oz/½ cup walnuts, toasted
* 2 garlic cloves
* 50g/1¾oz/½ cup Pecorino, finely grated
* Juice of ½ lemon
* 60ml/2fl oz/¼ cup extra virgin olive oil
* Salt and pepper, to taste

Make the Dough: On a clean work surface, combine the spelt and 00 flours in a mound. Create a well in the centre and gradually add the water, mixing with your fingers or a fork to incorporate the flour until a rough dough forms. Knead for 5–7 minutes until smooth and elastic. Cover with a dish towel and let rest for 30 minutes.

Prepare the Kale Pesto: Bring a pot of salted water to the boil. Blanch the kale for 2 minutes, then immediately transfer it to a bowl of iced water to cool. Drain and squeeze out any excess water. In a food processor, combine the blanched kale, toasted walnuts, garlic, Pecorino and lemon juice. Pulse until coarsely chopped. Gradually add the olive oil while processing, until the pesto reaches your desired consistency. Season with salt and pepper to taste. Set aside.

Shape the Strozzapreti: Lightly dust a tray and a wooden board or work surface with flour. Cut off a small piece of the rested dough. Roll it into a rope about 1cm/⅓in thick. Cut the rope into shorter lengths, about 4cm/1½in. Take one piece at a time and place it on the board. Using the side of your hand, press and roll the piece away from you in a single motion. As you roll, the dough will twist and stretch slightly into an irregular, elongated shape. You're not looking for a tight spiral, just a loose, natural twist with uneven edges. This gives strozzapreti their typical rustic look, broader and flatter than trofie and not tapered at the ends. Set aside on the tray and keep covered as you work.

Cook the Strozzapreti: Bring a large pot of salted water to the boil. Add the strozzapreti and cook for 3–4 minutes, or until they float and the texture is al dente.

Combine and Serve: Using a slotted spoon, lift the strozzapreti directly into a large bowl with the pesto. Toss gently to coat, adding a splash of cooking water if needed to help the sauce cling evenly. Adjust the seasoning with salt and pepper if necessary and serve immediately.

CRUXIONIS: SARDINIAN RAVIOLI WITH RICOTTA & SAFFRON

Cruxionis de arrascottu e zaffaranu

A traditional pasta from southern Sardinia, shaped with care and filled with scented ricotta, served in a sauce that gently bends the rules. *Cruxionis* are Sardinia's answer to ravioli, varying in name and shape depending on where you are on the island. In some areas, they're called *culurgiones* and sealed with a decorative pleat; in others, they're known as *cruxionis* and cut with a serrated wheel. What they all share is a focus on the making. Each one is shaped by hand, sealed with care and made in batches.

This version is filled with ricotta and saffron, a fragrant pairing that feels special and humble. Like many Sardinian dishes, this isn't fast food. The shapes are made one by one. The sauce takes time. But there's a calm sort of joy in the repetition and a real sense of satisfaction when it all comes together.

Serves: 4

Preparation time: 1 hour, plus 30 minutes resting

Cooking time: 35 minutes

For the Dough:

* 400g/14oz/3 cups 00 flour
* 4 eggs

For the Filling:

* Pinch of saffron threads, infused in 2 tbsp hot water for a few minutes
* 500g/17½oz/2 cups ricotta, well drained
* 2 tbsp grated Pecorino or Parmigiano Reggiano
* Salt and pepper, to taste

For the Sauce:

* 3 tbsp extra virgin olive oil
* 1 garlic clove
* 200g/7oz/2 cups cauliflower florets, cut into small pieces
* ½ tsp smoked paprika
* 400g/14oz/2 cups tomato passata or polpa di pomodoro
* 1 tsp sugar
* A few fresh basil leaves
* Salt, to taste

To Finish:

* 125g/4⅓oz/½ cup smoked burrata (optional)

Make the Dough: On a clean work surface, make a mound with the flour and create a well in the centre. Crack in the eggs and whisk gently with a fork, gradually incorporating the flour until a rough dough forms. Knead for 5–7 minutes until smooth and elastic. Cover with a dish towel and let rest for 30 minutes.

Prepare the Filling: In a bowl, mix the ricotta with the saffron threads with their water, Pecorino and some salt and pepper. Taste and adjust the seasoning, if needed. The filling should be smooth and not too wet. Keep chilled until needed.

Make the Sauce: In a wide pan, heat the olive oil over a medium heat. Add the garlic clove and cauliflower florets and sauté for 5–6 minutes until the cauliflower is lightly golden in spots. Stir in the smoked paprika and cook for another 30 seconds. Add the passata, sugar, basil and a pinch of salt. Reduce the heat and simmer gently, uncovered, for 20–25 minutes until the sauce thickens slightly. Remove the garlic before serving.

Roll and Fill the Cruxionis: Lightly dust a tray and work surface with flour. Divide the rested pasta dough into 4 pieces and keep them covered. Roll each piece into a thin sheet, about 1mm thick (setting 5 on a Marcato). Place small teaspoons of filling evenly spaced along the sheet. Fold the sheet over the filling to cover, gently pressing around each mound to remove any air. Use a ravioli cutter or serrated wheel to cut into rounds or squares. I used a flower-shaped brass cutter, but you can use what you have or simply cut with a knife. Press the edges to seal. Place the shaped cruxionis on the floured tray and cover while you repeat with the remaining dough.

Cook the Cruxionis: Bring a large pot of salted water to the boil. Cook the cruxionis in batches for 3–4 minutes, or until they float and the texture is al dente.

Combine and Serve: Using a slotted spoon, add the cruxionis directly to the warm sauce, folding gently to combine. Spoon the cruxionis onto plates with the cauliflower-tomato sauce. Optionally, spoon some smoked burrata on top, then serve.

SPIZZULUS WITH YELLOW DATTERINO SAUCE, ROBIOLA & CRISPY GARLIC

Spizzulus con salsa di datterini gialli, robiola e aglio croccante

A traditional Sardinian pasta formed into a teardrop shape, served with sweet yellow tomatoes, creamy Robiola and crisp garlic. The name *spizzulus* comes from the Sardinian word for "pinch", which refers to the final gesture that gives this pasta its distinctive teardrop shape. It's a handmade form, once common in the province of Oristano, and still made today for festive or Sunday meals. Like many island pastas, it's shaped without tools beyond a board and a bit of time. Each piece is made individually, with a movement that's simple, repetitive and satisfying.

The sauce is light and balanced with its gentle yellow datterino tomatoes cooked down with olive oil, finished with basil and a spoonful of soft-ripened Robiola for creaminess. The final touch is crisp garlic slices, fried until golden and scattered on top.

This is a dish that doesn't call attention to itself, but everything about it works.

Serves: 4

Preparation time: 1 hour, plus 30 minutes resting

Cooking time: 30 minutes

For the Dough:

* 400g/14oz/3 cups semola
* 200ml/7fl oz/scant 1 cup lukewarm water

For the Sauce:

* 3 tbsp extra virgin olive oil
* 1 garlic clove, unpeeled
* 500g/17½oz/3½ cups yellow datterino tomatoes, halved
* A few fresh basil leaves, torn
* Salt and sugar, to taste

To Finish:

* Olive oil, for frying
* 3 garlic cloves, thinly sliced
* 100g/3½oz/½ cup Robiola, brought to room temperature
* Fresh basil leaves, to serve

Make the Dough: On a clean work surface, make a mound with the semola and create a well in the centre. Gradually add the water, mixing with your fingers or a fork to incorporate the semola until a rough dough forms. Knead for 5–7 minutes until smooth and elastic. Cover with a dish towel and let rest for 30 minutes.

Make the Sauce: Heat the olive oil in a wide pan over a medium heat. Add the whole garlic clove and sauté gently for 1–2 minutes until fragrant, then remove and discard. Add the halved tomatoes and a pinch of salt. Cook for 15–20 minutes, stirring occasionally, until the tomatoes soften and release their juices. Add a pinch of sugar to balance the acidity if needed. Stir in the torn basil and transfer to a blender. Blend until smooth, then return to the pan, keeping the sauce warm.

Shape the Spizzulus: Lightly dust a tray and work surface with semola. Cut off a portion of the rested dough and keep the rest covered. Roll it into a rope about 1cm/⅓in thick and cut it into lengths of 7–8cm/3¼in. One by one, roll each piece along a gnocchi board to create ridges, then gently bring the two ends together and pinch them firmly to form a closed teardrop shape. Place the finished spizzulus on the tray and cover lightly with a dish towel while you continue shaping the rest.

Fry the Garlic: Heat a little olive oil in a frying pan over a medium heat. Add the sliced garlic and fry for 30–60 seconds until golden and crisp. Remove with a slotted spoon and drain on paper towels.

Cook the Spizzulus: Bring a large pot of salted water to the boil. Add the spizzulus and cook for 4–5 minutes, or until they float and the texture is al dente.

Combine and Serve: Using a slotted spoon, lift the pasta directly into the pan with the tomato sauce. Toss gently to coat, adding a splash of cooking water if needed to help the sauce cling evenly. Divide the dressed spizzulus between plates. Dot each portion with small spoonfuls of Robiola, scatter with the crispy garlic and finish with a few basil leaves.

CAVATELLI WITH TOMATO SAUCE, STRACCIATELLA & RAGUSANO

Cavatelli col sugo di mamma, stracciatella e ragusano dop

A southern classic with depth, where simple ingredients come together with confidence and care. This dish takes me straight back to the kitchen where I grew up. My mum would start with a pan of gently sweating onions, then add tomatoes, a handful of torn basil and a pinch of salt . . . nothing more. When summer jars of fresh tomato sauce ran out, or when time was short, she'd make this quicker version with canned tomatoes. It had the same care and flavour, just done in less time with what was on hand. It was the sauce for everything: pasta, rice, even bread when there was nothing else. It didn't need explaining.

Here, that sauce is tossed with cavatelli. Stracciatella is stirred through just before serving, softening the flavour and giving the dish a little richness. On top, Ragusano DOP, grated generously: salty, sharp and full of depth. If you don't have Ragusano, aged Pecorino will do. It's not a dish that shows off. But every part of it has purpose.

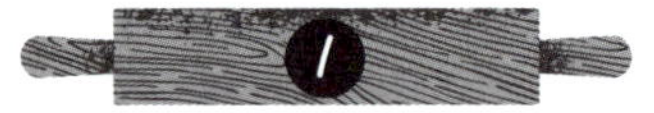

Serves: 4

Preparation time: 45 minutes, plus 30 minutes resting

Cooking time: 35 minutes

For the Dough:

* 400g/14oz/3 cups semola
* 200ml/7fl oz/scant 1 cup lukewarm water

For the Sauce:

* 3 tbsp extra virgin olive oil
* 1 large onion, finely chopped
* 400g/14oz/2 cups tomato passata or polpa di pomodoro
* A few fresh basil leaves, torn
* Salt, to taste

To Finish:

* 100g/3½oz/½ cup stracciatella
* 40g/1½oz/⅓ cup Ragusano DOP or aged Pecorino, finely grated

Make the Dough: On a clean work surface, make a mound with the semola and create a well in the centre. Gradually add the water, mixing with your fingers or a fork to incorporate the semola until a rough dough forms. Knead for 5–7 minutes until smooth and elastic. Cover with a dish towel and let rest for 30 minutes.

Make the Sauce: Heat the olive oil in a saucepan over a medium-low heat. Add the onion and a pinch of salt. Cook gently until softened and translucent, about 10–12 minutes. Add the passata and the torn basil leaves. Simmer, uncovered, for 15–20 minutes, stirring occasionally, until the sauce thickens and the flavour has rounded. Taste and adjust the salt. Keep warm.

Shape the Cavatelli: Lightly dust a tray and work surface with semola. Divide the rested dough into 4 portions and roll each into ropes about 1cm/⅓in thick. Cut into small pieces, roughly 3cm/1¼in long. Using a cavatelli board, press and drag each piece toward you with your thumb to create a curled shape. Set aside on the tray and keep covered as you work.

Cook the Cavatelli: Bring a large pot of salted water to the boil. Cook the cavatelli for 3–4 minutes, or until they float and the texture is al dente.

Combine and Serve: Using a slotted spoon, lift the cavatelli directly into the pan with the sauce. Toss gently to coat, adding a splash of cooking water if needed to help the sauce cling evenly, then gently fold in the stracciatella. Divide between plates and finish with a generous grating of Ragusano DOP or your preferred cheese. Serve immediately.

BUSIATE WITH ROASTED PEPPER & WALNUT PESTO

Busiate con pesto di peperoni arrostiti e noci

A vibrant pesto of sweet roasted peppers and toasted walnuts, wrapped around the gentle twists of handmade Sicilian pasta. Busiate are one of Sicily's most recognizable pasta shapes, especially in the west of the island where they're paired with Pesto Trapanese (page 39). The dough is rolled into long ropes and twisted around a skewer or *ferretto* creating light spirals that hold their shape beautifully when cooked. Their texture gives them just the right amount of surface area to carry a loose sauce without being overwhelmed by it.

This roasted pepper and walnut pesto is a softer alternative to the more assertive Trapani style made with raw tomatoes and almonds. The peppers are roasted until the skins blacken, then blended with toasted walnuts, olive oil and a touch of garlic. A little lemon juice brings freshness, and the result is smooth, rich and slightly sweet. It settles into the pasta spirals without overpowering them.

Serves: 4

Preparation time: 1 hour, plus 30 minutes resting

Cooking time: 35 minutes

For the Dough:
* 400g/14oz/3 cups semola
* 200ml/7fl oz/scant 1 cup lukewarm water

For the Pesto:
* 2 large red peppers
* 60g/2oz/⅔ cup walnuts, toasted
* 1 small garlic clove (optional)
* 2 tbsp lemon juice
* 4 tbsp extra virgin olive oil
* 30g/1oz/¼ cup Pecorino or smoked ricotta salata, grated
* Salt, to taste

To Finish:
* Finely grated smoked or regular ricotta salata
* Fresh basil leaves, torn, or microbasil
* Chopped walnuts, toasted (optional)

Make the Dough: On a clean work surface, make a mound with the semola and create a well in the centre. Gradually add the water, mixing with your fingers or a fork to incorporate the semola until a rough dough forms. Knead for 5–7 minutes until smooth and elastic. Cover with a dish towel and let rest for 30 minutes.

Roast the Peppers: Preheat the oven to 220°C/425°F/Gas Mark 7. Place the whole peppers on a baking sheet and roast for 25–30 minutes, turning occasionally, until the skins are blistered and blackened. You can also do this step over an open flame if using a gas hob/stovetop. Transfer the peppers to a bowl and cover with a plate or cling film/plastic wrap. Let steam for 10 minutes, then peel and deseed. Tear the flesh into strips.

Shape the Busiate: Lightly dust a tray and work surface with semola. Cut off a small portion of the rested dough and keep the rest covered. Roll it into a thin rope, about 4–5mm/¼in thick. Cut it into lengths of around 10–12cm/4½in. Wrap each piece around a skewer or *ferretto*, rolling it gently to form a spiral. Slide it off and place it on the tray, and keep covered as you work. Repeat with the remaining dough.

Make the Pesto: In a food processor, blend the roasted pepper flesh with the toasted walnuts, garlic, if using, lemon juice, olive oil and Pecorino until smooth. Season with salt to taste. Adjust the consistency with a little more oil or a splash of warm water if needed.

Cook the Busiate: Bring a large pot of salted water to the boil. Cook the busiate for 4–5 minutes, or until al dente.

Combine and Serve: Using tongs, lift the pasta directly into a large bowl with the pesto. Toss to combine, adding a splash of cooking water if needed to help the sauce cling evenly. Divide between plates and top with grated smoked ricotta salata, torn basil leaves or microbasil and a few extra chopped walnuts, if you like. Serve warm or at room temperature.

CHICCHE DELLA NONNA WITH SUMMER VEGGIES

Chicche della nonna con verdure estive

A dish that tastes like summer without trying too hard. Chicche, also known as gnocchetti, are nothing but gnocchi, only smaller and rounder. They have been present in various Italian regions, including northern Tuscany and Emilia-Romagna, for quite some time. For example, in Piacenza, green chicche made with spinach are a traditional dish often served with gorgonzola sauce. While chicche may not have the same historical prominence as other gnocchi varieties, they are not a modern invention. They've been part of regional Italian cuisine for generations, and their popularity has grown thanks to their quick cooking time and adaptability. We didn't grow up making gnocchi at home, but I've come to enjoy how this particular shape suits modern kitchens: quick, unfussy and just right for seasonal vegetables.

Serves: 4

Preparation time: 30 minutes

Cooking time: 1 hour

For the Dough:

* 500g/1lb floury potatoes (about 2 medium)
* 100g/3½oz/¾ cup plain/all-purpose flour
* 1 egg

For the Sauce:

* 3 tbsp extra virgin olive oil
* 1 garlic clove, unpeeled
* 1 small courgette/zucchini, thinly sliced
* 6–8 asparagus tips, chopped
* 100g/3½oz/⅔ cup yellow and red datterino tomatoes, halved
* 1 tbsp single/light cream or crème fraîche
* A generous handful of finely grated Pecorino, plus extra to serve
* A few fresh mint leaves, finely chopped, plus extra to garnish
* Salt, to taste

Make the Dough: Peel and boil the potatoes whole for around 40–45 minutes, or until completely tender. Mash until smooth using a potato ricer or masher. Leave to cool slightly. Add the flour and egg. Mix until a soft, workable dough forms.

Shape and Cook the Chicche: Roll the dough into ropes about 1.5cm/½in thick, then cut into marble-size pieces. Roll each piece lightly between your palms to form a smooth ball. Bring a large pot of salted water to the boil. Cook the chicche in batches for 2–3 minutes, until they float to the surface. Remove with a slotted spoon and set aside in a warm place. Reserve a ladleful of the water.

Make the Sauce: In a wide pan, warm the olive oil over a medium heat. Add the whole garlic clove and let it infuse for 1–2 minutes. Add the courgette/zucchini and cook gently for 5–7 minutes until softened. Add the asparagus and tomatoes and continue cooking for 3–4 minutes until the tomatoes begin to collapse and release their juices. Discard the garlic, stir in the cream and season with salt. Let the sauce simmer gently for a couple of minutes.

Combine and Serve: Add the cooked chicche to the sauce. Sprinkle with the Pecorino and chopped mint and toss gently to combine. If the sauce is too thick, add a splash of the reserved cooking water. Serve immediately with extra Pecorino and mint to finish.

TROFIE WITH PUMPKIN & RICOTTA

Trofie con salsa "piciocia"

Serves: 4

Preparation time: 45 minutes, plus 30 minutes resting

Cooking time: 15 minutes

For the Dough:

* 400g/14oz/3 cups semola
* 200ml/7fl oz/scant 1 cup lukewarm water

For the Sauce:

* 2 tbsp extra virgin olive oil
* 1 small white onion, finely grated
* 350g/12oz/2½ cups pumpkin or butternut squash, peeled, deseeded and diced
* about 500ml/17fl oz/2 cups vegetable stock
* 250g/9oz/1 cup ricotta
* 4 tbsp finely grated Pecorino, plus extra to serve
* Salt and pepper, to taste
* A few fresh marjoram leaves, to garnish

A soft tangle of handmade pasta from Liguria meets a local sauce from Sicily to celebrate autumn's best flavours. This is a comforting dish featuring the rich, creamy flavours of pumpkin, fresh ricotta and Sicilian Pecorino. "Autumn carries more gold in its pocket than all the other seasons", said the American journalist Jim Bishop, and it's a sentiment I feel deeply in the kitchen. There's something about autumn's gentle decay that reminds us of the fleeting nature of things: a time to let go, like trees releasing their leaves. This traditional autumn recipe, known in Ragusa as *pasta con salsa piciocia*, embodies the warmth and simplicity of Sicilian cooking, and refers to a dish made with pumpkin, ricotta, Pecorino and an aromatic broth.

I've chosen to pair the sauce with trofie, though many families use casarecce. Trofie are small, hand-rolled pasta twists from Liguria; you often see them paired with basil pesto, but their tight shape works beautifully here. The result is a dish that's mellow, savoury and comforting; the kind of thing you'd eat after a morning at the market or while watching the season begin to turn.

Make the Dough: On a clean work surface make a mound with the semola and create a well in the centre. Gradually add the water while mixing with your fingers or a fork to incorporate the semola until a rough dough forms. Knead for 5–7 minutes until smooth and elastic. Cover with a dish towel and let rest for 30 minutes.

Prepare the Sauce: In a wide sauté pan, heat the olive oil over a medium heat and add the grated onion. Cook gently for 2–3 minutes until softened. Add the pumpkin and season with salt and pepper. Pour in a couple of ladlefuls of the hot stock, cover and simmer for about 10 minutes until the pumpkin softens but still holds its shape.

Shape the Trofie: Lightly dust a tray and work surface with semola. Cut the rested dough into small pieces, about the size of a hazelnut. Working one at a time, place a piece on a wooden board or work surface. Using the side of your palm, especially the outer edge near your pinkie finger, press down and roll the dough diagonally across the surface, dragging it gently toward you. This creates a tapered, twisted shape with pointed ends and a thicker middle. It takes a bit of practice, but once you find the right pressure and angle, it becomes second nature. Place the finished trofie on the tray and keep covered as you work.

Cook the Trofie: Bring a large pot of salted water to the boil. Cook the trofie for 2–3 minutes, or until they float and the texture is al dente.

Combine and Serve: Using a slotted spoon, lift the trofie directly into the pan with the pumpkin. Toss gently to combine. In a bowl, whisk together the ricotta, Pecorino and a splash more of the stock. Add the mixture to the cooked trofie and pumpkin and stir to combine, adding a splash of cooking water if needed to help the sauce cling evenly. Plate and finish with fresh marjoram and more grated Pecorino. Serve warm.

CORZETTI WITH CHILLI OIL, ANCHO CHILLI & HAZELNUTS

Corzetti bicolore al peperoncino e nocciole

Serves: 4

Preparation time: 40 minutes, plus 30 minutes resting

Cooking time: 10 minutes

For the Classic Dough:

* 200g/7oz/1½ cups semola
* 1 tsp extra virgin olive oil
* 100ml/3½fl oz/scant ½ cup water

For the Spinach Dough:

* 200g/7oz/1½ cups semola
* 1 tsp extra virgin olive oil
* 100ml/3½fl oz/scant ½ cup spinach purée (made from about 200g/7oz/4 cups spinach, wilted and blended)

For the Chilli Oil Seasoning:

* 4 tbsp extra virgin olive oil
* 1 garlic clove, smashed
* 1 dried ancho chilli, crumbled
* 40g/1½oz/⅓ cup hazelnuts, lightly toasted and roughly crushed
* Smoked sea salt or flaky salt, to finish
* Fresh basil leaves, to garnish (optional)

A pasta shape that brings its own elegance to the table: no sauce needed to make a statement. Corzetti aren't just pasta: they're small emblems of craftsmanship. Originally from Liguria and parts of northern Tuscany, these medallion-shaped discs are pressed with carved wooden stamps, often bearing coats of arms, floral or geometric patterns. For this recipe, I made mine with two batches of dough – one plain, one with spinach – to echo the visual tradition of contrast and ornament. The raised design isn't only decorative, it helps grip the seasoning, which here is no more than good oil, mellow heat and the crunch of hazelnuts. Minimal in ingredients, but memorable in flavour and form.

Make the Doughs: For each dough, place the semola on a clean work surface and create a well in the centre. Add the olive oil, then gradually add the water or spinach purée, mixing with your fingers or a fork to incorporate the semola until a rough dough forms. Knead for 5–7 minutes until smooth and elastic. Cover both doughs with a dish towel and let rest for 30 minutes.

Roll and Stamp the Corzetti: Lightly dust a tray and work surface with semola. Roll out the rested doughs into thin sheets, about 2–3mm/⅛in thick (setting 3 on a Marcato). Cut out rounds using a corzetti stamp or a round cutter (about 4cm/1½in in diameter). If using a stamp, press the patterned side onto each round to emboss the design. Lightly dust with semola and set aside on the tray, and keep covered as you work.

Make the Chilli Oil: In a small saucepan, gently warm the olive oil with the garlic clove for 30–60 seconds over a low heat. Add the crumbled ancho chilli and let it infuse for 2–3 minutes, until aromatic. Remove from the heat and discard the garlic. Stir in the crushed hazelnuts and set aside.

Cook the Corzetti: Bring a large pot of salted water to the boil. Cook the corzetti for 3–4 minutes, or until al dente.

Combine and Serve: Using a slotted spoon, lift the corzetti directly into the pan with the warm chilli oil and hazelnuts. Toss gently to coat, adding a splash of cooking water if needed to help the sauce cling evenly. Divide among plates and finish with a pinch of smoked salt. Serve immediately with fresh basil, if using.

RAVIOLI WITH WILD GREENS, NUTMEG RICOTTA & PARSLEY PESTO

Ravioli alle erbe di campo, ricotta e pesto al prezzemolo

This is a dish that honours the simplicity of wild herbs and fresh cheese, wrapped in tender pasta and brought to life with a vibrant green sauce. Gathering or selecting wild greens can feel grounding: nettles, dandelion, chard, sorrel or any tender leaves that the season offers. In my family, these greens were never wasted. They were wilted, chopped, made into soups or stir-fried. This ravioli brings that tradition to the table: a filling of softly cooked wild greens and nutmeg-scented ricotta, wrapped in golden sheets of semola dough. Served with a bright parsley pesto, it's a celebration of all things green.

Serves: 4

Preparation time: 30 minutes, plus 30 minutes resting

Cooking time: 10 minutes

For the Dough:

* 400g/14oz/3 cups semola
* 4 eggs

For the Pesto:

* 40g/½oz/1½ cups packed fresh flat-leaf parsley leaves
* 30g/1oz/¼ cup pine nuts, lightly toasted, plus extra to serve (optional)
* 1 small garlic clove, minced (optional)
* 60ml/2fl oz/¼ cup extra virgin olive oil, plus extra to serve
* 2 tbsp finely grated Parmigiano Reggiano
* 2 tbsp finely grated Pecorino
* Salt and pepper, to taste

For the Filling:

* 300g/10½oz/6 cups packed wild greens (nettles, dandelion, sorrel, spinach, chard), etc, washed and trimmed
* 250g/9oz/1 cup ricotta, well drained
* 30g/1oz/¼ cup Parmigiano Reggiano, finely grated, plus extra to serve (optional)
* A good pinch of freshly grated nutmeg
* Salt and pepper, to taste

Make the Dough: On a clean work surface, make a mound with the semola and create a well in the centre. Crack in the eggs and whisk gently with a fork, gradually incorporating the semola until a rough dough forms. Knead for 5–7 minutes until smooth and elastic. Cover with a dish towel and let rest for 30 minutes.

Make the Pesto: In a food processor or using a mortar and pestle, combine the parsley, pine nuts, a pinch of salt, and the garlic, if using. Blitz or pound to a paste. Slowly add the olive oil, blending until smooth. Stir in both cheeses and adjust the seasoning to taste. Set aside.

Prepare the Filling: Blanch the wild greens in a pan of salted boiling water for 2–3 minutes until tender. Drain well and squeeze out as much liquid as possible, then finely chop. In a bowl, mix the greens with the ricotta, Parmigiano, nutmeg and some salt and pepper until well combined.

Roll and Fill the Ravioli: Lightly dust a tray and work surface with semola. Roll out the rested dough into a thin sheet, about 1mm thick (setting 5 on a Marcato). Cut out circles using a 6–8cm/3¼in ravioli stamp or cookie cutter. Place a teaspoon of filling in the centre of half the discs, brush the edges lightly with water, then top with another pasta disc. Press out any air and seal the edges well. Place on the tray and cover with a dish towel.

Cook the Ravioli: Bring a large pot of salted water to the boil, then lower to a simmer. Cook the ravioli for 3–4 minutes, or until they are al dente and float to the surface.

Combine and Serve: Using a slotted spoon, lift the cooked ravioli into a large bowl with the pesto. Toss to coat, adding a splash of cooking water if needed to help the sauce cling evenly. Serve with a drizzle of extra virgin olive oil and an extra sprinkle of cheese and some toasted pine nuts, if you like.

Ch. 7

HEALING Through Food

Food nourishes in multiple ways. Beyond sustaining the body, it also steadies the mind, fills a silence and carries us through. This chapter is where the heart of this book lives: the in-between moments, when life hasn't gone to plan and cooking becomes the only way to make sense of things.

I didn't always cook to create. During my toughest moments – my diagnosis, 16 rounds of chemo, 20 rounds of radiotherapy and two surgeries; and later, watching my parents deteriorate within the same year – I found myself in the kitchen, simply because I didn't know where else to be. Grief made everything feel distant. The future felt terrifying. But a pan heating on the hob/stovetop demanded attention. Rinsing vegetables, peeling garlic or slicing onions gave my hands purpose.

The kitchen became a place where I could be with my feelings without naming them. I've stirred tomato sauce while crying so hard I could barely see the spoon. I've made pasta because folding dough helped me feel capable of making something with care. When I lost my mum, I remember washing the dishes she used the last time she cooked for me, not because they needed cleaning, but because I needed to touch something that had touched her. These small acts helped me survive.

It wasn't always dramatic. Some days, healing looked like a bowl of pasta with olive oil, eaten in silence. Other times, it was a slow return to colour: the day I finally cooked for someone else, or tried a new recipe not for distraction, but pleasure. These moments arrived silently, gradually stitching me back together.

Then came the Pasta Therapy workshops. Through them, I met people who had similar experiences. They came for the pasta but stayed for the pause: that moment their hands were in dough and their thoughts weren't racing. In those workshops, no one had to explain why they were there. You could feel it in the room, that mix of fragility and strength, of not knowing what tomorrow will bring but choosing to make something today.

Each recipe here holds a thread of those moments. They aren't extravagant or technical. They're the dishes you reach for when you're too tired to think or when you need something gentle.

VERONICA'S ORECCHIETTE WITH BEANS & SHIITAKE MUSHROOMS

Orecchiette funghi e fagioli

This recipe carries the memory of my dear friend Veronica, whom I met through the Future Dreams community. We became close during a time of shared vulnerability and struggle, and over the years she came to embody strength, grace and determination. Even when she was going through the hardest moments, she had a word of care, a gesture of thoughtfulness, a way of making you feel seen. When she heard I was writing this book, she told me about this orecchiette dish her mum used to make and described it with such warmth that I knew it had to be here. She followed every step of this project with genuine interest, always asking if she could help in any way.

This dish now feels like a small tribute to her. It is calm, steady and nourishing. The kind of bowl that brings a bit of comfort when everything feels too heavy.

Serves: 4

Preparation time: 50 minutes, plus 30 minutes resting

Cooking time: 25 minutes

For the Dough:

* 300g/10½oz/2¼ cups semola
* 150ml/5fl oz/⅔ cup lukewarm water

For the Soup:

* 2 tbsp extra virgin olive oil
* 1 small onion, finely diced
* 1 carrot, finely diced
* 1 celery stalk, finely diced
* 150g/5¼oz/1¾ cups shiitake mushrooms, sliced
* 150g/5¼oz/¾ cup cooked adzuki beans, drained
* 150g/5¼oz/¾ cup cooked black-eyed peas, drained
* 100ml/3½fl oz/scant ½ cup vegetable stock or pasta cooking water
* 1 tbsp plant-based butter or extra virgin olive oil
* Pinch of freshly grated nutmeg
* Salt and pepper, to taste
* Fresh thyme or parsley, chopped, to garnish

Make the Dough: On a clean work surface, make a mound with the semola and create a well in the centre. Gradually add the water, mixing with your fingers or a fork to incorporate the semola until a rough dough forms. Knead for 5–7 minutes until smooth and elastic. Cover with a dish towel and let rest for 30 minutes.

Prepare the Soup: Heat the olive oil in a large pan over a medium heat. Add the onion, carrot and celery. Cook for 5–7 minutes, until softened and fragrant. Add the sliced shiitake mushrooms and cook for another 5 minutes, stirring occasionally, until tender and beginning to brown.

Add half the adzuki beans and half the black-eyed peas to the pan. Purée the remaining beans with some of the vegetable stock to form a smooth cream. Add more stock if needed to adjust the consistency. Pour the purée into the pan and stir to combine, letting the mixture heat and thicken gently for about 10 minutes.

Shape the Orecchiette: Lightly dust a tray and work surface with semola. Cut the rested dough into 4 pieces and roll each piece into a long rope about 1cm/⅓in thick. Cut the ropes into short lengths, roughly the size of a thumbnail. Press each piece of dough with a butter knife, dragging it slightly toward you to form a coin-size disc, then turn it inside-out to create the traditional "ear" shape. Place the orecchiette on the tray and keep covered as you work.

Cook the Orecchiette: Bring a large pot of salted water to the boil. Cook the orecchiette for 4–5 minutes or until they float and the texture is al dente.

Combine and Serve: Using a slotted spoon, lift the cooked orecchiette directly into the soup, along with the plant-based butter and nutmeg. Mix, adding a little pasta water or stock if needed to create a silky consistency. Season with salt and pepper to taste. Serve the orecchiette hot, garnished with fresh thyme or parsley for a burst of colour and a touch of freshness. Enjoy the comfort and warmth of this hearty, healing dish.

RICKY'S SPAGHETTONI WITH PEAR, GOAT'S CHEESE & WALNUTS

Spaghettoni pere e formaggio di capra

A little sweet, a little salty, totally comforting. This recipe was inspired by Ricky, Veronica's wonderful husband. Like me, they're both Italian, though from the north in the Lombardy region, and over the years we've shared conversations about food, family and everything in between. One afternoon, while I was on the phone with Veronica, I heard Ricky shout in the background, "Tell her to make a pasta with pear and cheese for the book!" and the idea stuck with me.

This dish is a small tribute to that moment. The sweetness of the pear melts into the sauce, balancing the tang of the goat's cheese. The spaghettoni, rolled by hand, give the dish its warmth and texture, rustic and satisfying. It's an unexpected pairing, but it works, much like the best conversations with friends. I think of Ricky whenever I make it. His generosity, humour and love for Veronica are folded into every bite.

Serves: 4

Preparation time: 30 minutes, plus 30 minutes resting

Cooking time: 15 minutes

For the Dough:
* 400g/14oz/3 cups semola
* 200ml/7fl oz/scant 1 cup water
* Salt, to taste

For the Sauce:
* 2 tbsp unsalted butter
* 2 ripe blush pears, peeled, cored and diced
* 120g/4¼oz/½ cup fresh goat's cheese
* 50g/1¾oz/½ cup walnuts, lightly toasted and roughly chopped
* Salt and pepper, to taste
* Fresh parsley, chopped, to garnish

Make the Dough: On a clean work surface, make a mound with the semola and a pinch of salt and create a well in the centre. Gradually add the water, mixing with your fingers or a fork to incorporate the semola until a rough dough forms. Knead for 5–7 minutes until smooth and elastic. Cover with a dish towel and let rest for 30 minutes.

Prepare the Sauce: Melt the butter in a wide frying pan over a medium heat. Add the diced pears and cook gently for 4–5 minutes, until softened but not mushy. Crumble in the goat's cheese and stir gently until melted and combined. Set aside.

Shape the Spaghettoni: Lightly dust a tray and work surface with semola. Divide the rested dough into small portions, roughly the size of a golf ball. Roll each into ropes about 4–5mm/¼in thick, then cut into lengths of 25–30cm/12in. Roll each piece lightly under your palms to form thick strands, similar to thick spaghetti or pici. Lightly dust with semola and set aside on the tray, and keep covered as you work.

Cook the Spaghettoni: Bring a large pot of salted water to the boil. Cook the spaghettoni for 4–6 minutes, or until al dente.

Combine and Serve: Using tongs, lift the pasta directly into the pan with the goat's cheese sauce, tossing gently and adding a splash of cooking water if needed to help the sauce cling evenly. Fold in the toasted walnuts, then season with salt and add plenty of freshly ground black pepper. Divide between the plates and scatter with chopped fresh parsley. Serve immediately, with an extra twist of pepper, if you like.

QUINOA FLOUR FIORELLI WITH SWEET POTATO & MISO

Fiorelli di farina di quinoa con patate dolci e miso

A dish of warmth, depth and gentle surprise. Healing through food sometimes means embracing the unexpected, be it in flavour, texture or technique. Sometimes, something unfamiliar can become deeply comforting. This recipe does just that. Sweet potatoes are blended into a smooth, savoury filling, wrapped in dough made with quinoa flour for a subtle nutty lift. A white miso butter sauce brings umami depth, and a light dusting of coffee powder at the end sharpens everything with contrast. Fiorelli are small, flower-shaped pasta bundles, their ruffled edges resembling petals gathered around a soft centre of filling. You can, of course, use any other shape for this stuffed pasta.

For me, this dish is a reminder of how unexpected combinations, like the interplay of sweet, salty and bitter, can create something truly comforting and transformative. Each fiorello is a small bundle of warmth and care, a perfect way to nourish both the body and soul.

Serves: 4

Preparation time: 40 minutes, plus 30 minutes resting

Cooking time: 1 hour

For the Dough:
* 150g/5¼oz/1¼ cups quinoa flour
* 250g/9oz/scant 2 cups 00 flour
* 4 eggs

For the Filling:
* 3 medium-large sweet potatoes (approx. 500–600g/17⅓–21oz)
* 1 tbsp fine breadcrumbs
* 30g/1oz/¼ cup Parmigiano Reggiano, finely grated
* ¼ tsp ground nutmeg
* Salt and pepper, to taste

For the Sauce:
* 3 tbsp unsalted butter
* 1 tbsp white miso paste

For Garnish:
* A sprinkle of espresso coffee powder (optional but recommended)

Make the Dough: On a clean work surface, combine the quinoa and 00 flours and form a well in the centre. Crack in the eggs and whisk gently with a fork, gradually incorporating the flour until a rough dough forms. Knead for 5–7 minutes until smooth and elastic. Cover with a dish towel and let rest for 30 minutes.

Prepare the Filling: Preheat the oven to 200°C/400°F/Gas Mark 6. Pierce the sweet potatoes with a fork and bake them whole for about 45–50 minutes, or until soft. Once cool enough to handle, remove the skins and mash the flesh until smooth. Mix in the breadcrumbs, Parmigiano, nutmeg and some salt and pepper. Adjust the seasoning to taste, ensuring the filling is well balanced between sweet and savoury. Keep the filling in the refrigerator while you roll the dough.

Shape the Fiorelli: Lightly dust a tray and work surface with flour. Divide the rested dough into 4–6 portions. Roll each piece into a thin sheet, about 1mm thick (setting 5 on a Marcato). Place small spoonfuls of the filling on the sheet, leaving about 4–5cm/2in between each mound to allow space for sealing and cutting. Fold the dough over and press gently around the filling to seal. Use a fiorelli or ravioli stamp to cut out flower shapes. Transfer to the floured tray and cover with a dish towel as you roll and fill the remaining dough.

Make the Sauce: Melt the butter in a small saucepan over a medium-low heat. Add the white miso and whisk for 1–2 minutes until smooth and slightly bubbly. Keep warm.

Cook the Fiorelli: Bring a large pot of salted water to the boil. Cook the fiorelli for 3–4 minutes, or until they float and the texture is al dente.

Combine and Serve: Using a slotted spoon, gently transfer the fiorelli to the miso butter, tossing lightly to coat. Plate the fiorelli and garnish with a light dusting of coffee powder just before serving, if you like.

Note: For an extra layer of nutty flavour, toast the quinoa flour in a dry pan over a low heat for 2–3 minutes before mixing it into the dough.

CHESTNUT FLOUR FETTUCCINE WITH LENTIL RAGÙ

Fettuccine di farina di castagne con ragù di lenticchie

Serves: 4

Preparation time: 30 minutes, plus 30 minutes resting

Cooking time: 50 minutes

For the Dough:

* 200g/7oz/1½ cups chestnut flour
* 200g/7oz/1½ cups 00 flour
* 4 eggs

For the Lentil Ragù:

* 3 tbsp extra virgin olive oil
* 1 small onion, finely chopped
* 1 small carrot, finely chopped
* 1 celery stalk, finely chopped
* 1 garlic clove, minced
* 1 bay leaf
* 2 tbsp tomato purée/paste
* 120ml/4fl oz/½ cup dried red wine
* 400g/14oz/2 cups canned diced tomatoes
* 150g/5¼oz/¾ cup brown or green lentils, rinsed
* 500ml/17fl oz/2 cups vegetable stock, plus more as needed
* Salt and pepper, to taste
* Fresh basil, chopped, to garnish
* Parmigiano Reggiano, finely grated, to serve (optional)

A deeply satisfying bowl, shaped by tradition and resourcefulness. Chestnuts were once a staple in mountainous regions, where they helped families survive harsh winters. This dish draws from that history. The pasta, made with chestnut flour, has a subtle sweetness and rustic character, while the lentil ragù is hearty and deeply savoury: a meatless version of a sauce that has fed generations.

For me, this recipe is a reminder that even the most modest ingredients can come together to create something special. The textures are full, the flavours familiar yet layered. It's the kind of meal that fills you up in more ways than one, without being heavy or overdone.

Make the Dough: On a clean work surface, make a mound with the chestnut and 00 flours and create a well in the centre. Crack in the eggs and whisk gently with a fork, gradually incorporating the flour until a rough dough forms. Knead for 5–7 minutes until smooth and elastic. Cover with a dish towel and let rest for 30 minutes.

Prepare the Lentil Ragù: Heat the olive oil in a large saucepan over a medium heat. Add the onion, carrot, celery and garlic. Cook gently for 5–7 minutes until softened. Stir in the bay leaf and tomato purée/paste and cook for another minute. Deglaze with the red wine and let it reduce slightly, increasing the heat to high for 30 seconds, then bringing it back down to medium. Add the canned tomatoes, lentils and stock. Season with salt and pepper. Bring to a gentle boil, then reduce the heat and simmer, uncovered, for 30–40 minutes, or until the lentils are tender and the sauce is thickened. Add more stock to loosen the sauce if it becomes too thick or starts to stick.

Shape the Fettuccine: Lightly dust a tray and work surface with flour. Divide the rested dough into 4–6 portions. Roll each piece into a thin sheet, about 1mm thick (setting 5 on a Marcato). Cut into fettuccine strips about 1cm/⅓in wide. Lightly dust with flour and set on the tray, and keep covered as you work.

Cook the Fettuccine: Bring a large pot of salted water to the boil. Cook the fettuccine for 2–3 minutes, or until al dente.

Combine and Serve: Before you combine the pasta and sauce, remove the bay leaf from the sauce. Then, using tongs, lift the fettuccine directly into the pan with the ragù and toss gently to coat. Add a splash of cooking water if needed to help the sauce cling evenly. Serve hot, garnished with fresh basil and grated Parmigiano, if desired.

Note: For a deeper, toastier flavour, dry toast the chestnut flour in a pan over a low heat for 2–3 minutes before using it to make into the dough.

GLUTEN-FREE TRIANGLES, GREEN TOMATO PESTO & COURGETTE/ZUCCHINI

Triangoli gluten-free, pesto ai pomodori verdi e zucchine

Soft, fragrant dough meets sharp green tomato: the smell of summer in the kitchen. My second cousins Serena and Gianni run Sine Glutine, a beautiful fully gluten-free bakery in Ragusa, one of the few in Sicily. During one of my visits, they gave me a bag of their flour blend to try; soft, pale and fragrant with the smell of corn and rice. I wanted to make something that would let the flour speak for itself, so I used it for a basic dough and cut the sheets into triangles. No fancy tools needed. Just a knife or a cutter will do.

The pesto is what brings everything to life. Made with raw green tomatoes, basil, almonds, pine nuts, garlic and Parmigiano, it has that unmistakable smell of summer: green, sharp and full of light. The courgettes/zucchini are cooked separately and added at the end, still holding their shape, just kissed by olive oil. The whole dish comes together in a way that feels honest. No flourishes, just good ingredients and a sense of when to stop.

Serves: 4

Preparation time: 45 minutes, plus 30 minutes resting

Cooking time: 10 minutes

For the Dough:
* 400g/14oz/3 cups gluten-free flour blend
* 5 eggs (this ratio may vary according to the flour blend; please check package directions)

For the Pesto:
* 150g/5¼oz/1 cup green tomatoes, roughly chopped
* 30g/1oz/¼ cup Parmigiano Reggiano, finely grated
* 2 tbsp almonds, blanched
* 2 tbsp pine nuts
* 1 small garlic clove
* A handful of fresh basil leaves
* 4 tbsp extra virgin olive oil
* Salt, to taste

For the Courgettes/Zucchini:
* 2 tbsp extra virgin olive oil
* 1 small green courgette/zucchini, finely diced
* 1 small yellow courgette/zucchini, finely diced
* Salt, to taste

Make the Dough: On a clean work surface, make a mound with the gluten-free flour and create a well in the centre. Crack in the eggs and whisk gently with a fork, gradually incorporating the flour until a rough dough forms. Knead for 5–7 minutes until smooth and cohesive. Cover with a dish towel and let rest for 30 minutes.

Prepare the Pesto: In a food processor, combine the green tomatoes, Parmigiano, almonds, pine nuts, garlic and basil. Pulse until combined. With the motor running, stream in the olive oil and blend until smooth but still textured. Season with salt to taste. Set aside.

Shape the Triangles: Lightly dust a tray and work surface with gluten-free flour. Divide the rested dough into 4–6 portions. Roll each piece into a thin sheet, about 1mm thick (setting 5 on a Marcato). Cut into 5cm/2in triangles using a knife, cutter or triangle stamp. Lightly dust with gluten-free flour and set on the floured tray, and keep covered as you work.

Cook the Courgettes/Zucchini: In a wide pan, heat the olive oil over a medium heat. Add the sliced courgettes and sauté for 5–6 minutes until just tender and lightly golden. Season with salt and set aside.

Cook the Triangles: Bring a large pot of salted water to the boil. Add the pasta triangles and cook for 2–3 minutes, or until they float and the texture is al dente.

Combine and Serve: Using tongs or a slotted spoon, lift the pasta directly into a large bowl with the pesto. Toss gently to coat, adding a splash of cooking water if needed to help the sauce cling evenly. Gently fold in the sautéed courgettes and serve immediately.

PAGLIA E FIENO WITH CAJUN & CHARRED SWEETCORN

Paglia e fieno con mais alla fiamma e cajun

Bright, buttery and just the right amount of messy. I took two work-related trips to New Orleans just weeks before the world shut down with Covid-19. The food was unforgettable: bold, fearless, built on layers of flavour mixing French, Spanish and African influences, but never fussy. Before flying home, I picked up a book called *Creole Italian* by Justin A Nystrom, which explores the overlooked influence of Sicilian immigrants on the city's food culture. It reminded me that Sicilian identity has always travelled well, and it stays in the food long after the journey ends.

***Paglia e fieno* means "straw and hay": a traditional Italian pasta made with two colours of tagliatelle: one plain (typically made with 00 flour and eggs), the other green (usually spinach-based). The visual contrast gives it its name: golden and green, intertwined like a just-cut field.**

This pasta has nothing to do with that book, but I used the Cajun spice I brought back. It feels like a summer evening, just after the heat breaks, when you're cooking with whatever's left from the barbecue, eating outside, music playing, maybe with a small group of friends or family. It evokes garden energy, cooking barefoot, a bit of butter on your cheek and no one minds. The charred corn and Cajun butter give it a kind of "American barbecue meets Italian comfort" vibe.

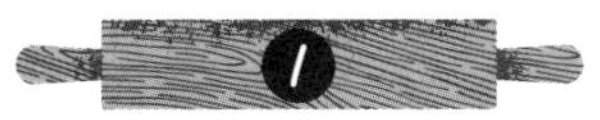

Serves: 4

Preparation time: 45 minutes, plus 30 minutes resting

Cooking time: 20 minutes

For the Plain Dough:

* 200g/7oz/1½ cups 00 flour
* 2 eggs

For the Spinach Dough:

* 200g/7oz/1½ cups 00 flour
* 100g/3½oz/⅔ cup cooked spinach, squeezed dry and finely chopped
* 2 eggs

For the Corn:

* 2 large corn cobs, husked
* 2 tbsp unsalted butter
* 1 tsp Cajun spice mix
* Salt, to taste

To Finish:

* 1 tbsp unsalted butter
* A small bunch of fresh parsley, roughly chopped
* Cajun spice mix, to taste

Make the Dough: For each dough, place the flour on a clean work surface and create a well in the centre. For the spinach dough, mix the spinach with the eggs. For both, add the eggs to the wells. Gently whisk with a fork, gradually incorporating the flour until a rough dough forms. Knead for 5–7 minutes until smooth and elastic. Cover both doughs with a dish towel and let rest for 30 minutes.

Prepare the Charred Corn: Boil the corn cobs in a pan of salted water for 5–6 minutes. Remove and pat dry. Char directly over an open flame or in a hot dry pan over a medium-high heat for about 10 minutes, turning frequently, until blackened in spots. While hot, spread with the butter and sprinkle with the Cajun spice mix and some salt. Leave to cool slightly, then slice the kernels off in large chunks using a sharp knife.

Roll and Cut the Tagliatelle: Lightly dust a work surface with flour. Divide the rested dough into 4–6 portions (2–3 portions for each colour). Roll each piece into a thin sheet, about 1mm thick (setting 5 on a Marcato). Cut into tagliatelle with a machine attachment or fold the sheet gently into thirds and slice into ribbons of 6–8mm/⅓in using a sharp knife. Lightly dust with flour and toss the two colours together to combine.

Cook the Tagliatelle: Bring a large pot of salted water to the boil. Cook the tagliatelle for 2–3 minutes, or until al dente.

Finish and Serve: At the same time, melt the butter in a wide pan over a medium-low heat. Add the charred corn and toss briefly to warm through. Using tongs, lift the pasta directly into the pan with the corn. Toss gently to coat, adding a splash of cooking water if needed to help the sauce cling evenly. Stir in the chopped parsley and taste for seasoning. Add a little more Cajun spice or butter, if you like. Serve immediately, piled high, without over-arranging. It's meant to feel loose, full of life.

CAROB FLOUR TAGLIATELLE, MUSHROOMS, CAMEMBERT & LEMON

Tagliatelle di farina di carrube con funghi, camembert e limone

Serves: 4

Preparation time: 30 minutes, plus 30 minutes resting

Cooking time: 20 minutes

For the Dough:

* 300g/10½oz/2¼ cups 00 flour
* 100g/3½oz/¾ cup carob flour
* 4 eggs

For the Sauce:

* 2 tbsp extra virgin olive oil
* 1 small shallot, finely chopped
* 250g/9oz/3 cups mixed mushrooms (such as chestnut/cremini, oyster, shiitake), sliced
* 100g/3½oz Camembert, rind removed and chopped
* Salt and pepper, to taste

For Garnish:

* Zest of 1 unwaxed lemon, to garnish
* 2 tbsp ffesh lat-leaf parsley, roughly chopped, to garnish

Carob is one of those flavours that lives deep in my memory. In Sicily, its trees grow sturdy and generous, their pods used to sweeten desserts, feed livestock and even weigh gold. But for me, carob recalls two specific things. One is the unmistakable smell (pungent, sweet, earthy) wafting through the car window whenever we passed by the factory in the small town of Rosolini that made carob syrups, molasses and flour, on our way to visit my father's hometown, Noto. The other is of one summer spent building a treehouse with my cousins in the arms of a giant carob tree.

Carob flour is an not uncommon ingredient for pasta in Sicily. It gives the tagliatelle a subtle, sweet depth that works beautifully with mushrooms and soft, creamy Camembert. A little lemon and parsley lift the dish and bring it into balance. It's both rustic and refined, and for me, it carries the scent of a childhood drive and the branches of a long-forgotten tree. Carob itself is said to help regulate blood sugar and support digestion: small reminders that food can comfort the body as much as the heart.

Make the Dough: On a clean work surface, make a mound with the 00 and carob flours and create a well in the centre. Crack in the eggs and whisk gently with a fork, gradually incorporating the flour until a rough dough forms. Knead for 5–7 minutes until smooth and elastic. Cover with a dish towel and let rest for 30 minutes.

Make the Sauce: Heat the olive oil in a wide pan over a medium heat. Add the shallot and cook gently for 3–4 minutes until soft. Increase the heat to high and add the mushrooms. Sauté until golden and all the moisture has evaporated, about 6–8 minutes. Season with salt and pepper. Lower the heat and add the Camembert, stirring gently until melted.

Roll and Cut the Tagliatelle: Lightly dust a tray and work surface with flour. Divide the rested dough into 4–6 portions. Roll each piece into a thin sheet, about 1mm thick (setting 5 on a Marcato). Cut into tagliatelle with a machine attachment or fold the sheet gently into thirds and slice into ribbons of 6–8mm/⅓in using a sharp knife. Lightly dust with flour and transfer to the floured tray. Cover with a dish towel to prevent drying as you prepare the remaining dough.

Cook the Tagliatelle: Bring a large pot of salted water to the boil. Cook the tagliatelle for 2–3 minutes, or until al dente.

Combine and Serve: Using tongs, lift the pasta directly into the pan with the sauce. Toss to coat, adding a splash of cooking water if needed to help the sauce become glossy and cling evenly. Garnish with the lemon zest and parsley. Serve immediately.

CAVATELLI RIGATI WITH POTATO, TOMATO & PECORINO

Comfort food from the southern countryside. In Sicily and across the south, pasta and potatoes often share the same pot, stretching simple ingredients into a full meal. This is pure comfort cooking. The potatoes release starch into the sauce and turn buttery, and the Pecorino adds just the right edge. During a time when even the idea of food felt distant, when grief dulled my appetite and everything felt too much, this was the one thing I could eat. Simple, familiar, nourishing. A spoonful of Pecorino adds sharpness just when it's needed. Not heavy, not showy. Just enough.

Serves: 4

Preparation time: 45 minutes, plus 30 minutes resting

Cooking time: 35 minutes

For the Dough:

* 400g/14oz/3 cups semola
* 200ml/7fl oz/scant 1 cup lukewarm water

For the Sauce:

* 3 tbsp extra virgin olive oil, plus extra to serve
* 1 onion, finely chopped
* 1 small carrot, finely chopped
* 1 small celery stalk, finely chopped
* 2 potatoes (about 300g/10½oz), peeled and cut into small cubes
* 300ml/10½fl oz/1¼ cups tomato passata
* 200ml/7fl oz/scant 1 cup water or vegetable stock, plus extra as needed
* Salt and pepper, to taste
* Finely grated Pecorino, to serve
* Handful of fresh flat-leaf parsley, roughly chopped, to serve

Make the Dough: On a clean work surface, make a mound with the semola. Gradually add the water, mixing with your fingers or a fork to incorporate the semola until a rough dough forms. Knead for 5–7 minutes until smooth and elastic. Cover with a dish towel and let rest for 30 minutes.

Make the Sauce: Heat the olive oil in a pan over a medium heat. Add the finely chopped onion, carrot and celery. Sauté for 6–8 minutes until soft and fragrant. Add the diced potatoes and cook for another 2–3 minutes until slightly browned. Pour in the passata and water. Season with salt and pepper. Let it simmer gently, uncovered, for 15–20 minutes, until the potatoes are tender and the sauce has thickened slightly.

Shape the Cavatelli: Lightly dust a tray and work surface with semola. Divide the rested dough into 4 portions. Roll each into a rope about 1cm/⅓in thick. Cut into small nuggets, each the size of a hazelnut. Using a cavatelli board, gnocchi paddle or the tines of a fork, drag each piece toward you to create ridges. Place the shaped pasta on the tray and keep covered as you go.

Cook the Cavatelli: Tip the cavatelli directly into the simmering sauce. Stir gently and let cook for 4–5 minutes, adding more water if needed. The pasta will cook through as the sauce thickens, and the starch from the dough will help everything come together.

Serve: Ladle into bowls and finish with plenty of grated Pecorino and parsley and a drizzle of olive oil. Eat immediately while hot.

SPAGHETTI WITH VEGAN "MEATBALLS"

Spaghetti con polpette vegane

Serves: 4

Preparation time: 20 minutes, plus cooling

Cooking time: 1 hour (pressure cooker) or 1 hour 20 minutes (hob/stovetop)

For the Lentil Meatballs:

* 200g/7oz/1 cup dried brown lentils, rinsed
* 500ml/17fl oz/2 cups vegetable stock or water
* 1½ tsp salt (divided)
* 1 small banana shallot, chopped
* 2 garlic cloves, minced
* A handful of sun-dried cherry tomatoes, soaked and drained
* ½ tsp black pepper
* 2 tbsp finely chopped fresh parsley
* 2 tbsp pine nuts or chopped walnuts
* 1 tsp tomato purée/paste
* 2 tbsp pomegranate molasses
* 1 tbsp sesame seeds
* 2 tbsp extra virgin olive oil

For the Sauce:

* 2 tbsp extra virgin olive oil, plus extra to serve
* 1 small onion, finely chopped
* 2 garlic cloves, minced
* 400g/14oz/2 cups canned cherry tomatoes
* 1 tbsp tomato purée/paste
* ½ tsp salt
* 1 tsp sugar (optional)
* 2 tsp ground coriander
* 1 tsp ground cumin
* ½ tsp black pepper
* Fresh parsley, to garnish

To Serve:

* 400g/14oz spaghetti
* Salt, to taste

Lentils, spice and a little kitchen magic. This is a dish where the sauce is the protagonist, not the pasta. We all have dishes that mark our childhood. For many in Sicily, that dish is *polpette al sugo*: soft meatballs simmered in tomato sauce, eaten with pasta or mopped up with bread. This has been my vegan version for years, and though it may not have the meat, it has everything else: richness, texture and the kind of flavour that makes you want seconds.

The polpette are made with lentils, nuts, spices and two unexpected ingredients that take them to another level: pomegranate molasses and a little tomato purée/paste are mixed straight into the dough adding a little sweetness and acidity. I serve them with spaghetti and a slow-cooked cherry tomato sauce, full of warmth and body. They're just as comforting as the original, maybe even more so.

Cook the Lentils: Pressure-cook the lentils in the vegetable stock with ½ teaspoon of the salt for 20 minutes on high pressure. Let the pressure release naturally. If you don't have a pressure cooker, you can cook them in a pot over a medium heat for 40 minutes. Leave to cool. If there is excess water, drain well. The lentils should be soft enough to mash but still hold their shape.

Make the Meatballs: Add the cooked lentils to a food processor with all the other meatball ingredients, including the remaining 1 teaspoon salt, except the sesame seeds and olive oil. Pulse until coarse but combined. Stir in the sesame seeds. With damp hands, form the mixture into 16 small balls. If too wet, add 1 tablespoon plain/all-purpose flour.

Fry the Meatballs: Warm the olive oil in a wide pan over a medium heat. Shallow-fry the meatballs in batches for 5–6 minutes until golden on all sides. Remove and set aside.

Make the Sauce: In the same pan, add the olive oil and sauté the onion for 5–6 minutes, until golden. Add the garlic and sauté for another 30–60 seconds. Then add the canned tomatoes, tomato purée/paste, salt, sugar, if using, and spices. Cook over a low heat, covered, for 20 minutes. Add a splash of water if the sauce gets too thick.

Add the Meatballs: Add the fried polpette to the sauce. Simmer gently, uncovered, for 3–5 minutes so the flavours come together.

Cook the Spaghetti: Bring a large pot of salted water to the boil. Cook the spaghetti according to the package directions. Drain and add to the sauce or serve with the polpette and sauce spooned over the top.

Serve: Finish with a sprinkling of parsley and an extra drizzle of olive oil. Serve hot.

FREGOLA WITH PEAS, MOZZARELLA, BRIE & LEMON

Fregola con piselli, mozzarella, brie e limone

Serves: 4

Preparation time: 10 minutes

Cooking time: 30 minutes

Ingredients:

* 3 tbsp extra virgin olive oil (divided), plus extra to serve
* 1 onion, finely chopped
* 250g/9oz/1¼ cups fregola, preferably toasted
* 750ml/26fl oz/3¼ cups hot vegetable stock, or as needed
* 1 tbsp unsalted butter
* Zest of 1 unwaxed lemon
* Freshly ground black pepper, to taste
* 150g/5¼oz/1 cup frozen peas
* 1 ball of mozzarella, torn
* 80g/2¾oz brie, rind removed and chopped
* Salt, to taste
* Fresh dill or other herbs, to garnish

Small pasta, big comfort. Fregola comes from Sardinia, where it's traditionally toasted and cooked like rice. It's similar in size and shape to *maftoul*, the hand-rolled couscous found in Palestinian and Jordanian cooking and has close relatives across North Africa and the Levant, always somewhere between pasta and grain, familiar and filling. This version uses peas for sweetness, mozzarella for stretch and brie for a creamy richness that melts gently into the sauce. Lemon zest lifts the softness, keeping it fresh and balanced. It's the kind of dish you want to eat from a bowl, warm and unhurried.

Cook the Fregola: In a wide sauté pan, heat a tablespoon of the olive oil over a medium heat. Add the onion and cook gently for 4–5 minutes until translucent. Stir in the fregola and toast for 1–2 minutes, coating the grains in the oil. Begin adding the hot stock a ladleful at a time, stirring often and allowing each addition to absorb before adding the next. Continue this way for about 15–18 minutes, until the fregola is tender but still has a slight bite.

Make the Sauce: In a wide pan, melt the butter with the remaining olive oil over a low heat. Add most of the lemon zest (reserving some for garnish) and a grind of black pepper. Stir in the fregola and the peas. Add the mozzarella and brie, letting them melt gently into the pasta. Stir to coat, adding an extra splash of stock to loosen if needed. Taste and adjust the seasoning with salt, and more pepper, if needed.

Serve: Spoon into bowls and finish with the reserved lemon zest and a drizzle of olive oil. Garnish with fresh dill and serve hot.

ORZO WITH SPICED MINESTRONE

Minestrone speziato con orzo (aka risoni)

Serves: 4

Preparation time: 10 minutes

Cooking time: 35 minutes (pressure cooker) or 1 hour (hob/stovetop)

Ingredients:

* 3 tbsp extra virgin olive oil, plus extra to serve
* 1 small onion, finely chopped
* 1 carrot, finely chopped
* 1 celery stalk, finely chopped
* 1 bay leaf
* 150g/5¼oz/¾ cup brown lentils, dried or canned, rinsed and drained
* 1 tsp ground turmeric
* ½ tsp ground cumin
* ½ tsp sweet paprika
* Freshly ground black pepper, to taste
* 400g/14oz/2 cups tomato passata or polpa di pomodoro
* 750ml/26fl oz/3¼ cups vegetable stock or water
* 250g/9oz/2¼ cups orzo (*risoni*)
* A few fresh thyme sprigs, leaves picked
* 2 tbsp chopped fresh parsley
* Salt, to taste

There are days when even stepping into the kitchen feels like a daunting task, and all you crave is something warm, simple and deeply comforting. For those moments, this spiced orzo (also known as *risoni*) minestrone is the perfect go-to. With the hearty depth of lentils, the aromatic warmth of spices like cumin and turmeric, and the freshness of herbs, this dish offers a satisfying meal that nourishes without the fuss of homemade pasta.

This recipe can be prepared in a pressure cooker for speed or on the hob/stovetop if you prefer a slower, more leisurely approach. Either way, it's a simple one-pot dish that's full of flavour and nourishment; the kind of meal that wraps you in warmth when everything else feels overwhelming. The blend of spices and herbs adds an uplifting twist to the classic minestrone, turning it into something special, while still delivering the comfort we often seek on rainy or tough days.

Cook the Soffritto: In a large pot or pressure cooker, heat the olive oil over a medium heat. Add the chopped onion, carrot and celery, along with the bay leaf. Sauté gently until softened and fragrant, about 8–10 minutes.

Add the Lentils and Spices: Stir in the lentils (if using dried, but if using canned, add in the next step after the tomatoes), turmeric, cumin, paprika and a generous crack of black pepper. Cook for another 2–3 minutes to allow the spices to release their aroma.

Add the Passata and Stock: Pour in the passata and vegetable stock, stirring well to combine. If you're using a pressure cooker, close the lid and cook on high pressure for 10 minutes. Let the pressure release naturally. If cooking on the hob/stovetop, bring to the boil, then reduce to a simmer and cook for 25–30 minutes, or until the lentils are tender.

Cook the Orzo: Once the lentils are cooked through, add the orzo directly into the pot. Continue to cook, stirring occasionally, for another 10–12 minutes, or until the orzo is tender but still holds its shape. Add more water or stock if needed to achieve a loose, soupy consistency.

Add the Fresh Herbs and Serve: Remove the bay leaf, then stir in the fresh thyme leaves and chopped parsley and season with salt to taste. Drizzle with extra olive oil for added richness and comfort.

MUM'S BROWN LENTIL MINESTRONE WITH QUADRATINI

Minestrone di lenticchie della mamma con quadratini integrali

Serves: 4

Preparation time: 25 minutes, plus 30 minutes resting

Cooking time: 50 minutes

For the Dough:

* 200g/7oz/1½ cups wholemeal/whole-wheat flour
* 100ml/3½fl oz/scant ½ cup lukewarm water

For the Soup:

* 3 tbsp extra virgin olive oil, plus extra to serve (optional)
* 1 small onion, finely chopped
* 1 carrot, finely chopped
* 1 celery stalk, finely chopped
* 1 bay leaf
* 1 tbsp tomato purée/paste
* 200g/7oz/1 cup dried brown lentils, rinsed
* 1.2l/40½fl oz/5 cups vegetable stock or water, plus more as needed
* Salt and pepper, to taste

A bowl that fed us in more ways than one. My mum made this soup exactly the same way every time. Always with pasta. Always on a cold day when one of us wasn't feeling well. She didn't like lentils much – something about being forced to eat them as a child – so she made this only when she felt she had to. But to me, it never felt reluctant. I've loved lentils since I was little, and this was one of those dishes that brought comfort without asking for attention.

I now make it with homemade wholemeal/whole-wheat *quadratini*: tiny pasta squares, just 5mm/¼in across, and I like how they hold their shape in the broth. It's the same soup she made, carried forward with this one small change.

Make the Dough: On a clean work surface, make a mound with the flour and create a well in the centre. Gradually add the water, mixing with your fingers or a fork to incorporate the flour until a rough dough forms. Knead for 5–7 minutes until smooth and elastic. Cover with a dish towel and let rest for 30 minutes.

Make the Soup: Heat the olive oil in a heavy pot. Add the onion, carrot, celery and bay leaf. Cook gently for 8–10 minutes until soft and fragrant. Stir in the tomato purée/paste and cook for another minute. Add the lentils and pour in the stock. Season with salt and pepper. Bring to the boil, then reduce the heat and simmer, covered, for 30–35 minutes, or until the lentils are tender but still hold their shape.

Shape the Quadratini: Lightly dust a tray and work surface with flour. Divide the rested dough into 4–6 portions. Roll each piece into a thin sheet, about 1mm thick (setting 5 on a Marcato). Cut into strips, then into small squares about 5mm/¼in wide. A dough cutting wheel or pizza cutter makes this step really quick. Lightly dust with flour and set on the tray.

Cook the Quadratini: Once the lentils are ready, bring the soup back to a gentle boil. Add the quadratini and cook for 3–4 minutes, or until al dente. Add a splash more stock if needed to adjust the consistency.

Serve: Taste and adjust the seasoning. Serve hot, with an extra drizzle of olive oil, if you like.

FRASCATULA (SICILIAN POLENTA/ CORNMEAL WITH WILD GREENS)

Frascatula (polenta siciliana con erbe spontanee)

A soft, sustaining dish from the old kitchen garden. This dish was suggested to me by my mum's cousin Gino and his lovely wife Pina, who remembered it from our family table when they were young. *Frascatula* has ancient and humble roots. Its name likely comes from the French *flasque*, meaning soft or loose, and it's thought to have been introduced during the 13th-century French occupation of Sicily, when soldiers made it as sustenance.

Across the island, it goes by different names: *paniccia* and *picciotta* being some of them. It can be made with semola, chickpea, fava or any cereal flours depending on the province and what's available. It's always cooked slowly in water with seasonal wild greens: borage, wild fennel, mustard leaves, bitter chicory/endive, beetroot/beets, asparagus. A dish made to use what was growing nearby.

For this version, I used chickpea flour, wild fennel and *lassini* (mustard greens). It's soft, gently bitter and deeply nourishing.

Serves: 4

Preparation time: 10 minutes

Cooking time: 15 minutes

Ingredients:

* 200g/7oz *lassini* or sprouting broccoli
* 25g/1oz/1 cup wild fennel or fresh dill
* 3l/101fl oz/12½ cups water
* 400g/14oz/3 cups chickpea flour
* 2 tbsp extra virgin olive oil
* Dried chilli/hot pepper flakes, to taste (optional)
* Salt, to taste

Prepare the Greens: Remove the toughest stems from both greens, wash thoroughly and chop coarsely.

Cook the Frascatula: Bring the water to the boil in a large pot. Add some salt, then parboil the greens for 3–4 minutes. Lower the heat slightly and begin adding the chickpea flour through a sieve/fine-mesh strainer, a little at a time, whisking constantly to avoid lumps. Continue whisking as it thickens. Cook over a medium-low heat for 8–10 minutes, or until soft and it can coat the back of a spoon.

Serve: Ladle into bowls and finish with the olive oil and a pinch of dried chilli/hot pepper flakes, if desired. Serve hot.

BULGUR SALAD WITH FETA & ROASTED VEGGIES

Insalata di bulgur con feta e verdure arrostite

Serves: 4

Preparation time: 15 minutes

Cooking time: 35 minutes (pressure cooker) or 40 minutes (hob/stovetop)

For the Bulgur:

* 200g/7oz/1 cup bulgur wheat
* 400ml/14fl oz/1⅔ cups water or vegetable stock
* Salt, to taste

For the Roasted Vegetables:

* 2 carrots, sliced
* 2 parsnips, chopped
* 200g/7oz baby potatoes, halved
* 2 tbsp extra virgin olive oil
* 1 tsp honey or maple syrup
* ½ tsp smoked paprika
* Freshly ground black pepper, to taste

For the Salad:

* 2 spring onions/scallions, finely chopped
* 2 tbsp finely chopped fresh dill
* 2 tbsp finely chopped fresh parsley
* 2 tbsp walnuts, toasted and chopped
* 2 tbsp sultanas/golden raisins or dried cranberries (or a mix of both), roughly chopped
* 2–3 peeled cooked chestnuts, crumbled or chopped

For the Dressing:

* 3 tbsp extra virgin olive oil
* Juice of ½ lemon
* Salt and pepper, to taste

To Finish:

* 100g/3½oz/½ cup feta, crumbled

This salad is a steady workhorse. I make it all the time. Cook the bulgur, leave it to cool and everything else happens in the meantime. The roasted vegetables bring sweetness and warmth, the chopped herbs and nuts keep things bright and textural, and the lemony emulsion ties it all together. It's the kind of dish that comes together slowly, almost without noticing. It's nourishing and I could eat it every day.

I cook the bulgur in a pressure cooker which makes it fast, efficient and hands-free. While that's going, I chop the herbs, toast the nuts and roast whatever vegetables I have on hand. Here I used carrots, baby potatoes and parsnips; but squash, beetroot/beets or sweet potatoes would work just as well.

Cook the Bulgur: Rinse the bulgur, then pressure-cook with the water and a generous pinch of salt for 8 minutes on high pressure. Let the pressure release naturally. Fluff with a fork and set aside to cool. Alternatively, simmer in a covered pot on the hob/stovetop for 12–15 minutes.

Roast the Vegetables: Preheat the oven to 200°C/400°F/Gas Mark 6. Toss the vegetables in the olive oil, honey, smoked paprika and some black pepper. Spread out on a baking sheet and roast for 20–25 minutes, or until golden and soft. Stir once halfway through. Leave to cool slightly.

Prepare the Salad Base: In a large bowl, mix the cooled bulgur with the spring onions/scallions, herbs, walnuts, sultanas/golden raisins and chestnuts.

Make the Dressing: In a small bowl or jar, whisk the olive oil with the lemon juice and some salt and pepper until emulsified. Pour over the salad and toss well to coat.

Assemble and Serve: Spoon the salad onto a serving plate or bowl. Top with the roasted vegetables, then crumble the feta over the top. Serve at room temperature.

CICERI E TRIA (CHICKPEAS/GARBANZO BEANS WITH TWICE-COOKED TRIA PASTA)

Ciceri e tria (ceci con pasta fritta e bollita)

A dish from Salento with texture at its core. *Ciceri e tria* is more than just pasta and chickpeas/garbanzo beans. It's a celebration of texture and simplicity, an iconic dish of cucina povera that is still little known beyond the region.

The pasta, tria, is made with just semola and water, rolled and cut into ribbons that are wider, shorter and thicker than tagliatelle. A third of it is fried until golden and the rest is boiled and stirred into soft, seasoned chickpeas/garbanzo beans. At the table, the two are mixed together: creamy, chewy and crisp all at once.

Traditionally eaten on San Giuseppe in March (Italian Father's Day), it's the kind of dish that fits any moment of the year when comfort is called for. Rustic, generous, deeply satisfying.

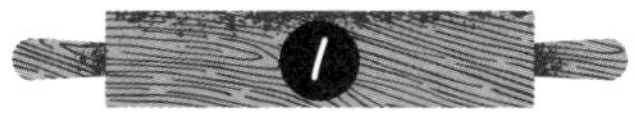

Serves: 4

Preparation time: 20 minutes, plus overnight soaking

Cooking time: 1 hour (pressure cooker) or 2 hours (hob/stovetop)

For the Chickpeas/Garbanzo Beans:

* 250g/9oz/1¼ cups dried chickpeas/garbanzo beans
* 1 onion, halved
* 1–2 carrots, chopped
* 1–2 celery stalks, chopped
* 1 bay leaf
* 1 fresh thyme sprig
* Salt, to taste

For the Dough:

* 300g/10½oz/2¼ cups semola
* 150ml/5fl oz/⅔ cup lukewarm water

To Finish:

* 3 tbsp extra virgin olive oil, plus extra for frying
* 1–2 dried red chillies, to taste, or a pinch of dried chilli/hot pepper flakes
* Salt and pepper, to taste

Cook the Chickpeas: Soak the chickpeas/garbanzo beans in cold water overnight, or for at least 8 hours, then drain. Place in a large pot with the vegetables, herbs and a generous pinch of salt. Cover with water by several centimetres. Bring to a gentle simmer and cook for about 1½ hours, or until tender. (Alternatively, cook in a pressure cooker for 25–30 minutes on high pressure. Let the pressure release naturally.) Remove the herbs.

Make the Dough: On a clean work surface, make a mound with the semola and create a well in the centre. Gradually add the water, mixing with your fingers or a fork to incorporate the semola until a rough dough forms. Knead for 5–7 minutes until smooth and elastic. Cover with a dish towel and let rest for 30 minutes.

Make the Sauce: Heat the olive oil in a large pan. Sauté the chilli gently for 30 seconds until fragrant, then add the cooked chickpeas with a little of their liquid and simmer for 12–15 minutes, crushing some of them with a spoon to thicken the sauce slightly. Season with salt and pepper to taste.

Roll and Cut the Pasta: Lightly dust a work surface with semola. Divide the rested dough into 4–6 portions. Roll each piece into a sheet, about 3mm/⅛in thick (setting 3 on a Marcato). Cut into ribbons about 1cm/½in wide and 10–15cm/6in long.

Fry a Portion of the Pasta: Heat 3–4 tablespoons of olive oil in a wide pan over a high heat. Once it's heated, fry a quarter of the pasta for 1–2 minutes until crisp and golden, in batches if needed. Drain on paper towels and set aside.

Cook the Remaining Pasta: Bring a large pot of salted water to the boil and cook the rest of the pasta for 3–4 minutes, until al dente. Using a slotted spoon, lift the pasta directly into the chickpea sauce. Add more chickpea broth if needed to help the sauce cling evenly.

Serve: Spoon into bowls and top with the fried pasta ribbons. Serve immediately.

Ch. 8

BEYOND Nourishment

Sundays in our house didn't creep up quietly; you heard them coming. The clatter in the kitchen started early, before the rest of the world had woken up. Someone was already peeling, stirring, shouting for kids to get ready. The table had to be extended, fold-out chairs taken down from the attic. Somewhere between the third coffee and the fourth phone call, relatives started arriving and lunch began to take shape. We always knew who would arrive first (my cousin Giusy and her family), and last (my cousin Carmen and her family). In between . . . nonne, zia Rita, cousin Elena, each bringing something.

This took place every Sunday, and the whole week orbited around it. My mamma Giovanna, my nonna Maria and my zia Rita would start plotting the menu days in advance, usually during another meal. There were rules, traditions and always too much food. Always a pasta, two second courses, a tray of vegetables, a salad no one ate, two or three desserts and coffee served at least six times.

These gatherings were messy, loud, overflowing. Children running all over the place, someone arriving late because they *had* to get that dessert from that special *pasticceria* on the other side of town, someone else shouting: "*Chi vuole un altro caffè?*" ("Who wants another coffee?") for the hundredth time before lunch had even begun. The table was the anchor, but it was everything around it that made it whole: the teasing, the interruptions, the last-minute garnish.

This chapter is about those meals. The ones that asked for time, effort and a bit of chaos. The kind you couldn't pull off alone. Dishes that took hours because they were meant to. They were labours of love, but also of pride, habit and sometimes stubbornness. Meals that didn't aim for elegance; they aimed to feed 12 people, each with an opinion. That was the point: not perfection, but abundance. The kind of abundance that made people linger. That left you full in more ways than one.

If you cook from this chapter, do it with company. Or noise. Or both. Call someone to argue about the menu. Use the good pot. Make too much. And leave the dishes for later.

PEA & LEMON RICOTTA RAVIOLONI WITH MINT OIL

Ravioloni ricotta e piselli con olio alla menta

A festive spring pasta, perfect for long lunches and full tables. Larger than life in size and flavour, these ravioloni bring together the sweetness of peas, the brightness of lemon and the uplifting aroma of mint, served with a warm, fragrant oil that's made for celebratory tables. This is the kind of pasta you make when the table's going to be full, and the menu has been debated for days.

I use a hand-carved, clover-shaped wooden stamp for these, which means cutting and shaping each one by hand. The result is worth it. You can use any ravioli stamp or simply cut them by hand. What matters is the generosity: the spring peas, the sharp lemon, the creamy ricotta, all wrapped in silky sheets of pasta. A warm mint oil with an optional flicker of chilli adds freshness and flair. This is a dish for the centre of the table, best made when the kitchen is crowded, the music's on and the glasses are full.

Serves: 4

Preparation time: 45 minutes, plus 30 minutes resting

Cooking time: 5 minutes

For the Dough:

* 400g/14oz/3 cups 00 flour
* 4 eggs

For the Filling:

* 250g/9oz/1 cup ricotta, well drained
* 150g/5¼oz/1 cup peas, lightly blanched and mashed
* Zest of 1 unwaxed lemon
* 2 tbsp finely chopped fresh mint
* Pinch of freshly grated nutmeg
* Salt and pepper, to taste

For the Mint Oil:

* 20g/¾oz/1 cup loosely packed fresh mint leaves
* 100ml/3½fl oz/scant ½ cup extra virgin olive oil
* ½ green chilli, thinly sliced (optional)

To Serve:

* Fresh mint leaves
* Finely grated Pecorino or ricotta salata (optional)

Make the Dough: On a clean work surface, make a mound with the flour and create a well in the centre. Crack in the eggs and whisk gently with a fork, gradually incorporating the flour until a rough dough forms. Knead for 5–7 minutes until smooth and elastic. Cover with a dish towel and let rest for 30 minutes.

Make the Filling: In a bowl, mix the ricotta, mashed peas, lemon zest (reserving some for garnish), mint, nutmeg and some salt and pepper until smooth. Taste and adjust the seasoning. Cover and refrigerate until needed.

Roll and Fill the Ravioloni: Lightly dust a tray and work surface with flour. Divide the rested dough into 4–6 portions. Roll each piece into a thin sheet, about 1mm thick (setting 5 on a Marcato). Cut the sheets into large squares or circles, depending on your stamp. Place a heaped teaspoon of the filling in the centre of each. Brush the edges with a little water if needed, then top with another square or circle of dough. Press gently to seal, making sure to remove any air pockets. Stamp out each raviolone using a mould or cutter. Transfer to the floured tray and keep covered as you work. Repeat with the remaining dough and filling.

Make the Mint Oil: Blanch the mint leaves in boiling water for 5 seconds, then transfer immediately to a bowl of iced water to cool. Drain and pat dry. In a blender, blitz the mint with the olive oil until smooth. If using the chilli, gently warm it in a small pan with the blended oil for 1–2 minutes over a very low heat. Strain through a fine sieve/fine-mesh strainer or muslin cloth/cheesecloth for a fragrant oil.

Cook and Serve: Bring a large pot of salted water to the boil. Cook the ravioloni for 3–4 minutes, or until they float and the texture is al dente. Using a slotted spoon, lift the ravioloni directly onto the serving plates. Drizzle with the mint oil and garnish with fresh mint, the reserved lemon zest and grated Pecorino, if using. Serve immediately.

ORECCHIETTE TIMBALE WITH ROOT VEGETABLES & CARAMELIZED ONIONS

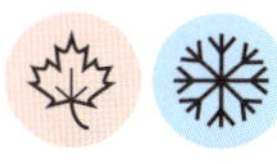

Timballo di orecchiette con tuberie cipolla caramellata

Serves: 4

Preparation time: 45 minutes, plus 30 minutes resting

Cooking time: 50 minutes

For the Dough:

* 400g/14oz/3 cups semola
* 200ml/7fl oz/scant 1 cup lukewarm water

For the Timbale:

* 1 golden beetroot/beet, peeled and diced
* 1 Chioggia/candy cane beetroot/beet, peeled and diced
* 1 carrot, peeled and diced
* 1 small turnip or 4–5 radishes, peeled and diced
* 1 smoked or regular garlic clove, minced
* 2 tbsp extra virgin olive oil, plus extra for drizzling
* 2 fresh rosemary sprigs, stalks removed, leaves finely chopped
* 5–6 fresh sage leaves, finely chopped
* 1 tsp smoked paprika
* ½ tsp ground nutmeg
* 200g/7oz/2 cups Gruyère, half grated and half cubed
* A handful of fresh parsley, plus extra to finish the bake (optional)
* 3 tbsp grated Grana Padano or Parmigiano Reggiano
* Salt and pepper, to taste

For the Caramelized Onions:

* 4–5 tbsp extra virgin olive oil
* 2 onions, thinly sliced
* Salt and sugar, to taste

A hearty baked dish for colder days, full of roasted roots, golden cheese and soft handmade orecchiette. This homemade orecchiette timbale brings together the comforting textures of roasted root vegetables with the rich creaminess of Gruyère cheese. The caramelized onions add a sweet, delicate flavour that contrasts beautifully with the earthiness of the vegetables, while the delicate herbs brighten the entire dish.

I chose colourful beetroot/beets, radishes and carrots, but you could go with swede/rutabaga, sweet potato or even fennel . . . the options are endless. The versatility of this dish makes it a perfect, nourishing meal for colder days when you still want to celebrate. It's grand and holds its shape beautifully thanks to the Gruyère keeping everything together.

Homemade orecchiette add an extra layer of texture and flavour, making it a true labour of love.

Make the Dough: On a clean work surface, make a mound with the semola and create a well in the centre. Gradually add the water, mixing with your fingers or a fork to incorporate the semola until a rough dough forms. Knead for 5–7 minutes until smooth and elastic. Cover with a dish towel and let rest for 30 minutes.

Prepare the Vegetables: Preheat the oven to 200°C/400°F/Gas Mark 6. Toss the diced vegetables and the garlic with the olive oil, rosemary, sage, smoked paprika, nutmeg and some salt and pepper. Spread it all out on a baking sheet and roast for 20–25 minutes, or until tender and slightly caramelized.

Make the Caramelized Onions: While the vegetables roast, heat the olive oil in a pan and gently cook the onions over a low heat with a pinch of salt and sugar for 20–25 minutes, stirring occasionally, until golden and sweet.

Shape the Orecchiette: Lightly dust a tray and wooden board or work surface with semola. Roll the rested dough into long ropes about 1cm/⅓in thick. Cut them into small pieces and, using a butter knife or your thumb, drag each piece against the board to form small, concave discs. Flip them inside-out onto your thumb for the traditional "ear" shape. Set on the tray and keep covered as you work. Repeat with the remaining dough.

Cook the Orecchiette: Bring a large pot of salted water to the boil. Cook the orecchiette for 2–3 minutes, or until they float and the texture is al dente.

Assemble the Gratin: Preheat the oven to 210°C/410°F/Gas Mark 6½. Using a slotted spoon, lift the orecchiette into a greased springform tin and combine with the roasted vegetables, half the caramelized onions, the grated Gruyère, the parsley, a splash of pasta water and a drizzle of olive oil if needed to coat the pasta evenly.

Bake the Gratin: Top with the remaining cubed Gruyère, grated Grana Padano and a little more parsley, if desired. Bake for 15–20 minutes, or until the top is golden and bubbling. Let it rest for a few minutes before serving. Garnish with the remaining caramelized onions.

VEGETARIAN WHITE CHRISTMAS (EGGLESS) LASAGNA

Lasagne bianca vegetariana di natale

A festive showstopper of handmade eggless semola sheets, Romanesco cream and pink peppercorn béchamel. This vegetarian white lasagna is the ultimate festive dish, bringing all the seasonal colours and flavours to your table.

Romanesco's pointy, bright green florets resemble little Christmas trees. The pink peppercorns add an unexpected, subtle spice that complements the broccoli's nuttiness. This dish is a festive tribute to the season, perfect as an individual centrepiece to make your Christmas meal feel even more special.

Serves: 4 (individual portions)

Preparation time: 45 minutes, plus 30 minutes resting

Cooking time: 35 minutes

For the Dough:

* 400g/14oz/3 cups semola
* 200ml/7fl oz/scant 1 cup lukewarm water
* 2 tbsp extra virgin olive oil, plus extra for greasing

For the Filling:

* 2 heads of Romanesco broccoli
* 4 tbsp extra virgin olive oil
* 6 garlic cloves, minced
* 2 heaped tbsp capers, rinsed
* 60g/2oz/⅔ cup Pecorino, finely grated, plus extra to finish
* 160g/5⅔oz/⅔ cup provolone, thinly sliced or cubed
* 2 tbsp garlic confit oil or extra virgin olive oil
* A few pink peppercorns, to garnish
* Salt, to taste

For the Béchamel:

* 60g/2oz/4 tbsp unsalted butter
* 60g/2oz/4 tbsp plain/all-purpose flour
* 800ml/28fl oz/scant 3½ cups whole milk
* 2 tsp crushed pink peppercorns
* Salt, to taste

Make the Dough: On a clean work surface, make a mound with the semola and create a well in the middle. Gradually add the water and olive oil, mixing with your fingers or a fork until a rough dough forms. Knead for 5–7 minutes until smooth and elastic. Cover with a dish towel and let rest for 30 minutes.

Prepare the Romanesco: Cut the Romanesco broccoli into small florets, reserving a handful of the nicest ones for garnish. Blanch the remaining florets in boiling salted water for 1 minute, then drain and set aside. Reserve the blanching water.

In a large pan, warm the olive oil over a medium heat and sauté the garlic for 30–60 seconds until fragrant. Add the blanched Romanesco, capers and a pinch of salt. Cook for 3–4 minutes, adding a couple of ladlefuls of the reserved cooking water to help soften the broccoli. Once tender, transfer to a blender, add the Pecorino and blend into a thick, creamy purée. Set aside.

Make the Béchamel: In a saucepan, melt the butter over a low heat. Add the flour and whisk into a smooth paste, then cook for 2–3 minutes until lightly golden. Gradually add the milk, whisking constantly to prevent lumps. Add the crushed pink peppercorns and a pinch of salt. Simmer gently, stirring often, for 6–8 minutes until the sauce thickens to a light coating consistency. Remove from the heat and cover.

Roll and Cut the Lasagna Sheets: Lightly dust a tray and work surface with semola. Divide the rested dough into quarters. Roll each piece into a thin sheet, about 1mm thick (setting 5 on a Marcato). Cut out 28 discs using a 9cm/3½in pastry ring or cutter. Set on the tray. This will make four lasagnas with 5 discs each (plus extras).

Assemble and Bake the Lasagnas: Preheat the oven to 210°C/410°F/Gas Mark 6½. Line a baking sheet with baking parchment. Lightly grease four 9cm/3½in pastry ring moulds with oil and place them on the sheet.

Spread a thin layer of béchamel in the bottom of each ring. Add a pasta disc, then layer with more béchamel, a spoonful of Romanesco cream and a few pieces of provolone. Repeat until you have five pasta layers per lasagna, finishing with a final layer of béchamel and a generous sprinkle of grated Pecorino.

Bake for 12–15 minutes, or until the top is golden and the filling is hot and bubbling.

Garnish and Serve: While the lasagnas are baking, heat the garlic confit oil in a small pan and sauté the reserved Romanesco florets with a pinch of salt for 1–2 minutes until slightly golden brown. Carefully remove the moulds by running a knife around the edges to loosen. Top each lasagna with a few Romanesco florets and a few pink peppercorns for garnish. Serve immediately.

MUSHROOM-FILLED TORTELLI WITH CREAM, MINT & GARDEN PEAS

Tortelli ai funghi con panna, menta e piselli

Serves: 4

Preparation time: 40 minutes, plus 30 minutes resting

Cooking time: 25 minutes

For the Dough:

* 400g/14oz/3 cups 00 flour
* 4 eggs

For the Filling:

* 1 tbsp extra virgin olive oil
* 1 tbsp unsalted butter
* 1 shallot, finely chopped
* 250g/9oz/3 cups mixed mushrooms (like chestnut/cremini, button and porcini), finely chopped
* 2 tbsp finely grated Parmigiano Reggiano
* 2 tbsp fine breadcrumbs, or as needed
* A few fresh thyme leaves
* 1 egg yolk
* Salt and pepper, to taste

For the Sauce:

* 200g/7oz/1½ cups fresh or frozen peas
* 1 tbsp unsalted butter
* 200ml/7fl oz/scant 1 cup single/light cream
* 1 tbsp finely chopped fresh mint
* Salt and pepper, to taste

For Serving:

* Extra mint leaves
* Freshly ground black pepper
* Finely grated Parmigiano Reggiano

A light and comforting pasta inspired by my mum's love of cream sauces. Cream sauces have fallen out of fashion in Italian cooking, but in our family, they were the height of elegance. In the 80s and 90s, when my mother wanted to make a dish feel elegant or festive, she would almost always reach for a dash of cream. One of our family favourites was tortellini with cream, peas and mushrooms (sometimes with ham too) served on birthdays, holidays or simply because she felt like making something a little more refined.

This dish is a fresh take on that classic. The tortelli are filled with sautéed mushrooms and shallots, then served with a light cream sauce, peas and a touch of mint. It's soft, fragrant and gently nostalgic. Use fresh peas if they're in season, or frozen ones if that's what you have.

Make the Dough: On a clean work surface, make a mound with the flour and create a well in the centre. Crack in the eggs and whisk gently with a fork, gradually incorporating the flour until a rough dough forms. Knead for 5–7 minutes until smooth and elastic. Cover with a dish towel and let rest for 30 minutes.

Prepare the Filling: Warm the olive oil and butter in a pan over a medium heat. Add the shallot and cook for 2–3 minutes until soft. Add the chopped mushrooms and a pinch of salt and pepper and cook over a medium heat until the mixture is tender and dry, about 8–10 minutes. Remove from the heat, stir in the grated Parmigiano, breadcrumbs and thyme. Leave to cool completely, then transfer to blender or food processor. Add the egg yolk, season to taste and blitz everything to a smooth consistency.

Roll and Fill the Tortelli: Lightly dust a tray and work surface with flour. Divide the rested dough into 4–6 portions. Roll each piece into a thin sheet, about 1mm thick (setting 5 on a Marcato). Cut them into strips about 6–7cm/2¾in wide. Pipe or spoon small mounds of the mushroom filling at intervals of 4–5cm/2in along one strip. Brush the edges lightly with water, lay a second strip on top and press gently to seal. Cut into squares using a pasta wheel, stamp or knife. Press the edges firmly to ensure they are sealed. Transfer to the floured tray, cover with a dish towel and repeat with the remaining dough and filling.

Make the Sauce: Blanch the peas in a pan of boiling salted water for 2–3 minutes, until just tender, then drain. In a wide pan, melt the butter and add the cream to gently warm. Add the peas, chopped mint and some salt and pepper. Simmer for 2–3 minutes until slightly thickened, then remove from the heat.

Cook the Tortelli: Bring a large pot of salted water to the boil. Cook the tortelli for 2–3 minutes, or until they are al dente and float to the surface.

Combine and Serve: Using a slotted spoon, lift the tortelli directly into the pan with the warm cream sauce and toss gently to combine. Serve with extra mint leaves, black pepper and grated Parmigiano.

POLENTA/CORNMEAL GNOCCHI WITH MONTASIO CHEESE & BUTTER

This dish hails from the Alpine kitchens of northern Italy, where polenta/cornmeal wasn't just a staple but a source of comfort and creativity. Here, it's transformed into tender gnocchi, cut into rounds and baked with butter and Montasio cheese until golden on top and crisp at the edges. If Montasio is hard to find, you can substitute with a young Asiago, Piave, or even a mild Gruyère . . . literally, any cheese that melts well and has a nutty, milky sweetness. Rich, satisfying and surprisingly elegant, the gnocchi make a beautiful first course or light main. It's a humble dish, but one that brings a sense of celebration.

Serves: 4

Preparation time: 20 minutes, plus 30 minutes chilling and cooling

Cooking time: 1 hour

For the Dough:

* 800ml/28fl oz/scant 3½ cups water
* 200g/7oz/1 cup coarse polenta/cornmeal
* 2 tbsp unsalted butter
* 1 tbsp grated Grana Padano
* Salt, to taste

To Assemble and Bake:

* 100g/3½oz/1 cup Montasio cheese, grated
* 2 tbsp finely grated Parmigiano Reggiano
* 2 tbsp unsalted butter, plus extra for greasing
* Freshly ground black pepper, to taste (optional)
* Neutral oil, for greasing

Cook the Polenta: Lightly grease a tray with oil. In a medium saucepan, bring the water to the boil with a generous pinch of salt. Gradually pour in the polenta/cornmeal, whisking constantly to prevent lumps. Lower the heat to medium-low and cook, stirring frequently, until the mixture thickens and pulls away from the sides, about 30–35 minutes. Stir in the butter and Grana Padano. Spread the hot polenta evenly on the prepared tray to a thickness of about 1cm/½in. Leave to cool completely at room temperature, then refrigerate for at least 30 minutes until firm.

Shape the Gnocchi: Once the polenta is cold and firm, preheat the oven to 200°C/400°F/Gas Mark 6 and cut out small rounds of polenta using a floured glass, pastry cutter or ravioli stamp. Re-shape any offcuts into discs. You should have 20–24 pieces.

Assemble and Bake: Grease a baking dish with a little butter. Arrange the polenta gnocchi in slightly overlapping rows in the dish. Sprinkle with the Montasio and Parmigiano, dot with small pieces of the butter and season with black pepper, if you like.

Bake and Serve: Bake for 20–25 minutes, or until golden and bubbling on top. Let rest briefly before serving.

AGNOLOTTI DEL PLIN WITH CHEESE FONDUTA, MUSHROOMS & SAGE

Agnlotti del plin ripieni alla fonduta, con funghi e salvia

Delicate hand-pinched agnolotti filled with a silky cheese fonduta, served with golden mushrooms sautéed in butter and sage. These agnolotti come from the hills of Langhe and Monferrato in Piedmont, a region where pasta is shaped as carefully as it is named. *Plin* means "pinch" in the local dialect, and that's exactly how each agnolotto is sealed with a neat pinch of the fingers, forming a distinctive shape that has become a symbol of northern Italian craftsmanship. Traditionally, they are stuffed with roasted meat leftovers and served *al tovagliolo*, nestled in a warm cloth to preserve their softness.

Here, the filling is lighter: a soft fonduta made from Fontina cheese, allowing the flavour of the pasta and topping to shine. The mushrooms, sautéed in butter and sage, bring texture and depth, while the pasta holds it all together. This dish isn't everyday fare. It's a celebration of simplicity done well.

Serves: 4

Preparation time: 35 minutes, plus 30 minutes resting

Cooking time: 30 minutes

For the Dough:

* 350g/12oz/2⅔ cups 00 flour
* 8 egg yolks

For the Filling:

* 200g/7oz Fontina cheese, rind removed and diced
* 100ml/3½fl oz/scant ½ cup whole milk
* 1 egg yolk
* A small grating of nutmeg
* Salt, to taste

For the Mushroom & Sage Butter:

* 3 tbsp unsalted butter
* 6–8 fresh sage leaves
* 250g/9oz/3 cups mixed mushrooms (such as porcini, chestnut/cremini or button), chopped
* Salt and pepper, to taste

To Finish:

* Extra grated Fontina or Parmigiano Reggiano (optional)

Make the Dough: On a clean work surface, make a mound with the flour and create a well in the centre. Add the egg yolks and whisk gently with a fork, gradually incorporating the flour until a rough dough forms. If needed, add a splash of water to make the dough come together. Knead for 5–7 minutes until smooth and elastic. Cover with a dish towel and let rest for 30 minutes.

Prepare the Fonduta Filling: In a heatproof bowl set over a saucepan of barely simmering water (bain-marie), over a low heat, warm the diced Fontina and milk until melted, stirring often. Once smooth, stir in the egg yolk, nutmeg and a pinch of salt. Continue to stir gently for 6–8 minutes until the mixture thickens slightly. It should coat the back of a spoon. Remove from the heat and leave to cool. The mixture will firm up as it cools, making it easier to use as a filling.

Roll and Fill the Agnolotti: Lightly dust a tray and work surface with flour. Divide the rested dough in half. Roll each piece into a very thin sheet, about 0.8mm thick (setting 6 on a Marcato). Place small teaspoons of the filling in a row about 2.5cm/1in apart, a few centimetres from the edge. Fold the dough over the filling and press gently to seal, removing any air pockets.

Using your fingers, pinch firmly between each mound (this pinch is called the *plin*) to define the individual bundles. Cut along the long top edge with a pasta wheel or knife, then cut between the pinches to separate each agnolotto. As you cut, flip each one so the sealed edge faces upward and forms a small lip, the traditional shape of *agnolotti del plin*. Place the finished agnolotti on the floured tray and keep covered as you work.

Make the Mushroom and Sage Butter: In a large pan, melt the butter over a medium heat. Add the sage leaves and let them crisp for 1–2 minutes, then remove and set aside. Add the mushrooms and sauté until golden and tender, about 8–10 minutes. Season with salt and pepper.

Cook the Agnolotti: Bring a large pot of salted water to the boil. Cook the agnolotti for 2–3 minutes, until they are al dente and float to the surface.

Combine and Serve: Using a slotted spoon, lift the agnolotti into the pan with the mushroom butter. Toss to coat, adding a splash of cooking water if needed to help the sauce cling evenly. Plate the agnolotti with a spoonful of the mushrooms and butter. Top with the crispy sage leaves and Fontina or Parmigiano, if desired.

RICOTTA & SPINACH RAVIOLINI WITH ROASTED CHERRY TOMATOES

Serves: 4

Preparation time: 40 minutes, plus 30 minutes resting

Cooking time: 25 minutes

For the Dough:

* 400g/14oz/3 cups 00 flour
* 4 eggs, plus 2 egg yolks

For the Filling:

* 200g/7oz/4 cups spinach
* 250g/9oz/1 cup ricotta
* 50g/1¾oz/½ cup Parmigiano Reggiano, finely grated
* Freshly grated nutmeg, to taste
* Salt and pepper, to taste

For the Sauce:

* 300g/10½oz/2 cups cherry tomatoes
* 2 garlic cloves, thinly sliced
* 4 tbsp extra virgin olive oil (divided)
* Fresh basil leaves, finely shredded
* Salt and pepper, to taste
* Freshly grated unwaxed lemon zest, to garnish (optional)

Tiny square ravioli filled with ricotta and spinach, served with a delectable sauce of caramelized roasted cherry tomatoes, garlic and basil. These raviolini bring me back to the kind of cooking that filled our kitchen with noise, colour and flour-dusted trays lined with pasta. The filling – ricotta, spinach, a grating of Parmigiano and nutmeg – is one of those eternal combinations that everyone in Italy loves. At home, we'd take turns shaping the tiny squares, barely larger than a coin, lined up like soldiers as they waited for the pot. The sauce comes together in the oven while you work: no fuss, just good olive oil, tomatoes and the kind of garlic-heavy scent that tells you dinner is close. If I'm feeling generous, I'll add a touch of lemon zest. It's not extravagant, but it tastes like home.

Make the Dough: On a clean work surface, make a mound with the flour and create a well in the centre. Crack in the eggs and add the yolks, then whisk gently with a fork, gradually incorporating the flour until a rough dough forms. Knead for 5–7 minutes until smooth and elastic. Cover with a dish towel and let rest for 30 minutes.

Prepare the Filling: Sauté the spinach in a pan with a splash of water over a medium-low heat for 1–2 minutes until wilted. Remove from the heat, cool slightly, then squeeze out any excess moisture. Chop the spinach finely and mix it with the ricotta, Parmigiano, nutmeg and some salt and pepper. Taste and adjust the seasoning.

Roll and Fill the Raviolini: Lightly dust a tray and work surface with flour. Divide the rested dough into 2–4 pieces. Roll each piece into a very thin sheet, about 0.8mm thick (setting 6 on a Marcato). Spread a very thin, even layer of filling across the sheet, leaving about 2cm/¾in around the edges to prevent spillage. Lay another sheet of pasta on top and press firmly to seal, working carefully around the filling to remove any air pockets. Cut into 3–4cm/1½in squares using a ravioli stamp or a pasta wheel. Transfer the raviolini to the floured tray and keep covered as you work.

Make the Sauce: Preheat the oven to 200°C/400°F/Gas Mark 6. Toss the cherry tomatoes and garlic with 3 tablespoons of the olive oil and some salt and pepper on a baking sheet. Roast for 15–20 minutes until soft and slightly caramelized. Transfer to a large bowl, gently mash a few of the cherry tomatoes and stir in the remaining tablespoon of olive oil.

Cook the Raviolini: Bring a large pot of salted water to the boil. Add the raviolini and cook for 2–3 minutes, or until they float and the texture is al dente.

Combine and Serve: Using a slotted spoon, lift the raviolini directly into the bowl with the sauce. Toss with the tomato mixture, adding a splash of cooking water if needed to help the sauce cling evenly. Stir in the finely shredded basil and adjust the seasoning. Finish with a touch of lemon zest, if using. Serve immediately.

OCCHI WITH CELERIAC/CELERY ROOT-COMTÉ FONDUTA & CHESTNUT-WALNUT RAGÙ

Occhi con fonduta di sedano rapa e comté, ragù di castagne e noci

Serves: 4

Preparation time: 45 minutes, plus 30 minutes resting

Cooking time: 1 hour

For the Dough:

* 400g/14oz/3 cups 00 flour
* 4 eggs

For the Filling:

* 200g/7oz/1⅓ cups celeriac/celery root, peeled and chopped
* 100g/3½oz/½ cup Yukon Gold or other yellow-flesh potato, peeled and chopped
* 1 tbsp unsalted butter
* 50g/1¾oz/½ cup Comté, grated, plus extra to serve
* 1–2 tbsp double cream/heavy cream
* Salt and pepper, to taste

For the Chestnut-Walnut Ragù:

* 2 tbsp extra virgin olive oil
* 1 small onion, finely chopped
* 1 small carrot, finely chopped
* 1 small celery stalk, finely chopped
* 2 tsp tomato purée/paste or 2 tbsp tomato passata
* 60ml/2fl oz/¼ cup white wine
* 100g/3½oz/¾ cup cooked (peeled) chestnuts, finely chopped
* 40g/1½oz/⅓ cup walnuts, toasted and finely chopped
* A handful of fresh marjoram leaves, chopped
* 1 tbsp unsalted butter
* Salt and pepper, to taste
* Fresh basil leaves, to garnish

A delicate filled pasta with a silky root vegetable and cheese centre, served with a nut-based ragù that captures the warmth of autumn. *Occhi* (literally "eyes") are a lesser-known filled pasta shape with a smooth, domed profile, traditionally found – in slightly differing versions – in both northern and southern Italy. Inspired by their elegant simplicity, I created this version with a roasted celeriac/celery root and yellow potato fonduta, lifted by the deep nuttiness of Comté, my favourite cheese. It's a dish that feels both refined and comforting, brought to life by a walnut and chestnut ragù delicately scented with fresh marjoram.

Make the Dough: On a clean work surface, make a mound with the flour and create a well in the centre. Crack in the eggs and whisk gently with a fork, gradually incorporating the flour until a rough dough forms. Knead for 5–7 minutes until smooth and elastic. Cover with a dish towel and let rest for 30 minutes.

Prepare the Filling: Steam or boil the celeriac/celery root and potato until soft, about 20–25 minutes. Mash or pass through a ricer while warm. In a pan, melt the butter over a low heat, add the mashed celeriac and potato and stir in the grated Comté and the cream. Mix for 4–5 minutes until smooth and thick, but not too runny. Season to taste. Leave to cool before using.

Roll and Fill the Occhi: Lightly dust a tray and work surface with flour. Divide the rested dough into 2–4 pieces. Roll each piece into a thin sheet, about 1mm thick (setting 5 on a Marcato). Pipe or spoon small mounds of filling evenly along a sheet, leaving a 4–5cm/1¾in space between each.

Lightly drape a second sheet of dough over the top. Press around the filling to seal and remove any air pockets. Then, using a round ravioli stamp with a domed base, press down firmly to cut and seal each piece in one motion. The result should be a thick, rounded shape (like a small button or eye) with no visible edges. If needed, dust your stamp with flour to prevent sticking. Lay the finished occhi on the floured tray and keep covered as you work. Repeat with the remaining dough and filling.

Make the Ragù: In a wide pan, warm the olive oil over a medium heat. Add the onion, carrot and celery and cook gently for 10–12 minutes until meltingly soft. Stir in the tomato purée/paste and cook for 1 minute. Deglaze with the white wine and let it reduce slightly for 30 seconds. Add the chopped chestnuts and walnuts, stir well, then cook over a low heat for another 5–10 minutes until it looks amalgamated and saucy. Add the marjoram, season to taste and finish with the butter.

Cook the Occhi and Serve: Bring a large pot of salted water to the boil. Add the occhi and cook for 2–3 minutes, until they float and the texture is al dente. Using a slotted spoon, lift the occhi directly into the pan with the warm ragù. Toss gently and serve immediately with a little extra Comté grated on top. Garnish with fresh basil.

GLUTEN-FREE CRESPELLE WITH CHARD & STRACCIATELLA

Crespelle senza glutine con bietole e stracciatella

Serves: 4

Preparation time: 15 minutes, plus 15 minutes resting

Cooking time: 40 minutes

For the Crespelle:

* 100g/3½oz/¾ cup oat flour
* 100g/3½oz/¾ cup rice flour
* 2 large eggs
* 350ml/12fl oz/scant 1½ cups whole milk
* Butter, melted, or olive oil, for cooking
* Salt, to taste

For the Filling:

* 2 tbsp extra virgin olive oil
* 1 garlic clove, lightly crushed
* 300g/10½oz rainbow chard, chopped
* 200g/7oz/¾ cup stracciatella cheese
* Salt and pepper, to taste

To Finish:

* 40g/1½oz/⅓ cup Parmigiano Reggiano, finely grated, plus extra to garnish
* 1 tbsp melted unsalted butter
* A handful of black or green olives, pitted
* A few sun-dried cherry tomatoes
* Fresh basil leaves, to garnish

A delicate dish with vibrant greens, melting cheese and golden edges. This recipe came together on one of those days when cooking needed to feel gentle. No rolling, no shaping, just a batter, a pan and a filling that spoke for itself. The *crespelle* are crêpes made with a blend of oat and rice flour, which gives them a soft, yielding texture and keeps them entirely gluten-free.

The filling is made from sautéed rainbow chard, garlicky and tender, and a spoonful of stracciatella, creamy, light and just the right contrast. Once folded and stacked in a baking dish, they're finished with Parmigiano, a little butter, some olives and tomatoes, then baked until golden. It's the kind of dish you make when you want something comforting but simple. Everything settles into place in the oven.

Make the Crespelle: In a bowl, whisk together the oat flour, rice flour, eggs and a pinch of salt until smooth. Add the milk gradually while whisking to avoid lumps. Let the batter rest for 10–15 minutes.

Heat a non-stick pan over a medium heat and brush with a little butter or olive oil. Pour a ladleful of the batter into the pan, swirling to coat the base thinly. Cook for about 1–2 minutes per side until golden and set. Remove to a plate. Repeat with the remaining batter to make 4 large crespelle. Set aside.

Prepare the Filling: In a wide pan, warm the olive oil over a medium heat and gently sauté the garlic for 30–60 seconds until fragrant. Add the chopped chard and cook for 5–7 minutes until wilted and tender. Season with salt and pepper. Remove the garlic.

Assemble and Bake: Preheat the oven to 200°C/400°F/Gas Mark 6. Fill each crespella with a spoonful of the chard mixture and a generous scoop of the stracciatella. Fold into quarters and arrange in a baking dish, overlapping the crespelle slightly. Sprinkle with the Parmigiano, drizzle with the melted butter and scatter the olives and sundred cherry tomatoes on top. Bake for 10–15 minutes, or until the top is golden and bubbling. Garnish with fresh basil leaves and extra Parmigiano and serve hot.

COFFEE-SPECKLED RICOTTA RAVIOLI WITH ESPRESSO BROWNED BUTTER

Ravioli ricotta al caffé con burro nocciola all'espresso

Serves: 4

Preparation time: 35 minutes, plus 30 minutes resting

Cooking time: 10 minutes

For the Dough:

* 400g/14oz/3 cups semola
* 1 tbsp finely ground espresso powder
* 4 eggs

For the Filling:

* 250g/9oz/1 cup ricotta, well drained
* 2 tbsp grated Parmigiano Reggiano
* ¼ tsp ground nutmeg
* ½ tsp sumac
* Salt and pepper, to taste

For the Espresso Browned Butter:

* 80g/2¾oz/⅓ cup unsalted butter
* 40g/1½oz/⅓ cup walnuts or pecans, roughly chopped
* 1 shot of brewed espresso
* Salt, to taste

A bit unexpected, deeply satisfying and exactly the kind of pasta you make when you want to surprise yourself. Okay. This one sounds a bit out there but hear me out. This recipe leans into contrast: bitter coffee powder in the dough, creamy ricotta inside, sharp sumac and warm nutmeg rounding out the filling. The sauce? Just browned butter but with a shot of espresso and a handful of toasted walnuts. I imagine pecans would work wonderfully too. It's complex, it's savoury and it just works. The coffee isn't there to dominate. It's there to deepen everything else.

Make the Dough: On a clean work surface, make a mound with the semola and mix in the ground coffee. Create a well in the centre, crack in the eggs and whisk gently with a fork, gradually incorporating the semola until a rough dough forms. Knead for 5–7 minutes until smooth and elastic. Cover with a dish towel and let rest for 30 minutes.

Make the Filling: In a bowl, combine the ricotta, Parmigiano, nutmeg, sumac and some salt and pepper. Mix well until smooth. Taste and adjust the seasoning. Chill while you roll out the pasta.

Roll and Fill the Ravioli: Lightly dust a tray and work surface with semola. Divide the rested dough into 4–6 portions. Roll each piece into a thin sheet, about 1mm thick (setting 5 on a Marcato). Place small mounds of filling onto one sheet, spacing them out by 3–4cm/1½in. Cover with another sheet, press around the filling to seal and remove air pockets and cut into squares or rounds. Set on the tray as you work and keep covered.

Make the Espresso Browned Butter: Melt the butter in a small pan over a medium heat. Add the walnuts and let them toast gently. Once the butter begins to brown and smell nutty, around 4–6 minutes, stir in the espresso. Let it bubble for 30 seconds, then remove from the heat. Season with a pinch of salt and keep warm.

Cook the Ravioli: Bring a large pot of salted water to the boil. Cook the ravioli for 2–3 minutes, or until they are al dente and float to the surface.

Combine and Serve: Using a slotted spoon, lift the pasta into the pan with the espresso browned butter. Toss carefully to coat. Plate the ravioli, spoon over any remaining butter and walnuts and serve immediately.

RAVIOLI ALLA PARMIGIANA (BURNT AUBERGINE/EGGPLANT IN TOMATO DOUGH)

Serves: 4

Preparation time: 45 minutes, plus 30 minutes resting

Cooking time: 1 hour 40 minutes

For the Tomato Dough:

* 400g/14oz/3 cups semola
* 2 tbsp tomato purée/paste
* 180ml/6fl oz/¾ cup lukewarm water

For the Filling:

* 2 aubergines/eggplants (about 600g/1lb 5oz)
* 2 tbsp extra virgin olive oil
* 100g/3½oz/¾ cup mozzarella, finely chopped
* 50g/1¾oz/½ cup Parmigiano Reggiano, finely grated
* A few fresh basil leaves, finely chopped, plus extra to garnish
* Salt and pepper, to taste

For the Sauce:

* 400g/14oz/2½ cups cherry or baby plum tomatoes
* 1 garlic clove, unpeeled
* 40g/1½oz/⅓ cup Pecorino, finely grated, plus extra to serve
* 1 tbsp extra virgin olive oil
* Salt, to taste

A tribute to the southern classic, reimagined as tomato-laced ravioli with a smoky, cheese-laced heart. Parmigiana was always a serious matter in our family and no one made it like zia Rita. Her version was rich, confident, unapologetically southern. Aubergines/eggplants fried just right, sauce full of depth and layers that somehow held together like a work of architecture. It was the kind of dish you smelled before you saw, and once you saw it, you knew there'd be seconds.

This ravioli takes that memory and reshapes it. The dough is coloured with tomato, the filling made from slow-roasted aubergines, melted mozzarella, Parmigiano and basil. The sauce is a blend of slow-roasted tomatoes and Pecorino, silky and sharp. Each triangle is a bite of nostalgia: compact, smoky, gorgeous.

Make the Dough: On a clean work surface, make a mound with the semola and create a well in the middle. In a small bowl, whisk the tomato purée/paste into the water until dissolved. Gradually add the liquid to the semola, mixing with your fingers or a fork to incorporate the semola until a rough dough forms. Knead for 5–7 minutes until smooth and elastic. Cover with a dish towel and let rest for 30 minutes.

Prepare the Filling: Preheat the oven to 220°C/425°F/Gas Mark 7. Prick the aubergines/eggplants all over and place on a baking sheet. Roast for 35–40 minutes, turning once, until the skin is charred and the flesh soft. Leave to cool slightly, then scoop out the flesh and discard the skin. Chop the aubergine flesh and then sauté it in the olive oil over a medium heat for 2–3 minutes to remove the excess moisture. Transfer to a bowl and mix in the mozzarella, Parmigiano, basil and some salt and pepper. Set aside to cool.

Make the Sauce: Reduce the oven to 160°C/320°F/Gas Mark 3. Place the tomatoes and garlic on a baking sheet lined with baking parchment and roast for 40–45 minutes until soft and lightly caramelized. Discard the garlic skin and blitz with the Pecorino and olive oil into a smooth sauce. Season to taste with salt and set aside.

Roll and Fill the Ravioli: Lightly dust a tray and work surface with semola. Divide the rested dough into 2–4 pieces. Roll each piece into a thin sheet, about 1mm thick (setting 5 on a Marcato). You can either use a triangle-shaped ravioli stamp or cut the sheets into squares of about 6–7cm/2¾in to fold each one into a triangle by hand. Place a small spoonful of the filling in the centre, then either press the stamp down to seal or fold and seal the square, pressing out any air pockets. Transfer the finished ravioli to the tray as you work and keep covered.

Cook the Ravioli: Bring a large pot of salted water to the boil. Cook the ravioli for 6–7 minutes, or until they float and the texture is al dente.

Combine and Serve: Meanwhile, gently warm the tomato sauce in a pan. Using a slotted spoon, lift the pasta directly into the sauce. Toss gently to coat, adding a splash of cooking water if needed to help the sauce cling evenly. Plate and serve with a few extra basil leaves and an extra grating of Pecorino.

SWEET FRIED RAVIOLI WITH HAZELNUT CREAM

Raviolo fritto dolce alla crema di nocciole

Serves: 4 (1 large raviolo per person)

Preparation time: 30 minutes, plus 30 minutes resting

Cooking time: 10–15 minutes

For the Dough:

* 200g/7oz/1⅓ cups 00 flour
* 1 tbsp caster/granulated sugar
* Zest of ½ unwaxed lemon or orange
* 1 egg
* 1½ tbsp melted unsalted butter
* 1–2 tbsp milk, as needed
* Salt, to taste

For the Filling:

* 4 heaped tsp chocolate hazelnut spread or pistachio spread

For Frying and Serving:

* 1l/35fl oz/4¼ cups neutral oil, for frying
* Icing/confectioners' sugar, to dust

A golden, sugar-dusted pastry filled with soft hazelnut cream, crisp on the outside and melting within. Throughout Italy, sweet fried ravioli mark moments of festivity. You'll find them at Carnevale in Tuscany, filled with ricotta and chocolate, or at Christmas in Calabria, where they might hide grape must, nuts or jam. In Sicily, similar shapes are made for San Giuseppe and other saints' days, often with chestnut cream or sweetened ricotta.

Each region has its version, but the feeling is the same: something indulgent, a little messy, best eaten warm with sugar still clinging to your fingertips.

This one is a modern take, filled with hazelnut cream and sealed in the same way we handle our savoury pies in Sicily: folded-and-pinched like we do for *impanate* (or *'mpanate*), where the edge is rolled and crimped inward, almost like a rope. The pastry puffs as it fries, and the centre turns molten. Serve warm with a dusting of icing/confectioners' sugar, and nothing else.

Make the Dough: On a clean work surface, mix the flour, sugar, citrus zest and some salt. Make a well in the centre, then crack in the egg and add the melted butter. Using your hands, slowly incorporate the flour, adding a spoonful or two of milk if needed to form a soft, pliable dough. Knead for 5–7 minutes until smooth and elastic. Cover with a dish towel and let rest for 30 minutes.

Roll and Fill the Ravioli: Lightly dust a tray and work surface with flour. Divide the rested dough in half. Roll each piece into a thin sheet, about 1–2mm thick (setting 4 on a Marcato). Cut out 8 circles about 10–12cm/4½in in diameter. Place a heaped teaspoon of chocolate hazelnut spread in the centre of 4 of the discs. Moisten the edge with water, then cover with a second disc. Press gently around the filling to seal, taking care to remove any air pockets. Seal by folding and pinching along the edge in a rolling motion to create a thick, hand-crimped border. Alternatively, press the edges with the tines of a fork to seal. Transfer to the floured tray and keep covered as you work.

Fry and Serve: Heat the oil in a deep pan until a small piece of bread dropped in sizzles and turns golden in 30–45 seconds (around 170°C/340°F). Fry one or two ravioli at a time for 2–3 minutes per side, until puffed and golden. Remove with a slotted spoon and drain briefly on paper towels. Dust generously with icing/confectioners' sugar and serve warm.

Ch. 9

RECIPES For a Lazy Day

There are days when even the thought of cooking feels like a stretch, when the clouds outside echo the weight within and making something from scratch feels more like a burden than a balm. On those days, I don't reach for flour or rolling pins. I reach for comfort in its simplest form.

This chapter is for those moments. The tired ones. The fragile ones. The ones where you're craving something warm and kind but haven't got the energy to do more than boil water or stir a pot. These recipes are not about achievement. They're about ease. Familiar flavours, quick methods and shortcuts that still feel like care.

Many of the recipes you'll find here are also the dearest to me; the ones my mum or dad would make on a weekday when they came home late from work, tired but still wanting to put something comforting on the table. They're the dishes my sister Paola and I learned to cook when we were still in school, when Mum had to travel home from afar and we'd take over lunch for the family before our parents walked through the door.

None of the recipes here involve fresh pasta. They're built on store-bought ingredients, forgiving techniques and the knowledge that sometimes just getting something nourishing on the table is enough. A bowl of spaghetti, a simple sauce, a pantry meal that surprises you with how satisfying it is.

There have been many days when cooking has saved me . . . but also days when even cooking felt like too much. These are the recipes I've turned to then. They ask little of you but offer plenty in return. Because sometimes, the kindest thing we can do for ourselves is make something warm to eat and keep going.

ASSASSIN'S SPAGHETTI

Spaghetti all'assassina

A bold one-pan spaghetti from Bari, cooked directly in tomato broth until spicy, crispy and full of character. We discovered *Spaghetti all'Assassina* shortly before my dad became ill, but it quickly became a staple at home. He loved its intensity. The chilli heat, the way the pasta crackled in the pan, the sticky richness of the sauce. It was one of those dishes that brought a bit of drama to the table.

It's made differently to most pasta. The spaghetti cooks directly in a spiced tomato broth, absorbing flavour as it softens. At the end, you let it catch just a little so the bottom crisps up. The result is a plate of pasta that's bold, satisfying and anything but boring.

Serves: 4

Preparation time: 10 minutes

Cooking time: 25 minutes

Ingredients:

* 4 tbsp extra virgin olive oil
* 2 garlic cloves, finely minced
* 1–2 red chillies, finely minced, to taste, plus extra to serve (optional)
* 400ml/14fl oz/1⅔ cups tomato passata or polpa di pomodoro
* 1 tsp salt
* 400g/14oz spaghetti
* 2 tbsp tomato purée/paste, diluted in 1l/35fl oz/4¼ cups water

Prepare the Sauce: Heat the olive oil in a wide pan over a medium heat. Add the garlic and chilli and cook for 2–3 minutes until fragrant but not browned. Stir in the passata and salt. Let it simmer for 5–7 minutes to thicken slightly.

Add the Pasta: Lay the uncooked spaghetti flat in the pan. Don't break it. Spoon a little of the tomato sauce over the top to help it soften.

Prepare the Broth: Bring the diluted tomato purée/paste to a gentle simmer in a separate saucepan. Keep warm over a low heat.

Cook the Pasta: As the spaghetti softens, add the tomato broth a ladleful at a time, like you would with risotto. Stir gently and let it absorb before adding more. Continue for about 12 minutes, until the pasta is al dente and coated in sauce.

Crisp the Bottom: Increase the heat slightly and leave the pasta untouched for 1–2 minutes to crisp underneath. Watch closely to avoid burning.

Serve: Serve straight from the pan while hot. Top with extra chilli, if you like.

VITTORIO'S RIGATONI

Rigatoni alla Vittorio

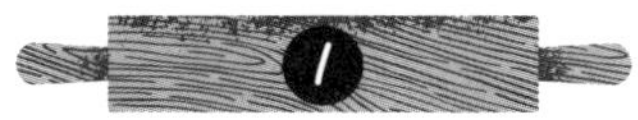

Serves: 4

Preparation time: 15 minutes

Cooking time: 50 minutes

Ingredients:

* 250g/9oz/1 cup San Marzano tomatoes, roughly chopped
* 250g/9oz/1 cup datterino tomatoes, halved
* 250g/9oz/1 cup beefsteak tomatoes, roughly chopped
* 400g/14oz rigatoni or other shape of your choice
* 50g/1¾oz/3½ tbsp unsalted butter, cubed
* 80g/2¾oz/¾ cup Parmigiano Reggiano, finely grated, plus extra to serve
* Salt, to taste
* A handful of fresh basil leaves, to garnish (optional)

A glossy tomato-butter sauce that is somehow both extravagant and understated. All comfort. No complications. I don't know Vittorio personally, but I owe him a thank you. (Okay, he has a three-star Michelin restaurant.) This recipe first popped up in my feed with no context, just a swirl of red sauce being finished with butter and an avalanche of cheese. I was intrigued. It looked simple, but something about it felt refined. When I tried it myself, I understood why.

It uses three kinds of tomatoes – San Marzano, datterino and beefsteak – blended into the smoothest purée, then pushed through a sieve/fine-mesh strainer and simmered to a velvety finish. If those are not available to you, any variety of tomatoes will work. That's it. No garlic, no onion, just basil. When the tomatoes are in season, they give you everything you need. It's both unfussy and sophisticated, a recipe that strips things back and lets the ingredients speak for themselves. Traditionally made with paccheri, I like it even better with rigatoni. The ridges catch just the right amount of sauce, and every bite feels complete. It belongs in this chapter because it proves that simplicity doesn't mean settling. Sometimes, it means perfection.

Make the Sauce: Place all the tomatoes in a large saucepan and cook over a medium heat for 25–30 minutes, until softened and collapsed. Remove from the heat and blend until smooth using a hand-held/immersion blender or food processor. Pass the purée through a fine sieve/fine-mesh strainer into a clean medium pan, pressing with the back of a spoon to extract as much smooth liquid as possible. Discard the skins and seeds. Return the sauce to a low heat and simmer for another 10 minutes to concentrate the flavour. Season with a little salt, if needed.

Cook the Pasta: Bring a large pot of salted water to the boil. Cook the rigatoni according to the package directions until al dente. Reserve a ladleful of the cooking water, then drain.

Finish and Serve: Off the heat, stir the butter into the warm tomato sauce until melted and glossy. Add the cooked rigatoni and toss to coat. Stir in the grated Parmigiano, mixing vigorously to emulsify the sauce. Add a splash of the reserved cooking water if needed. Divide between the plates and finish with an extra topping of Parmigiano, and some fresh basil, if you like.

SARDINIAN FLATBREAD LASAGNA

Pane frattau

A quick, rustic dish made with crispy bread, tomato sauce and a fried egg. Like lasagna, but faster, lighter and humbler. This isn't technically a pasta dish, but it belongs here. When I was putting this chapter together, I kept thinking about what we cook on the days we want comfort without effort. *Pane frattau* is exactly that. All the layering and softness of lasagna, without making or boiling anything.

It's made with *pane carasau*, the paper-thin Sardinian flatbread that dates back to shepherd culture. Baked twice to become crisp and dry, it was made to last through long seasons away from home. In *pane frattau*, these brittle sheets are dipped in broth to soften, then layered with tomato sauce, grated cheese and topped with a soft poached or fried egg.

It's a dish born out of resourcefulness. Simple ingredients, assembled quickly, and somehow greater than the sum of their parts. If you can open a can of tomatoes and make an egg, you can make this.

Serves: 4

Preparation time: 15 minutes

Cooking time: 25 minutes

Ingredients:

* 3 tbsp extra virgin olive oil, plus extra for frying and to serve
* 1 garlic clove
* 500ml/17fl oz/2 cups puréed tomatoes or passata
* 1–2 tsp white wine vinegar per 1 litre/34fl oz/4¼ cups of water
* 4 eggs
* 600ml/20fl oz/2½ cups vegetable stock or water
* 16 large sheets of *pane carasau* (Sardinian flatbread)
* 60g/2oz/¾ cup Pecorino Sardo or Pecorino Romano, finely grated
* Freshly fround black pepper, to garnish
* Salt, to taste

Make the Sauce: Warm the olive oil in a saucepan over a medium heat and gently fry the garlic for 2–3 minutes, making sure it doesn't burn. Add the puréed tomatoes and a pinch of salt. Simmer for 10–15 minutes, until slightly thickened. Remove the garlic and set the sauce aside.

Poach or Fry the Eggs: If poaching, bring a pot of water to a simmer with a splash of vinegar. Crack the eggs, one by one, into a small cup, then gently slide each into the water. Poach for about 3 minutes, until the whites are set and the yolks still runny. Remove with a slotted spoon and set aside on a warm plate. If frying, heat 1 tablespoon of olive oil in a pan and fry the eggs according to your preference. I like my yolk slightly runny.

Assemble the Pane Frattau: Warm the vegetable stock in a wide pan. Dip one sheet of *pane carasau* at a time into the hot liquid for just 2–3 seconds to soften, then transfer to a plate. Top with a few spoonfuls of the warm tomato sauce and a sprinkle of the Pecorino. Repeat with another softened sheet, more sauce and more cheese, then repeat twice more. Repeat for each person, using 4 sheets per portion.

Finish and Serve: Top each stack with an poached/fried egg and a final drizzle of olive oil and some black pepper. Serve warm, ideally eaten with a spoon to break into the soft layers.

FARFALLE WITH WALNUT SAUCE

Farfalle con salsa di noci

Serves: 4

Preparation time: 15 minutes

Cooking time: 10 minutes

Ingredients:

* 50g/1¾oz/2 slices of white bread, crusts removed
* 100ml/3½fl oz/scant ½ cup whole milk
* 150g/5¼oz/1½ cups walnuts
* 400g/14oz farfalle
* 1 small garlic clove
* 50g/1¾oz/½ cup mixed Parmigiano Reggiano and Pecorino, finely grated, plus extra to serve
* 3 tbsp extra virgin olive oil
* Salt, to taste
* A few fresh marjoram leaves or basil, to serve (optional)

A creamy walnut sauce from Genova: less famous than *pesto alla Genovese*, but just as traditional and deeply comforting. While basil pesto became iconic, this walnut sauce (*salsa di noci*) remained its lesser-known counterpart. Traditionally served with *pansotti*, a Ligurian ravioli filled with wild herbs, it's also excellent with dry pasta like farfalle, making it a weekday version: quick, reliable and still satisfying.

The method is simple: walnuts, milk-soaked bread, a bit of garlic, grated cheese and olive oil blended into a soft, mellow sauce. It's one of those sauces that feels like it should be more effort than it is. A handful of ingredients, a quick blitz and you're done.

Soften the Bread and Walnuts: Place the bread in a small bowl and cover with the milk. Let it soak until soft, about 5 minutes. Meanwhile, bring a small saucepan of water to the boil. Drop in the walnuts and blanch for 1 minute to help loosen the skins. Drain and rub them gently in a clean dish towel to remove most of the skins (this is optional but helps to reduce bitterness).

Cook the Pasta: Bring a large pot of salted water to the boil. Cook the farfalle according to the package directions until al dente. Reserve a ladleful of the cooking water, then drain.

Make the Sauce: While the pasta cooks, in a food processor or mortar and pestle, combine the soaked bread and milk, walnuts, garlic, cheese and olive oil. Blend or grind into a creamy paste. Add a spoonful of the reserved cooking water to loosen the sauce, if needed. Season with salt to taste.

Finish and Serve: Return the drained pasta to the pan and toss gently with the walnut sauce, adding more cooking water a little at a time to help it coat the farfalle evenly. Serve warm with extra grated cheese, and a few leaves of marjoram or basil, if you like.

BICOLOURED SPAGHETTI (PESTO & POMODORO)

Pasta portofino

Half pesto, half tomato. A pasta for the undecided. This was my mum's go-to lunch dish. Quick, satisfying and never boring. She'd mix one half of the spaghetti with pesto, the other with tomato sauce, and serve them side by side on the same plate: never mixed until the very last minute. It felt like two pastas in one. I used to think it was her invention. Only much later did I find out it has a name: *pasta portofino.*

The name likely comes from the Ligurian coast, where both tomatoes and pesto are household staples. In the original dish, the sauces are mixed together, but I much prefer the way my mum made it: split down the middle, no need to choose a side until you're ready to eat. It's colourful, comforting and very hard to mess up. Which is probably why we loved it so much. Making pesto is easy, but if you are short on time or can't be bothered, a good quality store-bought pesto will work just fine.

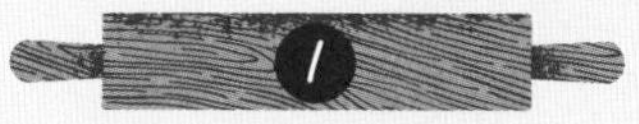

Serves: 4

Preparation time: 10 minutes

Cooking time: 20 minutes

For the Pesto:

* 30g/1oz/2 cups loosely packed fresh basil leaves
* 30g/1oz/4 tbsp pine nuts
* 1 small garlic clove
* 60ml/2fl oz/¼ cup extra virgin olive oil
* 40g/1½oz/⅓ cup Parmigiano Reggiano or Pecorino, finely grated, plus extra to serve
* Salt, to taste

For the Tomato Sauce:

* 2 tbsp extra virgin olive oil
* 1 garlic clove, unpeeled, lightly crushed (*in camicia*)
* 300ml/10½fl oz/1¼ cups puréed tomatoes or passata
* A few fresh basil leaves, plus extra to garnish
* ½ tsp sugar
* Salt, to taste

To Serve:

* 400g/14oz spaghetti

Make the Pesto: In a food processor, blend the basil, pine nuts, garlic and a pinch of salt. Slowly drizzle in the olive oil until smooth. Stir in the grated Parmigiano and adjust the seasoning if needed. Set aside.

Make the Tomato Sauce: In a small saucepan, warm the olive oil with the garlic over a low heat for 2–3 minutes until fragrant but not browned. Add the puréed tomatoes, basil, sugar and a pinch of salt. Simmer gently for 10–15 minutes, or until the oil separates and the sauce has thickened. Discard the garlic before serving.

Cook the Pasta: Meanwhile, bring a large pot of salted water to the boil. Cook the spaghetti according to the package directions until al dente. Reserve a ladleful of the cooking water, then drain.

Finish and Serve: Split the drained pasta into two pans or bowls. Mix one half with the pesto and a little of the reserved cooking water to loosen, and the other with the tomato sauce. Plate the two colours side by side and serve immediately, sprinkled with extra grated cheese and garnished with extra fresh basil.

SHORT BUSIATE WITH SICILIAN SUMMER GREENS

Busiate corte con tenerumi

A Sicilian dish that celebrates the fleeting season of these Sicilian greens, for a taste of late summer comfort. The end of summer in Sicily carries a special magic. The air cools just enough to bring you back into the kitchen, and for a fleeting moment, *tenerumi* (the tender leaves of the long squash plant) appear at the market. My parents would sit at the kitchen table, patiently sorting the tangled leaves from the shoots, knowing their season never lasted long.

Traditionally, tenerumi are cooked into a brothy soup with broken spaghetti. This version, sautéed in a pan and tossed with pasta and slow-roasted cherry tomatoes, is my own take. It's perfect for those in-between days, when summer starts to slip away and autumn hasn't fully arrived. If you can't find tenerumi, friarielli, rapini, broccoli rabe or mustard greens will do the job. What matters is the contrast: soft greens with a gentle bitterness alongside the sweetness of the tomatoes. The younger the shoot, the more tender and flavourful it will be.

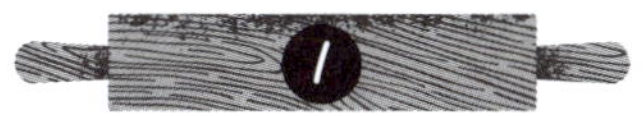

Serves: 4

Preparation time: 15 minutes

Cooking time: 40 minutes

For the Confit Cherry Tomatoes:

* 300g/10½oz/2 cups cherry tomatoes
* 2 tbsp extra virgin olive oil
* 1 tsp sugar
* 1 tsp salt
* A few fresh thyme sprigs

For the Greens & Pasta:

* 250g/9oz tender tenerumi leaves and shoots (or friarielli, rapini, broccoli rabe, mustard greens)
* 400g/14oz busiate corte or other shape of your choice
* 4 tbsp extra virgin olive oil
* 2 garlic cloves, thinly sliced
* ½ red chilli, finely chopped (optional)
* Salt, to taste

Clean the Greens: Clean the tenerumi by removing any tough stems and discoloured leaves, then rinse the greens thoroughly in cold water. Strip the leaves from the shoots and chop both finely.

Prepare the Confit Tomatoes: Preheat the oven to 140°C/275°F/Gas Mark 1. Halve the cherry tomatoes and place them cut-side up on a baking sheet lined with baking parchment. Drizzle with the olive oil and sprinkle with the sugar, salt and thyme. Bake for 40 minutes, or until softened and lightly caramelized.

Cook the Greens and Pasta: Meanwhile, bring a large pot of salted water to the boil. Add the chopped greens and cook for 2–3 minutes to soften. Remove with tongs and set aside. In the same pot, cook the pasta according to the package directions until al dente. Reserve a ladleful of the cooking water, then drain.

Prepare the Sauce: In a large frying pan, heat the olive oil over a medium heat and gently sauté the garlic and chilli, if using, for 30–40 seconds until fragrant but not browned. Add the cooked greens, a generous splash of the reserved cooking water and let them simmer together for 5–7 minutes. Add the cooked pasta and toss everything together. Season with salt and add more cooking water if needed to loosen the sauce.

Serve: Divide between the plates and top with the confit cherry tomatoes. Serve warm, without cheese, to let the flavour of the greens and tomatoes shine.

AGLIO E OLIO WITH SAMPHIRE & NORI PANGRATTATO

Aglio e olio "sapore di mare"

Serves: 4

Preparation time: 15 minutes

Cooking time: 15 minutes

Ingredients:

* 2 large sheets dried nori seaweed
* 6 tbsp fine breadcrumbs (pangrattato)
* 180g/6⅓oz/1¾ cups samphire
* 1 small piece dried kombu
* 400g/14oz spaghetti
* 4 tbsp rapeseed/canola oil
* 6 garlic cloves, finely chopped
* 2 tsp dried chilli/hot pepper flakes
* 100ml/3½fl oz/scant ½ cup sparkling water
* 4 tbsp chopped fresh parsley
* 2 tbsp chilli oil or dried chilli/hot pepper flakes
* Salt, to taste

A deeply savoury *aglio e olio*, scented with the sea and made entirely from plants. This is a dish I'm proud of. I created it during the pandemic on one of those weeks when I couldn't stop thinking about the sea. As someone who didn't grow up vegetarian, I sometimes still miss the flavour of meat and fish, but I don't like mock meats or overly processed food. I'd rather coax those same feelings out of vegetables and pantry staples.

Samphire brings the salinity. Nori and kombu bring depth. A splash of sparkling water lifts the sauce and softens the garlic just enough. But the nori pangrattato on top is what pulls it all together: umami-rich, crispy and completely addictive. It's proof that you don't need much to create something satisfying and complex. Just a few good ingredients, used with intention.

Make the Nori Pangrattato: Crumble the nori into a small bowl. Toast the breadcrumbs in a dry pan over a medium-low heat for 3–4 minutes, stirring frequently, until golden, then stir in the nori and toast for another 30 seconds. Set aside.

Cook the Samphire and Pasta: Bring a large pot of water to the boil. Blanch the samphire for 30 seconds, then lift it out and set aside. Add the kombu to the same water and simmer for 5 minutes to infuse. Taste the water: samphire and kombu are naturally salty, but you can add a little salt if needed. Bring the broth back to the boil and cook the spaghetti according to the package directions until al dente. Reserve a ladleful of the cooking water, then drain.

Prepare the Sauce: While the pasta cooks, warm the rapeseed/canola oil over a low heat in a large frying pan. Add the garlic and dried chilli/hot pepper flakes and cook gently for 2–3 minutes, until the garlic just begins to brown. Add the sparkling water in small splashes to loosen the mixture and create a light emulsion. Add a splash of the reserved cooking water too, to help everything come together.

Finish and Serve: Add the drained pasta and samphire to the pan. Toss quickly over a medium-high heat, then remove to add the parsley and chilli oil, stir again, and serve immediately with a generous handful of the nori pangrattato sprinkled on top.

SPAGHETTI WITH CHARRED ROMESCO

Spaghetti con salsa romesco veloce

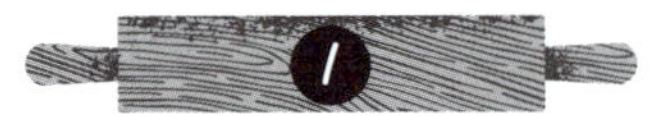

Serves: 4

Preparation time: 10 minutes

Cooking time: 10 minutes

Ingredients:

* 2 red peppers, deseeded and cut into strips
* 200g/7oz/1⅓ cups cherry tomatoes
* 1 garlic clove
* 400g/14oz spaghetti
* 50g/1¾oz/⅓ cup blanched almonds
* 1 slice of stale bread or 2 tbsp breadcrumbs
* 4 tbsp extra virgin olive oil, plus extra to serve
* 2 tbsp red wine vinegar
* Salt and pepper, to taste
* Pinch of smoked paprika or dried chilli/hot pepper flakes, to garnish (optional)
* Fresh basil leaves, to garnish

Smoky, sweet and ready in the time it takes to boil pasta. Some days you want bold flavour without the slow roast. This is a shortcut romesco sauce made in a pan, not the oven, and blitzed into something rich, nutty and deeply satisfying. The peppers and tomatoes get charred and softened in the same pan, while the pasta cooks alongside. All that's left is a quick blend and a swirl.

It's a sauce with Spanish roots and a Sicilian attitude. No drama, no fuss. Just staple ingredients and a frying pan.

Char the Vegetables: Heat a large frying pan over a high heat without any oil. When the pan is very hot, add the peppers, tomatoes and garlic. Cook for 8–10 minutes, turning now and then, until the skins are blackened in spots and the tomatoes have collapsed slightly.

Cook the Pasta: Meanwhile, bring a large pot of salted water to the boil. Cook the spaghetti according to the package directions until al dente. Reserve a ladleful of the pasta water, then drain.

Blend the Sauce: Transfer the charred vegetables to a blender or food processor. Add the almonds, bread, olive oil, vinegar and some salt and pepper. Blend until mostly smooth, leaving some texture, if you like. Add a spoonful or two of the reserved pasta water to loosen the sauce if needed.

Finish and Serve: Toss the cooked spaghetti with the romesco sauce and a splash more pasta water to help it cling evenly. Serve warm with an extra drizzle of olive oil, a pinch of smoked paprika, if using, and some fresh basil.

ARANCINI FROM LEFTOVER RISOTTO

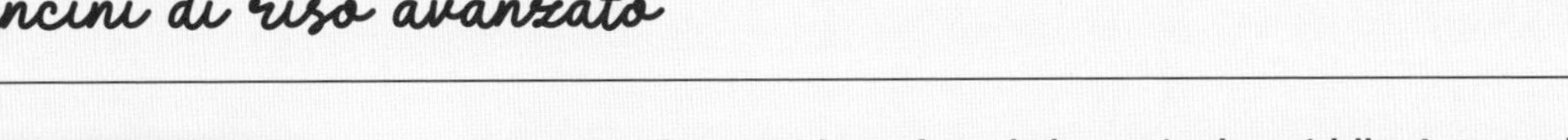

Arancini di riso avanzato

2

Serves: 4 (makes 10 arancini)

Preparation time: 20 minutes, plus 15 minutes chilling

Cooking time: 15 minutes (or longer if baking or air-frying)

Ingredients:

* About 500g/17½oz/2½ cups leftover cold risotto, ideally with saffron, courgette/zucchini and fiori di zucca
* 80g/2¾oz/¾ cup mozzarella, from a block or low-moisture package, or scamorza, cut into 10 small cubes
* 4 tbsp plain/all-purpose flour
* 2 eggs, beaten
* 100g/3½oz/1 cup breadcrumbs, plus extra if needed
* Salt and pepper, to taste
* 1l/35fl oz/4¼ cups vegetable oil, for shallow- or deep-frying (optional), or a drizzle or spray of olive oil, for baking or air-frying
* A spoonful of tomato sauce, to serve (optional)
* A spoonful of garlicky yogurt, to serve (optional)

Crispy on the outside, soft and cheesy in the middle. A second life for yesterday's risotto. In Sicily, arancini are a big deal. Even the name causes arguments. In Palermo, they say arancine, feminine, while in Catania, they're arancini, masculine. Let's just say they're gender-fluid and leave it at that. Whichever side you're on, the result is the same: crisp, golden rice balls with a molten centre and plenty of personality.

This version uses leftover risotto made with courgette/zucchini, *fiori di zucca* and saffron. The flowers melt into the rice, the courgettes stay soft and mild and the saffron gives everything a warm, fragrant lift. But honestly, any risotto will work. That's the beauty of this recipe. It doesn't ask for much. You just wrap yesterday's dinner around a cube of cheese, coat it well and fry, bake or air-fry until it's crackling and golden.

It's easy, satisfying and just dramatic enough to feel like you've pulled off something special with very little effort.

Shape the Arancini: Take a heaped tablespoon of the cold risotto and flatten it slightly in your palm. Place a cube of mozzarella in the centre, then close the rice around it to form a ball. Repeat until all the mixture is used and you've formed approx. 10 balls.

Coat the Arancini: Set up a breading station with one bowl of plain/all-purpose flour, one of beaten egg and one of breadcrumbs. Season each layer lightly with salt and pepper. Roll each rice ball in flour, then egg, then breadcrumbs. Chill in the refrigerator for 10–15 minutes to firm up.

If Frying: Pour the vegetable oil into a deep frying pan or saucepan to a depth of about 5cm/2in and heat to 170°C/340°F. If you don't have a thermometer, drop in a grain of rice; it should sizzle and turn golden in about 45 seconds. Fry the arancini in batches for 3–4 minutes, turning to brown evenly, until golden and crisp. Drain on paper towels.

If Baking: Preheat the oven to 200°C/400°F/Gas Mark 6. Place the arancini on a baking sheet lined with baking parchment. Drizzle with olive oil or spray lightly with the oil. Bake for 20–25 minutes, turning once, until golden and crisp.

If Air-frying: Preheat the air fryer to 200°C/400°F. Lightly spray the arancini with the olive oil and cook in batches for 10–12 minutes, shaking halfway through, until golden and crisp.

Serve: Serve hot, as they are, or with a spoonful of tomato sauce or garlicky yogurt on the side if you're feeling fancy.

LEFTOVER SPAGHETTI FRITTATA

Frittata di pasta

Serves: 4

Preparation time: 5 minutes

Cooking time: 15 minutes

Ingredients:

* 400g/14oz leftover cold, cooked spaghetti in tomato sauce
* 3 eggs
* 50g/1¾oz/½ cup Parmigiano Reggiano or Pecorino, finely grated (optional)
* 2 tbsp unsalted butter
* Salt and pepper, to taste

Crisp, golden and fiercely fought over. A proper second-day comfort dish. This was a regular in our house. My mum would make it with leftover spaghetti in tomato sauce, cooked again, this time in a pan with butter until the edges went crunchy and golden. It was one of the only times she used butter instead of olive oil, which in Sicily, I guess, always felt like a slightly northern move. But this dish needed it. The butter gave it flavour and bite. You could smell it as you rushed up the stairs back from school.

We had two teams in our family. My mum and sister liked theirs plain: just fried until crisp. But my dad and I would always crack in an egg or two (sometimes even throw in some grated cheese when no one was looking) and turn it into something more like a pasta omelette. This version follows our school of thought: spaghetti bound with egg, pan-fried until it gets that golden crust underneath. It's messy, indulgent and nearly impossible to share politely.

Prepare the Mix: Place the cold leftover spaghetti in a large bowl. Beat the eggs in a separate bowl with a pinch of salt and pepper. Add the eggs to the spaghetti and mix well. If using cheese, stir that in too.

Fry the Frittata: Heat the butter in a non-stick 24cm/9½in frying pan over a medium heat. Once melted and foaming, pour in the pasta mixture and press it down gently. Cook for 6–8 minutes, until the bottom is crisp and golden and the egg is mostly set.

Flip and Finish: Slide the frittata onto a plate, invert the pan over it and flip carefully back in. Cook the other side for another 4–5 minutes until golden all over and cooked through.

Serve: Cut into wedges and serve warm or at room temperature. Eat with your hands if you must. We always did.

FUSILLI CACIO E PEPE WITH RICOTTA SALATA

Fusilli cacio e pepe con ricotta salata affumicata

Serves: 4

Preparation time: 5 minutes

Cooking time: 15 minutes

Ingredients:

* 400g/14oz fusilli
* 1 tsp freshly ground black pepper, or to taste
* 2 tbsp extra virgin olive oil
* 60g/2oz/⅔ cup Pecorino, finely grated
* 40g/1½oz/⅓ cup smoked or regular ricotta salata (see page 270), finely grated, plus extra to serve
* Salt, to taste

This is what happens when you take *cacio e pepe* and let a Sicilian mess with it. Still just pasta, cheese, pepper and water, but instead of sticking strictly to Pecorino, this version uses a bit of ricotta salata, and it changes everything.

If you've never used it before, ricotta salata (use store-bought or make your own, recipe on page 270) is what happens when fresh ricotta is salted, pressed and aged until it's firm and sliceable. The smoked version adds depth without heaviness: it's sharp, savoury and just different enough to keep things interesting. You grate it like a hard cheese, but the flavour is gentler than Pecorino, with a subtle smokiness that lingers.

It's still a lazy dish. No sauce to make, no chopping, no stress. You cook the pasta, crack some pepper, grate some cheese and stir until it all comes together. But the result feels just a bit more special than it should.

Cook the Pasta: Bring a large pot of salted water to the boil. Cook the fusilli according to the package directions until al dente. Reserve about 250ml/9fl oz/1 cup of the pasta water, then drain.

Make the Sauce: In a large pan, gently toast the black pepper in the olive oil over a low heat for 1–2 minutes. Remove from the heat. Add a splash of the reserved pasta water to cool the pan slightly. In a bowl, mix both cheeses with a little hot pasta water to form a smooth paste.

Finish and Serve: Add the drained fusilli to the pan with the pepper. Stir in the cheese paste, tossing quickly to coat the pasta. Add more pasta water gradually until the sauce is glossy and clings evenly. Serve immediately, with a little extra smoked ricotta salata sprinkled over the top, if you like.

CREAMY SPINACH & LEMON BUCATINI

Bucatini con spinaci e crema al limone

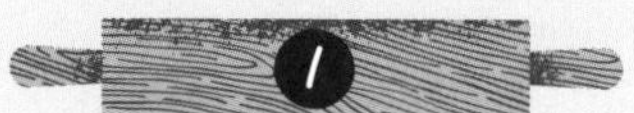

Serves: 4

Preparation time: 5 minutes

Cooking time: 10 minutes

Ingredients:

* 400g/14oz bucatini
* 2 tbsp extra virgin olive oil
* 200g/7oz/4 cups packed baby spinach
* 150g/5¼oz/⅔ cup cream cheese
* Zest and juice of ½ unwaxed lemon, plus extra zest to garnish
* Salt and pepper, to taste
* Finely grated Parmigiano Reggiano or Pecorino, to serve (optional)

Quick, green and silky. A pasta that feels like a hug and tastes like you made an effort. We've made it to the end . . . but we're not going out quietly. This one's fast, easy and far more luxurious than it has any right to be. The sauce is made with cream cheese and pasta water, and the spinach wilts right into it. The lemon gives it brightness, the bucatini gives it bounce. It's a proper lazy-day dish. No chopping, no layering, no slow cooking. Just a few ingredients stirred into something creamy and green that coats every strand. It's what I make when I want comfort but also want something a little fresh.

And yes, if it's the last main in the book, that means dinner is sorted; and so is everything else.

Cook the Pasta: Bring a large pot of salted water to the boil. Cook the bucatini according to the package directions until al dente. Reserve a ladleful of the pasta water, then drain.

Make the Sauce: While the pasta cooks, heat the olive oil in a large frying pan over a medium heat. Add the spinach and let it wilt for 2–3 minutes. Stir in the cream cheese, lemon zest and a splash of the reserved pasta water. Mix until smooth and creamy. Add more pasta water if needed to loosen the sauce.

Finish and Serve: Add the cooked pasta to the pan and toss well. Stir in the lemon juice and season with salt and pepper. Garnish with extra lemon zest and serve hot, with cheese if you fancy it, or leave it as is.

Ch. 10

THE PASTA Lover's Handbook

By now, your hands might know the feel of a good dough. You've shaped pasta into many shapes, prepared sauces using seasonal ingredients, cooked for yourself and maybe for others too. This last chapter steps away from the structure of recipes and focuses instead on the small things that support the whole practice. The things that often go unnoticed but are always doing the work in the background.

Some of them are practical, like how to store pasta properly so it doesn't clump, crack or spoil. How to freeze soffritto and have it handy when you need it. How to make a jar of pickled aubergines/eggplants or chilli oil that adds depth. Others are about building habits and mindset: how to plan a simple pasta night that doesn't feel like a performance, or how to create a pantry that's always stocked with what you need.

At the end, there's a glossary to help you look back over what you've learned or look up something that didn't quite stick the first time. This isn't a test, just a reference.

This chapter is less of a conclusion and more of a transition from learning by the book to cooking in your own way. The pages might stop here, but everything that follows is yours to shape, whether you keep things simple or start experimenting. The rest is practice, habit, instinct and appetite.

SECRET WEAPONS

Every cook has a few secret weapons up their sleeve: ingredients that don't shout for attention but change everything the moment they hit the pan. They're the jars, powders, oils and preserves I reach for instinctively, the ones that can take a dish from 10 to 100 with just a spoonful or sprinkle.

Some are rooted in tradition but adapted over time, others are entirely my own. Either way, these aren't the kind of things you find on a shopping list. They're built up slowly and used sparingly but with purpose. In this section, I'll share a few of my favourites: the flavour bombs that have become part of my everyday cooking. Keep them on hand and you'll always have something special to finish a dish, deepen a sauce or rescue a dull moment.

SICILIAN SUN-DRIED TOMATO MINCE

Capuliato

A rich, sun-dried tomato paste from Sicily, minced by hand and preserved in oil. This is a deeply savoury paste from the Vittoria Plain in the province of Ragusa, traditionally made with sun-dried tomatoes, herbs and olive oil. Use it to bring instant intensity to pasta, toast or soups. This is my version of *capuliato*, a condiment rooted in southern Sicily, where sun-dried tomatoes were once pounded by hand and stored in jars for winter. I use a mix of herbs, a little chilli and a splash of vinegar to brighten the flavours. A spoonful stirred through hot pasta with a little cooking water is all you need for a quick, intense dish. Keep a jar in the refrigerator and you'll always have a flavour bomb at the ready. Warning! May cause addiction.

Makes: 1 medium jar (about 275ml/9¼fl oz)

Preparation time: 20 minutes

Storage: Keeps for 1 month in the refrigerator, covered with olive oil

Ingredients:

* 200g/7oz/1½ cups sun-dried tomatoes, either dried (preferably) or packed in oil (drain well and skip soaking)
* 1 tsp fennel seeds
* 1–2 dried red chillies, crumbled, to taste
* 1 small garlic clove, finely chopped
* 1 tbsp capers, rinsed and chopped
* 1 tsp fresh thyme leaves
* 1 tsp fresh marjoram, mint or basil leaves
* 2–3 tbsp extra virgin olive oil, plus extra to cover
* 1 tbsp red wine vinegar
* Salt, to taste

Make the Capuliato: If using dried sun-dried tomatoes, soak them in warm water for 10 minutes to soften, then drain and pat dry. If using sun-dried tomatoes in oil, simply drain thoroughly. Finely chop the tomatoes by hand, or pulse briefly in a food processor if you prefer a finer texture. Transfer to a bowl and add the fennel seeds, chilli, garlic, capers and herbs. Stir in the olive oil and vinegar until combined. Taste and season with salt.

Store the Paste: Spoon into a clean, sterilized jar. Sterilizing helps it keep longer and safer. Press down gently to remove air pockets, and cover with a thin layer of olive oil. Seal and refrigerate. After each use, top up with oil to keep it preserved.

Use the Capuliato: Toss through hot pasta with a splash of cooking water, spread on toast or bruschetta, stir into sauces or dressings or use as a base for sandwich fillings.

SICILIAN RAW PICKLED AUBERGINES/EGGPLANTS

Melanzane sott'olio alla crudaiola

Makes: a 500ml/17fl oz jar

Preparation time: 30 minutes active, plus overnight salting, soaking and 4 hours drying

Storage: Keeps for 2–3 months in or out of the refrigerator, covered with olive oil

Ingredients:

* 2 large aubergines/eggplants
* 1 carrot
* 2 celery stalks
* 500ml/17fl oz/2 cups white vinegar
* 500ml/17fl oz/2 cups water
* 2 tbsp capers, rinsed
* A few fresh mint leaves
* 4–5 garlic cloves
* A few celery leaves (optional)
* Extra virgin olive oil, as needed
* Salt, as needed

My mum's raw pickled aubergines/eggplants, a family recipe from Ragusa passed down through generations. This is one of those recipes that's impossible not to love. Incredibly moreish and a regular fixture in my family's tradition, it's my mum's version of a classic Sicilian preserve. Unlike most recipes that involve blanching, in my family we leave the aubergines/eggplants raw and let vinegar do the work. The result is tender, very meaty strips layered with capers, garlic and herbs, then preserved in olive oil. They never last long in our house. We usually serve them piled onto good bread, or alongside cheese and other preserves as an accompaniment.

Salt the Aubergines: Peel the aubergines/eggplants and trim the ends. Slice them lengthways into 5mm/¼in-thick strips. Layer in a colander, sprinkling each layer generously with salt. Place a bowl underneath to catch the liquid and weigh down with a plate and something heavy. Leave for at least 5–6 hours, or overnight. Pat dry with paper towels, brushing off the excess salt.

Prepare the Vegetables: Peel and slice the carrot into 2–3mm/⅛in rounds. Slice the celery into 1cm/⅓in pieces. Cut the aubergine strips lengthways again so they're roughly finger-width.

Soak in Vinegar: Combine the aubergine, carrot and celery in a large bowl or pot. Combine the vinegar and water and pour it over the vegetables, making sure everything is submerged. Cover and leave to marinate overnight.

Dry Thoroughly: Drain the vegetables and spread them out on a clean dish towel. For a milder vinegar flavour, squeeze some liquid out of the aubergines as they will have absorbed the vinegar overnight. I personally like the vinegar flavour to be quite intense, so I skip this step. Cover with another dish towel and let dry at room temperature for 3–4 hours. They should feel completely dry before jarring to prevent spoilage.

Sterilize the Jar: Preheat the oven to 180°C/350°F/Gas Mark 4. Remove the rubber seal from a cleaned 500ml/17fl oz clip-top jar and place the jar on the oven rack for
5 minutes to sterilize. Leave to cool completely before using.

Pack the Jar: Layer the vegetables into the jar, alternating with the capers, mint leaves and garlic cloves. I like to add some celery leaves too, but that's optional. Press down gently and top up with olive oil until everything is completely submerged. Seal.

Store: Keep the sealed jar in a cool, dark place. Once opened, refrigerate and ensure the vegetables always remain under oil.

CAPER POWDER

Polvere di capperi

A salty, punchy seasoning made from dried salted capers. Intensely flavourful and shelf-stable for months. This is one of my favourites. I call it my gunpowder, because it takes only a pinch to fire up a dish. The flavour is bold, sharp and unmistakably Sicilian. I use salt-preserved capers for their intense flavour and lower moisture, which makes them perfect for drying slowly in the oven until they crumble into a powder. Sprinkle it on roasted aubergines/eggplants, stir into tomato sauce or dust over ricotta, pastas, salad, roasted potatoes . . . the combinations are endless! It's one of those things no one thinks to make, but once you do, you won't want to be without it.

Makes: 1 small jar (about 100ml/3½fl oz/scant ½ cup)

Preparation time: 10 minutes

Cooking time: 2–3 hours

Storage: Keeps for 6 months or longer in an airtight jar

Ingredients:

* 100g/3½oz/⅔ cup salted capers

Prepare the Capers: Rinse the salted capers well under running water to remove excess salt. Pat dry with a clean dish towel or paper towels.

Dry the Capers: Preheat the oven to 110°C/230°F/Gas Mark ½. Spread the capers out in a single layer on a baking sheet lined with baking parchment. Bake for 2–3 hours, or until completely dry. They should crumble easily between your fingers when ready.

Make the Powder: Allow the oven-dried capers to cool completely. Transfer to a mortar and pestle or spice grinder and grind to a fine or coarse powder, depending on your preference.

Store the Powder: Keep in a small, sterilized jar or spice jar in a cool, dry place. Use within 3 months for the best flavour.

Use the Powder: Dust over pastas instead of (or with) cheese, grilled vegetables, tomatoes or soft cheese. Stir into sauces or soups just before serving. It's also brilliant with eggs or mixed into breadcrumbs for coating vegetables or pasta.

CALABRIAN CHILLI OIL

Olio al peperoncino calabrese

For heat, depth and a flicker of bitterness. This is the jar you reach for when a dish needs waking up. It's hot, but not harsh. Fragrant with dried chilli/hot pepper flakes and rounded out with garlic, it lingers without overpowering. Stir into pasta, spoon over beans or drizzle onto pizza crusts. If you've got a jar of this in the refrigerator, you're never far from something flavourful.

Makes: 1 small jar (about 180ml/6fl oz/¾ cup)

Preparation time: 5 minutes

Cooking time: 2 minutes, plus at least 10 minutes infusing

Ingredients:

* 150ml/5fl oz/⅔ cup extra virgin olive oil
* 1 garlic clove, finely sliced
* 1 tbsp dried chilli/hot pepper flakes, or to taste
* Salt, to taste

Infuse for Oil: Warm the olive oil over a low heat in a small pan. Add the garlic and let it sizzle for 1–2 minutes, until golden and fragrant (be careful to avoid burning). Turn off the heat and stir in the dried chilli/hot pepper flakes and a pinch of salt. Let infuse for at least 10 minutes.

Cool and Store: Transfer to a clean, sterilized jar. Sterilizing helps it keep longer and safer. Once cool, store in the refrigerator. Use within 2 weeks and always use a clean spoon to avoid contamination.

FREEZER SOFFRITTO

Soffritto surgelato

A shortcut to the base of countless dishes. Every good sauce starts with a soffritto. This version gives you a head start whenever you need one. It's not fancy: just onion, carrot and celery blitzed and frozen in small portions. It will save you so much time when the pan is hot and you're in a hurry.

Makes: about 12–16 portions

Preparation time: 10 minutes

Storage: Keeps for 6 months or longer in the freezer

Ingredients:

* 4 onions
* 4 carrots
* 4 celery stalks

Blend the Base: Roughly chop the onions, carrots and celery. Add to a food processor and pulse until very fine, but not watery. You can chop these by hand if you prefer a coarser texture and have the time.

Portion and Freeze: Spoon into ice cube trays or small containers in manageable portions. Freeze until solid, then transfer to a large freezer bag. Use each portion straight from frozen as the base for sauces, stews or broths, and always use a clean spoon to avoid contamination.

TOASTED BREADCRUMBS

Pane atturrato

The original poor man's Parmigiano. A spoonful of this humble Sicilian staple can transform the simplest plate of pasta. Known locally as *pane atturrato*, this toasted breadcrumb topping was born out of necessity, when cheese was too expensive and home cooks relied on a handful of stale bread instead. Still used today, it brings texture, crunch and depth to a dish, especially when you want that extra something without reaching for grated cheese. This topping can be used throughout the book, whether scattered over a plate of pasta, or used as a crunchy garnish for baked dishes. It's a reminder that flavour doesn't have to be expensive, just honest.

Makes: 150g/5¼oz/1½ cups

Preparation time: 5 minutes

Cooking time: 8 minutes

For the Breadcrumbs:

* 2 tbsp extra virgin olive oil
* 150g/5¼oz/1½ cups fine breadcrumbs
* Salt, to taste

Optional (choose one or two):

* A handful of fresh herbs (parsley, mint, basil), chopped
* 1 tbsp crushed nuts (pistachios, almonds, walnuts)
* 1 tbsp sultanas/golden raisins, roughly chopped
* 1 garlic clove, finely grated

Toast the Breadcrumbs: Heat the olive oil in a frying pan over a medium-low heat. Add the breadcrumbs and stir immediately to coat them evenly. Keep stirring for 5–8 minutes, until golden brown and nutty in aroma. Don't walk away as they can catch easily.

Season and Cool: Add a pinch of salt and mix well. Leave to cool completely before storing and adding any optional flavourings, if using.

Store: Transfer to an airtight container or clean jar and keep in the refrigerator. It will keep for a couple of weeks. If you've added herbs, nuts or fruit, use within 2–3 days, and always use a clean spoon to avoid contamination.

HOMEMADE SALTED AGED RICOTTA

Ricotta salata fatta in casa

Salted, aged ricotta for grating: a key finishing touch in Sicilian cooking.

If Parmigiano is the king of the north, then ricotta salata is Sicily's answer. This homemade version takes time and patience, but the result is a firm, salty cheese you can grate over pasta, especially in classic dishes like *pasta alla norma*. All it requires is fresh ricotta and a lot of salt; nothing else. Over the course of a few weeks, it loses moisture, firms up and develops a concentrated, tangy flavour.

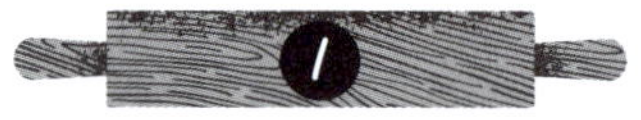

Makes: 1 small wheel (approx. 180g/6⅓oz once dried)

Preparation time: 20 minutes active, plus 3–4 weeks drying

Storage time: Keeps in the refrigerator for up to 2 months once dried and wrapped properly

Ingredients:

* 250g/9oz/1 cup ricotta
* 200–250g/7–9oz/¾–1 cup fine salt, as needed

Initial Draining: Spoon the ricotta into a small colander placed over a bowl. Leave to drain, uncovered, for 24 hours. If your kitchen is warm, keep it in the refrigerator, otherwise room temperature is fine.

First Salting: After the ricotta has drained, keep it in the colander and use a fork to gently flatten the surface, then cover it completely with a thin, even layer of fine salt. Be generous, and make sure every part is in contact with salt. Leave it to sit like this for 1–2 days. By this point, it should feel much firmer and have released more liquid.

Roll in Salt: Remove the ricotta from the colander. Spread more fine salt on a plate or piece of baking parchment and roll the cheese in it to coat all sides. Return it to the colander to continue drying.

Dry and Age: After 24 more hours, transfer the ricotta to a wooden or breathable surface (like a cheese board or wooden plate) and leave it to dry, uncovered, at room temperature for 2–3 weeks. Turn it every few days to help it dry evenly. It will slowly firm up and take on a pale-yellow colour.

Clean and Store: Once fully dried and hardened, scrape off the outer layer of excess salt using the flat side of a knife. Wrap the ricotta salata in baking parchment and store in the refrigerator. Use a microplane or fine grater to shave it over pasta. A little goes a long way.

FREEZER VEGGIE STOCK

Dadi di brodo surgelato

A flexible base for soups, sauces and risottos. This stock isn't precious. It's built from scraps and odds and ends, frozen until you're ready to simmer a batch. It's not meant to be crystal clear or delicately flavoured. It's meant to be there when you need it. Ideal for light broths, quick sauces or adding depth to a simple pasta dish.

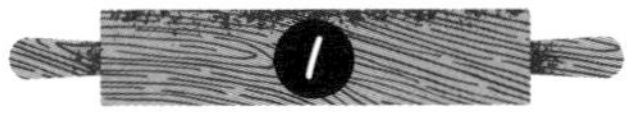

Makes: about 2l/70fl oz/ 8½ cups

Preparation time: 10 minutes

Cooking time: 1½ hour

Ingredients:

* 1 onion
* 2 carrots
* 2 celery stalks
* A handful of fresh parsley stalks or herb stems
* 1 bay leaf
* 1 garlic clove
* Any other clean veg scraps (courgette/zucchini tops, fennel fronds, leek greens, mushroom stalks, kale, broccoli or cauliflower stalks)
* Spices of your choice (I like about ½ teaspoon of black peppercorns, a few juniper berries and ½ teaspoon of coriander seeds as they give flavour without dominating)
* 2.5l/88fl oz/10½ cups cold water
* Salt, to taste

Make the Stock: Roughly chop the vegetables. Place them in a large pot, along with the herbs, garlic, any other veg scraps and spices, and cover with the water, making sure it sits a couple of centimetres above the vegetables. Bring to the boil, then simmer gently, uncovered, for 1–1½ hours. You shouldn't need to top up the water unless you notice the pot running very low, which usually only happens if the heat is too high. By the end, the liquid should have reduced by around a third and turned a light golden colour, with the vegetables soft and pale, having given up their flavour. Season with salt only at the end.

Cool and Freeze: Strain through a sieve/fine-mesh strainer and discard the vegetables, herbs, etc. Let the stock cool completely. Store in containers or ice cube trays and freeze for up to 3 months, and always use a clean spoon to avoid contamination. You can use directly from frozen.

STORAGE TIPS FOR FRESH AND DRIED PASTA

Fresh Pasta: Fresh pasta is best enjoyed immediately, but with the right storage methods, you can keep it fresh and delicious for later use. To prevent fresh pasta from sticking, lightly dust each piece or nest with semola or flour and place it on a baking parchment-lined tray. If you're cooking it within the next two days, cover loosely with a clean dish towel or cover in cling film/plastic wrap and refrigerate. For longer storage, freeze pasta nests or shapes on a tray until solid, then transfer them to clearly labelled airtight containers or freezer bags. Frozen fresh pasta keeps wonderfully for up to three months.

Dried Pasta: Properly storing dried pasta ensures it retains its flavour and texture for months. Keep dried pasta in a cool, dry, dark cupboard, away from direct sunlight or moisture. Airtight containers or resealable bags are perfect for preventing exposure to humidity, which can cause the pasta to become stale or attract pests. While dried pasta can technically last up to two years, it's at its best within one year.

TIPS FOR HOSTING A PASTA NIGHT: HOW TO FEED PEOPLE WITHOUT LOSING YOUR MIND

There is nothing more inviting than a table filled with bowls of steaming pasta, fresh bread and good company. Hosting a pasta night doesn't have to be complicated: the beauty of pasta is that it can be prepared ahead of time, with sauces simmering on the hob/stovetop while you enjoy a glass of wine with guests. Keep the menu simple, offering one pasta option with a simple, vibrant sauce. Serve an easy appetizer like marinated olives or a fresh salad and round off the meal with something light and sweet, like citrus granita or a slice of almond cake. Encourage guests to get involved in rolling, shaping or filling the pasta, as it turns dinner into an experience. Whether you're cooking for two or ten, these are the things that help make it enjoyable, both for you and everyone around the table.

Plan one pasta, not five. Choose a dish that can be mostly prepped ahead. A fresh pesto that needs no cooking, baked pasta or anything with a sauce that improves with time all work well.

Have a few first courses ready. I always make sure to have some simple appetizers on hand, along with a nice bottle of wine and a few soft drinks. The *capuliato* and aubergines/eggplants from this chapter, served on warm baguette slices, plus a few good cheeses, make everything feel thoughtful without any fuss.

Give people something to do. Let them grate cheese, fill water jugs or help serve. The best gatherings feel shared.

Set the mood, then let it go. Set the mood, then let it go. Dim lights, real napkins and a playlist are more than enough. No need for matching crockery or a perfect table.

Serve everything at once. In Sicily, pasta often comes first, but for a relaxed gathering, it's fine to bring out the salad, bread or side veg at the same time.

Finish simply . . . or with a bang. A bowl of fruit, a scoop of gelato or some special kind of chocolate is enough. But if you want to go the extra mile, tiramisu is always my go-to option: no-cook, easy and can be made ahead (even the day before).

SAMPLE MENUS: FOUR WAYS TO STRUCTURE A MEAL AROUND PASTA

These aren't prescriptive, just starting points. Pick based on the season, the occasion and your mood.

■ COMFORT IN A BOWL (AUTUMN/WINTER)

First course: Marinated aubergines/eggplants on toast

Main: Orecchiette Timbale with Root Vegetables & Caramelized Onions (page 213)

Side: Sicilian orange & fennel salad

Finish: Roasted pears with dark chocolate

■ PASTA & WINE WITH FRIENDS (ALL SEASONS)

Nibbles: Olives, nuts, selection of cheeses with crackers

Main: Spelt Tagliatelle with Sun-dried Tomato Pesto (page 62)

Side: Grilled courgettes/zucchini with mint and lemon

Finish: Almond biscotti & sweet wine

■ THE SICILIAN CELEBRATION (SPRING/SUMMER)

First course: Sicilian Sun-dried Tomato Mince (page 263)

Main: Busiate with Sicilian Red Pesto (page 39)

Side: Caponata

Finish: Seasonal fruit or a cup of lemon granita

■ THE SPRING GARDEN MENU (SPRING)

First course: Lolli col Macco/Broad/Fava Bean Soup (with no pasta) (page 90)

Main: Farfalle with Courgette/Zucchini, Peas & Mint (page 42)

Side: Grilled Artichokes with Lemon & Olive Oil

Finish: Tiramisu

CLOSING NOTE

This is the last page.

By now, you've shaped dough, simmered sauces, maybe made a bit of a mess. You've cooked with your hands, your senses and hopefully some joy. My hope is that this book has given you something lasting, not just recipes, but a new habit that fits into your life. A way to pause, to share, to return to yourself.

However pasta continues to live in your kitchen – be it once a week, once a season or every time you need grounding – I hope it brings you a little comfort and a lot of flavour.

Thank you for cooking with me.

STAY CONNECTED

If you'd like to keep cooking together, I share new recipes, stories and glimpses into the making of this book over on Instagram **@isabella.sicily**.

I'd love to see what you make, hear your stories and stay in touch as this journey continues.

Thank you.

ABOUT ME

I am a self-taught cook, chef and food writer whose roots run deep in the vibrant, multicultural soils of Sicily. Born under the sunny skies of Ragusa, my earliest memories are of big family gatherings around the table where the strong, passionate women in my family instilled in me a love for cooking that transcends mere sustenance.

Moving to Venice to study Languages and Cultures of Eurasia and the Mediterranean deepened my fascination with the diverse influences that have shaped Sicilian culture and cuisine. Inspired by the stories of my Libyan-born grandmother, I immersed myself in the studies of classical Arabic and the archaeology of the Mediterranean, unearthing the historical layers that have seasoned Sicilian cuisine with its distinctive, complex flavour.

Upon completing my studies, I embarked on a transformative decade-long journey in Southeast Asia, where I met my Indian husband and began blending the diverse cuisines and spices of Asia with my Mediterranean roots, creating a unique style that's evident in my cooking today. My kitchen, with its extensive spice collection, is a testament to this fusion of flavours.

Now based in London, I balance a thriving marketing career and my culinary pursuits. Through my Instagram community, blog, pasta-making workshops and supper clubs, I've created a platform to connect with people.

These experiences, combined with my passion for cooking and storytelling, have prepared me to bring *Pasta Therapy* to life, offering readers not just recipes, but a narrative of resilience, healing and the joy of cooking.

ACKNOWLEDGEMENTS

This book would not have been possible without the support, input and encouragement of many people, and I am deeply grateful to each of you.

To Akshay. My partner in every sense. You have been by my side through it all: the joy, the grief, the fear, the hope. When we moved to a new country with no family, no friends and no idea how to begin again, you held everything together. Through sickness and loss, you stood beside me with strength and determination, never letting me give up. You are the most talented, original thinker I know, a relentless problem-solver, the best cheerleader and the toughest (and usually constructive) critic. You push me to be better in the most loving way. This book has your fingerprints on every page, and I will never stop being grateful for you.

To my sister Paola, for being my sounding board and ever the wisest of the two of us. To my brother-in-law Federico, a brilliant cook and someone I've long admired in the kitchen. Your creativity and passion continue to inspire me. To my nieces, Irene and Beatrice, for always cheering me on and bringing so much light to our family.

To my extended family – in Sicily, India and around the globe – thank you for sharing your memories, ideas and family stories, and for reminding me how rich our heritage truly is.

To Charlotte, Anna and the team at Johnson & Alcock, thank you for believing in this project from the start and guiding it with care and insight.

To Ella and everyone at Nourish Books, thank you for taking a chance on a first-time author. You brought this vision to life with sensitivity and creativity, treating every word and recipe with care.

A heartfelt thank you to Sam Jacobs and Future Dreams for providing the platform that allowed me to run my *Pasta Therapy* workshops, and for the extraordinary support they offer to women and men affected by breast cancer. Your work changes lives, and I'm proud to be a small part of your mission.

To all the women who have participated in the *Pasta Therapy* workshops, thank you for your trust, openness and willingness to share. Your stories inspired more than you know. A special thank you to my friend Veronica and her husband Ricky, who inspired two of the recipes in this book.

To the friends who read drafts, tested recipes, helped with photos or simply asked "How's the book going?" – thank you. Your help, kindness and encouragement meant more than you know.

Finally, to every reader who picks up this book, thank you for inviting it into your kitchen. I hope it brings you comfort, inspiration and the joy of creating something by hand.

INDEX

Note: page numbers in **bold** refer to illustrations.